Strategic Marketing Planning

SECOND EDITION

Malcolm McDonald

Cranfield
UNIVERSITY
School of Management

KOGAN
PAGE

First published in 1992

Second edition 1996

Apart from any fair dealing for the purposes of research or private study, or criticism or review, as permitted under the Copyright, Designs and Patents Act, 1988, this publication may only be reproduced, stored or transmitted, in any form or by any means, with the prior permission in writing of the publishers, or in the case of reprographic reproduction in accordance with the terms of licences issued by the Copyright Licensing Agency. Enquiries concerning reproduction outside those terms should be sent to the publishers at the undermentioned address:

Kogan Page Ltd
120 Pentonville Road
London N1 9JN

©Malcolm McDonald, 1992, 1996

British Library Cataloguing in Publication Data
A CIP record of this book is available from the British Library.

ISBN 0 7494 2096 0

Typeset by Saxon Graphics Ltd, Derby
Printed and bound in Great Britain by Biddles Ltd, Guildford and Kings Lynn

CONTENTS

Contents

LIST OF FIGURES

LIST OF TABLES

Professor Malcolm HB McDonald
MA (Oxon), MSc, PhD, FCIM FRSA

Malcolm is Professor of Marketing Planning and Chairman of the International Marketing Planning Centre at the Cranfield School of Management.

He is a graduate in English Language and Literature from Oxford University, in Business Studies from Bradford University Management Centre, and has a PhD from the Cranfield University. He has extensive industrial experience, including a number of years as Marketing Director of Canada Dry.

In the past fifteen years he has run seminars and workshops on Marketing Planning in the UK, Europe, India, the Far East, South Africa, Australia, South America, the USA and Japan.

He has written twenty books, including the best seller *Market Plans; how to prepare them; how to use them* (Butterworth-Heinemann, 1995), and many of his papers have been published. He is editor of the *Journal of Marketing Practice*

His current interests centre around the development of computer based training programs in marketing and the development of expert systems in marketing planning.

THE CRANFIELD MANAGEMENT SERIES

The Cranfield Management Series represents an exciting joint initiative between the Cranfield School of Management and Kogan Page.

As one of Europe's leading post-graduate business schools, Cranfield is renowned for its applied research activities, which cover a wide range of issues relating to the practice of management.

Each title in the Series is based on current research and authored by Cranfield faculty or their associates. Many of the research projects have been undertaken with the sponsorship and active assistance of organizations from the industrial, commercial or public sectors. The aim of the Series is to make the findings of direct relevance to managers through texts which are academically sound, accessible and practical.

For managers and academics alike, the Cranfield Management Series will provide access to up-to-date management thinking from some of the world's leading academics and practitioners. The series represents both Cranfield's and Kogan Page's commitment to furthering the improvement of management practice in all types of organisations.

THE SERIES EDITORS

Frank Fishwick
Reader in Managerial Economics
Dr Fishwick joined Cranfield from Aston University in 1966, having previously worked in textiles, electronics and local government (town and country planning). Recent research and consultancy interests have been focused on business concentration, competition policy and the book publishing industry. He has been directing a series of research studies for the Commission of the

European Communities, working in collaboration with business economists in France and Germany. He is permanent economic adviser to the Publishers Association in the UK and is a regular consultant to other public and private sector organisations in the UK, continental Europe and the US.

Gerry Johnson

Professor of Strategic Management
Director of the Centre for Strategic Management and Organisational Change
Director of Research at Cranfield School of Management

After graduating from University College London, Professor Johnson worked for several years in management positions in Unilever and Reed International before becoming a management consultant. Since 1976, he has taught at Aston University Management Centre, Manchester Business School, and from 1988 at Cranfield School of Management. His research work is primarily concerned with processes of strategic decision making and strategic change in organisations. He also works as a consultant on issues of strategy formulation and strategic change at a senior level with a number of UK and international firms.

Shaun Tyson

Professor of Human Resource Management
Director of Human Resource Research Centre

Professor Tyson studied at London University and spent eleven years in senior positions in industry within engineering and electronic companies. For four years he was lecturer in personnel management at the Civil Service College, and joined Cranfield in 1979. He has acted as a consultant and researched widely into human resource strategies, policies and the evaluation of the function. He has published 14 books.

PREFACE

Already, the 1990s have forced dramatic changes in the ways organisations think, plan and behave. What caused success in the 1980s no longer worked towards the end of that decade, and those who clung doggedly to earlier policies disappeared with a suddenness and viciousness undreamed of in calmer times.

It wasn't just the growth of competition from the Pacific Rim countries, nor the ageing and declining populations of many parts of Europe. Nor was it the speed with which new technologies could be developed and commercialised and then transferred to less developed countries. More than anything else, it was rapidly changing consumer attitudes towards many of the things that had been taken for granted hitherto. The more sophisticated and environmentally aware consumers began to exercise their power, and individual life-styles, combined with technological breakthroughs that enabled institutions to offer more personal choice, challenged for the first time the long-established tenets of mass marketing.

This, combined with the sudden emergence of the concept of the single European market, had such a dramatic impact on all the established theories of management that some of the more traditional books on business management started to look increasingly suspect in this new, more chaotic and uncertain environment. On careful reflection, however, it became clear that the more fundamental tenets outlined in books on business strategy were still applicable in the 1990s, providing some effort could be applied in tailoring them to the new challenges raised by the new consumer and the new market in Europe.

The purpose of this book is quite simply to explain the concepts of strategic marketing and how to apply them to the new challenges facing organisations in the 1990s. In my years of consulting and in management education, there has appeared to be a substantial gap between theory and practice, even in the marketing field, where much of the theory has developed from observations of practice. I have reached a number of conclusions:

- the now large number of strategic concepts and principles that evolved during the 1980s are not widely known or their application understood;
- faced with an increasing number of concepts that are potentially relevant to any marketing strategy, it is not clear which are the ones to apply;
- a relatively simple, but practical, framework is necessary for the decision-maker or the strategist to understand the essence of what is required, so that the appropriate concepts and techniques are used.

This book is an attempt to address some of these issues, which have been written about by the author during recent years. This book is simply a compendium of some of these papers, each of which has been carefully selected to represent a major issue current to marketing practitioners.

The primary target of this book is marketing executives and students of marketing and business strategy courses. It should also be useful, however, to multinational corporations and foreign companies seeking to understand marketing strategy and the evolution and performance of businesses operating in a variety of markets.

Professor Malcolm McDonald
Cranfield School of Management
July 1996

ACKNOWLEDGEMENTS

A book of this type requires the help of many people. To all those executives who provided information and time, I am deeply indebted. I wish to thank them and their colleagues for their involvement and contributions. In particular, I should also like to thank Dr Linden Brown for his valuable advice and for his permission to publish Chapter 1 of our book. Also, to Hugh Wilson, for his contributions to other chapters in this book, I express my thanks.

Professor Malcolm McDonald
Cranfield School of Management

THE ROLE OF MARKETING PAST, PRESENT AND FUTURE*

Malcolm McDonald and Tim Denison

OVERVIEW

In a recent *McKinsey Quarterly* article, Brady and Davis (1993) expressed a concern that is surfacing in industry, questioning the contribution that marketing is making to businesses in the 1990s. They refer to the growing attention being paid to the typically large budgets associated with marketing departments and the doubts that are being cast in industry about its value for money. It seems that the halcyon, post-war decades of commercial marketing are going, and a new, 'lean and fit' era is beginning. Following on its heels, a Coopers and Lybrand survey of senior executives in large FMCG, retail and service sector organisations, fuelled the growing debate about the contribution of marketing to contemporary business.

*This paper was published in *The Journal of Marketing Practice: Applied Marketing Science*, Vol. 1, No 1, 1995, pp 54–76, MCB University Press, and is reproduced here with their kind permission.

The findings from the fieldwork summarised here are based on the CIM research carried out by the Cranfield School of Management Institute for Advanced Research in Marketing. Copyright in this report is held by CIM. The extracts in this article are used with kind permission from the CIM.

The purpose of this chapter is threefold: first, to outline the major issues and challenges that confront businesses today, which impact on marketing and have led to the current wave of criticism; second, to signal past failings in marketing that need to be addressed to secure its pivotal role in business success; and third, to illustrate the ways in which UK-based companies are responding to these issues. The latter draws on the results of a survey commissioned by the Chartered Institute of Marketing and carried out by the Cranfield School of Management Institute for Advanced Research in Marketing. This third objective represents the primary focus of the chapter. The other two, which put the primary research into context, have been the topic of many previous studies (see below), therefore warranting less attention in this chapter. The overall aim is to describe and comment on how marketing is evolving in British industry, as we approach the twenty-first millennium.

RESEARCH PROTOCOL AND METHODOLOGY

The research programme was carried out over the course of five months, beginning in September 1993. In essence, the study combines a catholic literature review of the state and contribution of marketing to businesses with an empirical, case-based approach, to generate and refine theories about the future evolution of marketing. This qualitative approach was the preferred means to develop forward-looking insight and substance, rather than a more quantitative study, geared at the statistical testing of narrow, deductive hypotheses, and constructed around reflective explanation. The remit was not to look back on marketing's performance, drawing on the past to address the future, but to take a visionary perspective of where marketing practices are heading and to be prescriptive in terms of how marketing should evolve. The study required a symbiotic relationship between the research team, leading academics and consultants and industry. Above all, it required a healthy respect for the experience and views of practitioners as an input to theory building.

Rather than cover all types of UK businesses in detail the study focuses on the industrial, consumer durables and services sectors, although not at the total exclusion of the FMCG sector. To date, the state of marketing in these sectors has been overshadowed by marketing practices in FMCG companies, generally acknowledged to be at the leading-edge of best practice. The scope of the study and sample frame is justified on two counts. First, FMCG manufacturers represent a relatively small proportion of British companies, bearing little resemblance, in a marketing sense, to common practices among the population as a whole. By concentrating the study outside the FMCG sector, we wanted to generate results and draw conclusions which would impact on Western industry at large. Second, in the past it has been assumed that the marketing lead taken by FMCG manufacturers is relevant and wholly transferable to others, and should set the precedent for those that follow in their wake. This assumption is now being questioned, particularly in the light of the growing competitive pressures that many FMCG companies have come under in recent years. Perhaps classical 4Ps marketing, with changes in emphasis to its constituent parts, is not as relevant a framework outside the FMCG domain as we have become prepared to accept all too easily?

The aim of the study is to fill the gaps in those areas that are not yet researched with the best knowledge available – namely, from those who operate where it is all happening. The science of marketing certainly needs the contribution of what Schon (1983) describes as 'the reflective practitioner'.

Several steps were taken to ensure that such practical experience and intuition were incorporated intelligently into scientific enquiry.

First, a literature review of the state of marketing practice in the UK was undertaken, so that we could build on the knowledge base that already exists. While this aspect of the study gave us some insights into the past performance of marketing, it was of limited value for helping us to project into the future, as the majority of previous papers and articles have taken a retrospective, normative approach. However, the literature was more helpful in determining the key challenges that are affecting businesses in the 1990s.

Second, the study features a series of in-depth, one-to-one interviews with leading marketing academics and consultants. In all, the views of 17 eminent thinkers were canvassed regarding the business challenges that organizations face, the past failings in marketing and the ways in which the organizations they work with are changing their approaches to marketing. In reality, this sample frame provides far more than the views and experiences of 17 individuals. Through the daily contact they all enjoy and the privileged information they share, with the practitioners they train and advise from all manner of companies, their collective perspectives represent a much wider and more valuable window on the world of current organizational practices and marketing issues. It is our belief that the broad base of knowledge generated in this way is equally valid, and perhaps even more so, than were we to have undertaken a large-scale quantitative survey of British-based companies, based on limited response questions, developed around our own mindsets and those exposed in past studies.

Third, in order to validate the findings from the first two stages of the study, and to add more depth, vision and clarity, a series of 15 case studies was undertaken with companies that were selected on the basis of their marketing competence and maturity. Targeting suitable companies presents its own set of difficulties. We chose not to select the sample purely on the grounds of current financial performance, because there is no absolute guarantee that this is a reflection of good marketing practice. Instead, we selected primarily on the basis of peer respect and marketing reputation. This was supported via referrals, made in conversation with the leading academics of companies that they consider to be strong and forward-thinking in their marketing approach and which is reflected in their market performance in their own industry sectors.

The case studies comprised five service-based, four industrial and six consumer goods companies, including one FMCG manufacturer. They included both large, multinational leaders and smaller niche players. The case studies were constructed around a series of iterative, in-depth, semi-structured interviews of key marketing and managing personnel within each company, ranging from CEOs to functional specialists. We relied on a 'snowballing' technique, cascading from the most senior marketing executive downwards, to identify the key people to interview. On average, approximately six hours were spent with employees from each of the 15 companies.

Our case-study approach is atypical of many past studies which have looked at the marketing effectiveness of British companies. The difference reflects our intent not to benchmark performance and develop key, general indicators of marketing success, but to look for guidance and vision over the ways in which companies will best meet customer needs in the future. The approach that we have chosen to compile this paper is to take holistic views of 'good marketing practices' in leading companies and then compare them with one another and with the perspectives of leading academics and consultants. It enables us to generalize analytically and to derive conclusions about where the future of marketing lies, built around a scaffold of previous thinking and explanation. (A list of the leading academics and companies interviewed is given in the appendix at the end of the chapter).

THE ACADEMIC PERSPECTIVE: LITERATURE REVIEW AND CONSULTATION

The State of Marketing in the UK

Research interest developed in this area during the 1980s, when a series of formative studies was undertaken, which set out to review the state of marketing practice in UK businesses. The investigation was led by a CIM-sponsored project by Hooley *et al* (1984), which surveyed, at a very general level:

- company management's internal attitudes towards marketing (its definition, role and function);
- the way that the function is organised (activities performed, involvement in strategic planning, level of co-ordination and information seeking across functions);
- the practices of the function (use of marketing research, planning, new product development input, etc).

This set the mould for other UK studies in the series reported in academic journals (Baker *et al*, 1986; Doyle, 1987; Doyle *et al*, 1988; Norbet *et al*, 1988; Piercy, 1985) which mirrored similar work done earlier in the USA (Barksdale and Darden, 1971; Griffin, 1982; Hise, 1965; Lusch *et al*, 1976; McDaniel and Hise, 1983; McNamara, 1972; Varadarajan, 1983).

The key conclusions that the UK studies reached were, first, that few British companies were marketing-oriented, or competent practitioners at the operational level, and second, that the minority that *were* performed better, in terms of return on investment (ROI) and market share. This series of studies in the mid-1980s, therefore, justified the importance of marketing in the contemporary business environment.

During the late 1980s and early 1990s, a second wave of like-style studies, conducted mainly by the same researchers in the UK, have revisited the scene, with the main intention of establishing if practices have changed over time (Doyle, 1992; Liu *et al*, 1991; Lynch *et al*, 1990; Shaw and Doyle, 1991; Wong *et al*, 1989). At the same time, a similar move was underway primarily in the USA, but also in other countries around the world (Avlonitis *et al*, 1992; Jaworski and Kohli, 1993; Mueller-Heumann, 1993; Narver and Slater, 1990; Wink, 1992).

The second phase of UK studies reconfirmed the importance of marketing to business success and, indeed, found signs that British companies were improving their marketing competence, although more in terms of organisational acceptance of the philosophy (ie, the need to be customer-oriented, market integrated and profit focused – see McGee and Spiro, 1988, for an example) than in their functional abilities. Marketing academics have remained largely critical of British marketing practitioners:

> It is now well accepted that poor marketing has been the single most important constraint on British companies' domestic and overseas market shares. But the transition to greater marketing effectiveness in British firms is slow and remains the major concern of UK CEOs, far outweighing all other factors combined. (Wong *et al* 1989)

The researchers generally agreed that the main inhibitor of marketing effectiveness in UK businesses in the late 1980s and early 1990s lay not in poor managerial acceptance of marketing thinking, but in poor implementation of basic marketing, (ie, in its functional activities).

On the evidence of past studies, we conclude that, despite the poor marketing ability of British companies in the 1970s and 1980s, the criticism remained external to industry. However, as the environment in which British industry competes has toughened over the late 1980s and into the 1990s, marketing has begun to attract heavy criticism from within industry.

The remainder of this article sets out to explore the three themes that we identified at the start: the business challenges that are facing marketing, the failings of marketing and the ways in which marketing can respond to perform more effectively as we move into the twenty-first century.

The Business Challenges Facing Marketing

Without appreciating the ways in which the business environment is changing, we cannot hope to propose ways in which marketing will evolve with any accuracy or credibility. The literature review, albeit limited, gave us a platform on which to build. Drawing on this, we conducted in-depth, personal interviews with 17 eminent academics and consultants. The purpose of this part of the research programme was to substantiate the views of previous writers and to gain peer consensus on the set of core challenges that are facing Western-world businesses in the 1990s, and which have an impact on the marketing discipline. As mentioned earlier, we were particularly concerned about capturing the challenges facing companies in the industrial, consumer durables and service sectors. The series of interviews confirmed the list of business challenges identified in the literature review, and provided greater depth and insight into the causes and consequences of these changes and challenges. Each of these challenges is outlined briefly below, to give context to the current debate about the role of marketing. We highlight the specific challenges that these trends present to marketing practices.

- *The internationalization of businesses.* Garda (1988) and Lazer (1993) cite globalisation as the challenge which will have the most impact on marketing. Buyers and suppliers of products and services are becoming more global in their approach to business. The concept of nationally separate markets is no longer relevant, except where strong differences in consumer tastes and cultural preferences exist and, as a consequence, competition among suppliers is intensifying. Industry deregulation and the creation of the single European market (bringing with it common standards, safety and technical requirements and the end of discrimination by public authorities) have served to hasten and encourage the trend. The challenge in marketing terms is one of restructuring domestic marketing operations to compete internationally in larger, more disparate markets. In effect, globalization complicates all aspects of the traditional 4Ps of the marketing mix.
- *Customer expertise, sophistication and power.* Customers, generally, are becoming more demanding as their expectations of quality, reliability and durability grow constantly. This is as true of the customers of consumer and industrial goods manufacturers as everywhere else. It stems partly from a better knowledge base, largely brought about through the developments in communications and IT, and partly from the concentration of buying into fewer hands, which is evident in many industries. Accompanying these changes, the development of buyer groups, networks and alliances are all

recent phenomena which have swung market control away from manufacturers in many industries. Their response, such as it is, has been to switch wherever possible to multichannelling, including the opportunity to sell direct either through established channels, such as the postal service or telesales, or through new ones, such as the television shopping channel and warehouse selling. The marketing challenge is twofold: first, of exploring ways to become closer to the consumer; second, of developing a means and experience base to cope with the complexity presented by multiple market channels.

- *Lack of market growth*. In many sectors, market maturity has been reached, characterised by overcapacity and exacerbated by current recessionary forces. Margins are being driven down, calling for greater operational efficiencies and 'value for money'. Under these conditions, the emphasis rests as much on customer retention as on catching new customers. It also presents a new challenge to marketing, namely, how to create and stimulate new-to-the-marketplace demand, rather than be satisfied simply by competing purely on a market-share basis. McKenna (1991) warns that the latter approach simply 'turns marketing into an expensive fight over crumbs, rather than a smart effort to own the whole pie'.

- *Process thinking*. A direct outgrowth of the technology explosion in information handling and communications has been the switch out of a single-product approach to business to systems thinking. The shift from selling ready-made, tangible products to selling by reputation and on capability to manufacture according to exact client specifications, on an 'as needed' basis, is one of the most fundamental challenges facing businesses today. It promotes the importance of forging longer term relationships with customers and being more customer committed.

- *Time-based competition*. Time horizons continue to become more compressed and the pace of change is still accelerating. The development of the likes of flexible manufacturing and control systems has encouraged companies to compete on time – ie, the speed with which they can deliver products to the marketplace. Concurrent with this is the growing transience in consumer preferences. As time has become a major determinant of competitive advantage, so businesses need to ensure that they are more closely in touch with their customers and the general marketplace. The need to hit the market early and recover the investment fast is very apparent. In this context, price-setting becomes vital.

These challenges present industry with the need to restructure and re-evaluate the way in which it undertakes marketing, in a functional sense, as well as to re-examine the ways in which marketing can be introduced and accepted as a business philosophy. These themes are addressed in the following section.

Garda (1988) suggests that marketing is becoming not only more complex as a function, as a result of these changes to the business environment, but more of an analytical science that uses logic, systematic data analysis and sophisticated market research. This, he comments, is far removed from the art form that marketing used to be in the 1950s and 1960s, when it was practised by the creative, intuitive and inspirational. If marketing, as a discipline, does little to respond to this set of new challenges, there is a very real danger that marketing, as a function at least, will be marginalized. The signs are there. 'Business process redesign', rather than marketing, has taken a major role in the corporate restructuring of the USA in recent times as the means for companies to become more customer focused (Hammer, 1990; Pallister *et al*, 1993).

Changing the Marketing Mindset

How is marketing evolving to respond to the changing business environment? Very few papers have been written which address this topic squarely. However, some of the most recent empirical studies which were mentioned earlier have made a contribution by identifying the criteria associated with the better performers over the last decade (Doyle, 1992; Liu and Wensley, 1991; Lynch *et al*, 1990; Whittington and Whipp, 1992). Lazer (1993) and McKenna (1991) and Hansen *et al* (1990) are other noteworthy contributors in this area. There are, however, weaknesses in flagging up the actions of the best performers as recommendations for others to follow. It is difficult to measure performance in any way other than retrospectively, so any deductions made about criteria associated with best performers, may be misleading. As Doyle (1992) observed, many of the leading companies of an age do not manage to continue there for very long. Perhaps one of the reasons for this is that if you are the market leader, you have a vested interest in maintaining the *status quo* and you can become guilty of not moving forward, only to be overtaken by the competition. With this in mind, we have drawn more on the thoughts and comments of leading academics and consultants, expressed during interview rather than rely heavily on the literature. Marketing academics in business schools are in the privileged position of seeing the changes underway in businesses on a day-to-day basis, through their close links and in-company work. We have drawn on this experience base to highlight and discuss the changes that are underway in companies that continue to lead from the front and are proactive in developing their markets, rather than include the actions of those current leaders whose future is geared solely to exploring their market position.

It is helpful to differentiate between changes that are occurring in the marketing function and those that relate to marketing's philosophical and strategic role in the company.

Strategic changes

- *Structure*. Common to many of the above papers is the notion that the organisational structure of the marketing department is having to change to accommodate the business challenges that we have described previously. In effect, leading companies appear to be moving away from a formal, top down, hierarchical structure, which is bureaucratic, but effective in terms of administrative costs as well as being risk-aversive, in so far as everyone is directly accountable for their actions. In the past, this structure served companies well, but it is now being criticised because it impedes the creation of innovative ideas and it hinders the company's ability to respond quickly to market opportunities. In its place, a move to a flatter, more flexible, open system structure is being adopted, in which traditional job titles and responsibilities are being replaced.

- *Focus*. As companies become more global in their outlook, the effectiveness of controlling marketing operations from a centralised position is being questioned. Many companies are disbanding their central function and establishing multiple cores, comprising multifunctional, customer-facing teams. Potentially, the move to decentralisation hinders marketing strategy cohesion. Companies overcome this problem in different ways; some use working groups or task forces (Unilever refer to them as category management teams), with representation from the various units, to steer strategic issues; others, such as P&G designate 'lead countries' to take lead roles in projects and then to disseminate the knowledge to the other units. This enables companies to take a focused search for areas of competitive advantage. Increasingly, companies are looking towards strategic alliances, other 'lock-in' relationships and more informal networks to expand their avenues for business growth.

- *Future driven*. To date, companies have assumed a largely reactive approach towards the way they conduct their business. There are signs that organisations are beginning to take a more proactive approach to the future and are becoming truly market-driven. McKenna (1991) describes this as changing culture from the 'tell us what colour you want' school of marketing to 'let's figure out together whether and how colour matters to your larger goal' marketing. In essence, it implies moving towards a position of genuine involvement with customers and, where necessary, becoming familiar with the customer's customer. It assumes a 'future backwards, market inwards' approach. Successful companies seemingly evolve with or in front of markets.

Operational and functional changes

Accompanying the strategic and philosophical changes is the need to implement changes at the functional level.

- *Professionalism.* There is an indication from the literature and discussions with academics that leading companies are becoming more professional in their marketing operations in a number of different ways. They attach more importance to formal marketing training and qualifications, and make greater use of marketing research and marketing planning, as well as heavier investment in market intermediary and internal analysis.
- *Market and performance assessment.* It is apparent that leading companies are moving away from discrete time assessments based around weekly, monthly or quarterly periods, towards continuous, ongoing monitoring and analysis, so that they can react quickly to market changes and prevent getting stuck in antiquated paradigms. Lazer (1993) thus described marketing as becoming a process of 'striving, but never arriving', of 'pursuing a journey, not reaching a destination'. In today's fast-changing marketplace, the traditional NPD process of getting an idea, developing a prototype, testing the market and launching, is judged to be 'slow, unresponsive and turf-ridden' (McKenna, 1991). The alternative is to nurture continuous innovation fed by monitoring the market wants and competitive activity on an ongoing basis.

In conclusion, it is apparent that marketing success is a matter of doing the right things as well as doing things right. This section has reviewed the lessons that have been drawn from the little empirical evidence that has been documented and reflects the current thinking of leading academics and consultants.

AN INDUSTRY PERSPECTIVE: FIELDWORK FINDINGS

How accurately do these thoughts and views reflect the practitioner's perspective? Fifteen case studies of leading marketing companies provide us with a unique window through which to observe current practices and experience live issues.

The Changing Business Environment

The views and opinions of senior managers in the 15 leading UK-based companies confirmed the main challenges to business as being those highlighted by academics and described above. Our intent here, however, is more about providing insight and depth of understanding than about generating a substantiated 'pecking order' of issues.

Internationalisation is undoubtedly one of the most important challenges currently facing organisations across the service, consumer-durable and industrial sectors. It is an issue to which they are reacting. It is now a key element of strategic planning for these excellent companies, although all of our sample companies acknowledge the need to 'think global, act local'.

Their motivations, however, are somewhat different. In the service companies we studied, the driving force is largely internal and centred around an inherent quest for fast growth (fast access to fast-growing markets). In effect, the consequence is that service companies can control their own destiny and speed of internationalisation to suit their own development. The service companies in our sample see internationalisation primarily as a growth opportunity, met primarily through alliances and acquisition. This is underlined by a comment made by Sir Colin Marshall of British Airways, in the 1993 accounts:

> We have been able to implement a significant part of our overall strategy for the future through major investments in the USAir Group Inc, the fourth largest of the US airlines in passenger number terms; in Quantas ... in TAT European Airlines, the second airline in France, and in Deutsche BA, operating both domestic and international routes in Germany.

Rentokil, another of our sample base, provide further evidence of this, having made 120 acquisitions in 10 years.

In the consumer-durables companies that we studied, the motivation is, once more, internally derived, rooted mainly in the opportunity for growth, but also in securing sustained performance, through insuring against local economic downturns. As one senior manager in our sample said: 'When one country falls over, usually one somewhere else is doing well'. Consumer markets are very susceptible to changes in discretionary spending levels.

In contrast, the main force behind internationalisation in industrial companies seems to be more externally driven. As their customers themselves are becoming more global, so customers expect their suppliers to be able to service them at a global, not just local, level. This is reflected in a comment from AT&T Global Information Solutions:

> One of the things that we are working on is to help customers who are themselves truly global players and deal with them as a single organisation. As customers become more international, either through acquisition or organic growth, they will expect us to be able to address them as one unit internationally.

A lack of ability to meet this demand is causing accounts to be lost, as buyers rationalise their numbers of suppliers.

In essence, we suggest that the challenge of internationalisation is a more pressing one for industrial companies than others, as the required pace of change is governed externally by their customers.

Increasing sophistication and power of customers is, without doubt, another key challenge to industrial companies at present. This increased sophistication, however, is not primarily technical among the companies we studied. It is rather the opposite; customers are less interested in purely technical matters, but are becoming more professional in their buying habits. This is illustrated by a comment from Rolls-Royce Aero Engines:

Product attributes are swamped by huge financial considerations ... Our customers have always been clever [but] ... they are not as engineering-oriented as they were. They are more concerned about the bottom line. Their area of sophistication has switched into finance and economics.

Product performance is increasingly becoming a given, not a cause of differentiation.

Likewise, consumer-durable manufacturers are equally concerned by the growing sophistication and importance of their customers and of end users. To them, this is less of a new challenge, but more of a continuing one, which now extends down to even the smallest of customers. The sophistication extends to buying systems and processes, requiring suppliers to respond more quickly.

It seems that customer power and sophistication has less impact on the service companies we studied. Perhaps this stems from the market growth that is still being enjoyed by many of them. It may stem also from the lower knowledge base that customers tend to possess when dealing with intangible products. Despite this challenge being less threatening, service companies do concede that customers are becoming more price sensitive and quicker to criticise and voice their opinion. One BA manager commented that 'passengers are increasingly telling us what they want'. Consolidation of suppliers and the concomitant concentration of their power is of more concern to leading service companies than the rise in customer power. 'Eat or be eaten' is the motto by which they survive and compete.

Industrial companies are the only group in our sample to cite lack of market growth as a high impact issue. This stems partly from the relative contribution that single customers and national markets can make to their businesses. If one or two of their customers slip into difficulties or one or two markets into recession, the whole of the business is more likely to suffer. It is encouraging the better performers to seek new markets more actively than ever before and place greater emphasis on new product development and innovation. To other companies in the sample, outside the industrial sector, the issue is more about increased competition rather than lack of market growth.

It is clearly evident from our study that good marketing companies are aware of the need to think more in terms of processes, particularly in relation to delivering customer value, than specific functional tasks. They are coming to understand and define their roles in terms of customer service and support. Some organisations have even gone so far as to change job titles and department names so that they explicitly mention customers.

One result of moving thinking away from functions towards processes seems to be a much clearer understanding of what makes the customer buy. Once organizations understand the customer's decision process, they are able to align their own processes and ways of doing things to the ways in which customers think and operate. This makes them much more sensitive to quality being seen as an 'end-to-end' process from the customer's service-delivery perspective, rather than in any abbreviated form.

Likewise, the challenge of time-based competition and the pace of change highlighted in the earlier stages of the study is impacting on all three sectors studied. This is typified by the experiences of Standard Life, another of the companies in our study. In the insurance business, traditional pension products, for example, have had 40- or 50-year lifespans. The kind of pension products that were being sold to customers in the 1980s would not have been unfamiliar to actuaries in the 1820s. Suddenly, however, the boom in unit-linked products and changes in regulation and taxation regimes means that product life-cycles for some products are down now to three or five years.

In order to respond to shorter product lives, the style of new product development is also changing: 'We are tackling this [shortening new product lead times] by bringing along more options ... keeping our options open for longer than we have done in the past ... if you have a failure with one, you have got a couple of others to go on with. In the past this was not the case; they did something, failed and then started all over again.' The whole process is driven by the desire to anticipate the service that customers will want next year and then to provide it today.

Past Failings in Marketing

Besides the changing environment in which businesses operate today, marketers are confronted by general low regard of their discipline, as a consequence of a number of longstanding weaknesses associated with it. It is beyond the scope of this chapter to describe these failings in depth. It is necessary, nevertheless, to mention them and to report their presence or absence in the companies we studied, so that we can take stock of all the challenges that face marketing today, before signalling where marketing is going.

Poor image, complacency, poor integration and lack of a secure knowledge base are all criticisms made about marketers, but which have been rarely conceded openly. Our case studies suggest that image and integration are failings less associated with marketing in the services sector, perhaps because of its relative youthfulness there, captured in a typical response from BT:

> Marketing in BT ... is in early adolescence. It has come through its childhood but it is not yet mature, and, like most adolescents, it is having an influence on the family – it is keeping the family young.

Elsewhere, even in the companies we studied, where marketing practices are considered to be better than most, the people we interviewed admitted that there are still problems, albeit that they are being eroded. In the industrial sector, for example, one spokesman testified that there is still 'a lot of scepticism in this organisation towards marketing and its values'. In the consumer goods companies that we approached, the signs are more encouraging. There is a belief that complacency and poor integration are becoming a thing of the past.

Yet poor image and lack of a secure skill and knowledge base continue to dog marketing and marketers in many organizations in the UK. The problem of poor image seems to arise where marketing has allowed itself to become merely a sales support function, or where companies have tried and failed to implement certain aspects of marketing. As one senior manager in a consumer-durable company reflected:

> Coming back to the UK from North America is like stepping back in a time warp. Management sciences are underdeveloped in this country and are paralysed by analysis, and UK companies are not performing as well as could be expected.

Only exceptionally do we find examples of companies in which marketing is becoming recognised as possessing a valued set of skills.

The effect of poor image and professional arrogance over time has created a cultural divide in many British companies between marketing and other functions. Poor integration with other parts of the organisation has been a common consequence. Such is the stigma that some marketers feel, they have become trapped in their vertical silos, frightened to step out, mingle and communicate with the other functions. The companies we studied, however, demonstrate a trend towards increasing integration of marketing with other departments.

The final weakness associated with marketing is that it is coming under attack for being increasingly risk-averse, for failing to recognise the opportunities of internationalisation and for generally losing its commitment to innovation. Nevertheless, as product life-cycles continue to shorten, the need to take risks in new product development will grow, as one manager from Boots pointed out: 'Now, you have to develop the ability to take risks, knowing that not everything will work. You have to be a bit risky and put a bit of life back into marketing'. Clearly, decisive steps have to be taken to overcome the persistency of the past failings in marketing.

It is evident, from our brief review, that marketing's achievements in British industry over the last few decades have not been impressive. Yet academics strongly reject the claims made by some commentators recently that marketing is failing. Research continues to show that those companies with a strong marketing focus perform better (Narver and Slater, 1990). The current criticism that marketing is attracting relates, we suggest, more to the function than the philosophy. However, only a minority of companies still achieve a strong marketing focus. Figures 1.1 and 1.2 summarise the evolution of marketing to date.

From our discussions with leading academics and practitioners, together with a review of the literature, we have highlighted the key business challenges that face British industry and to which marketing must respond. We have also

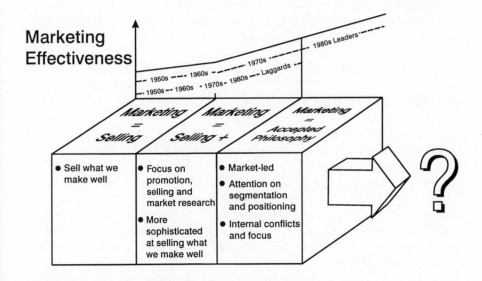

Figure 1.1 The evolution of marketing in industrial and service companies to the 1980s

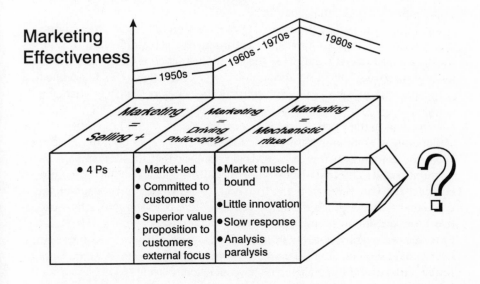

Figure 1.2 The evolution of marketing in fast-moving consumer goods companies to the 1980s

highlighted the failings that exist in current marketing practice. Armed with this background knowledge, where is marketing heading and how should it evolve to meet these business challenges?

DISCUSSIONS AND CONCLUSIONS

Marketing: the Way Forward

The strongest message to emerge from the companies that took part in this study is that they are redefining marketing. Marketing for the excellent companies is now about customer service in a very special sense. The excellent companies are talking not just about satisfying present customer needs, but about anticipating the customer needs of the future and delivering them today. This deceptively simple reorientation is beginning to have the most profound impact on the ways in which excellent companies do business.

The introduction of a customer-oriented business philosophy across the whole organisation is critical to effective marketing and business success. While many senior executives across different industries have come to accept that, over the last decade, the stumbling block has been how actually to implement it.

Corporate cultures are impossible to change overnight; no one denies that. And this is borne out among the companies that we studied. Even successful organisations like BT admit that there are still some attitudinal barriers to overcome before the marketing philosophy is embraced fully by all its personnel. If the case studies that we have analysed are a reasonable reflection of state-of-the-art practices across the three sectors, industrial companies have the most ground to cover. The signs, though, are very encouraging; leading industrial companies are moving in the right direction – the supertanker is changing its course.

According to the study, there are a number of ways which help organisations achieve an overarching business philosophy centred around the customer. From the evidence in the case studies, it is clear that these mechanisms are being adopted. The first is customer focus through leadership: the cultural change has to be driven from the top. Both in the service and consumer goods companies that we studied, the precedence here is to bring in senior executives from outside the company to drive the cultural change. There is a tendency to recruit senior managers from the FMCG sector, where customer culture has become second nature. Among the companies we spoke to, Allied Dunbar, British Airways and British Telecom have all taken this line.

The second mechanism that leading companies are adopting to become more customer focused is through the introduction of cross-functional mobility to their managers. This is particularly apparent in the service and consumer goods companies that we studied. Leading companies do seem to encourage mobility not just within the company, but also outside it as well. External secondment is becoming an accepted and useful means of encouraging new perspectives. As one British Airways manager pointed out: 'Anyone who comes in brings a new perspective ... I think that it is terribly important that we remain very open to new ideas and experiences'.

Company restructuring is the third mechanism to help to break down inherent cultures and reorientate around a customer focus. Whether the primary catalyst to restructuring has been the need to become market-led, or whether it has been to respond to the business challenges (such as internationalization) that confront industry today, we are left with little doubt that leading companies are in the throes of major reorganisations. There is a firm belief in the companies that we studied that restructuring around customers is necessary, both to become closer to customers and to be able to respond quickly to their needs. Company structures are becoming flatter, as hierarchies are being delayered, and responsibilities are being devolved.

In many of the companies that we spoke to, there is a move underfoot to restructure around markets. Currently, the standard practice is still to be organised around products and product categories. In industries where customer power has grown the quickest and become highly concentrated, leading companies are regrouping around key accounts and market segments, creating customer focus teams and equipping them with the necessary responsibility and authority. One company we studied, AT&T Global Information Solutions, has created 23 customer focus teams in the UK, as part of its restructuring, and has reduced the layers in its hierarchy to just three. This new organisation structure is being adopted worldwide, with the aim of creating a culture of market awareness. The company is striving to reach a point where there are no more than two organisational levels between the customer and the service solution. They are supported by centralised, functional, specialist departments. In other companies that we studied, cross-functional teams are being introduced to take on special projects. There is every sign, in these cases, that they are having great impact and will assume a more permanent and mainstream role in the future.

In the companies we studied which have adopted a marketing orientation, invariably marketing escapes from the traditional marketing department. This is being reflected in its size. The lead taken by good marketing companies to smaller functional marketing departments looks set to be followed by others. Crucially, however, its influence is growing, not diminishing, as companies recognise the pivotal role it plays in two-way communication with customers and in delivering customer satisfaction against their needs. The future role of centralised marketing departments is seen increasingly as being split between the policeman of corporate identity and the ombudsman of the customer.

Accompanying restructuring, a strong feature of the good marketing companies we studied is the heavy influence that the customer-facing divisions are having on strategy formulation. Unquestionably, the ways in which strategy is being developed are becoming more customer-sensitive and dynamic. Strong direction is being provided from the top, but this tends to be in outline form. Strategic detail, as well as tactics, are being developed lower down, or, at least, away from central HQ.

Besides restructuring, the largest, single initiative in strategic marketing today is the current emphasis being given to building relationships with customers and even customers' customers. This is apparent in all of the case studies that we made and is reflected in an obvious way by the restructuring that is underway.

In order to achieve marketing excellence at an operational level, there are three distinct trends that are emerging among the leading companies, irrespective of their industry sector. The first is the renewed emphasis that is being placed on the collection, analysis and use of marketing information. In particular, the companies that we studied are giving more emphasis on catching information which provides a better depth of understanding about their customers and their motivations to buy. Some leading companies believe that there is now too much emphasis being shown towards competitor analysis and benchmarking. By focusing on the competition, you can easily lose sight of the customer.

The quest for more, and better, market information is being met as new sources of information provision open up. Now, more than ever before, there are new third-party, industry-specific providers coming on-stream as a result of the growing amount of data that is being captured by IT systems. Suppliers are finding, also, more willingness on the part of their buyers to share more sales information with them, as relationships between buyers and suppliers strengthen.

The second trend that is developing at the operational end of marketing, is the growing use and importance being given to performance measurement and monitoring. This is, beyond doubt, a feature associated with leading companies. The number and scope of performance measures are growing, as companies establish and fine-tune the measures they need to take in order to deliver customer satisfaction end-to-end. The measures are not restricted to assessing external customer satisfaction levels, but, increasingly, are becoming more sophisticated to cover the whole value chain, including internal customers. In the industrial sector, there is, generally, more reliance on the vendor analysis and league tables provided by their customers, than on self-derived measures.

With the advent of performance measuring have come steps to relate performance to pay, right the way down the chain. One of the companies we studied now dispenses 25 per cent of its total bonus pay on the basis of customer satisfaction levels. This acts to reinforce the importance attached to customer satisfaction across the whole organisation.

The third and final trend that is helping leading companies to achieve marketing excellence is the investment made in the training and development of staff. All of the companies we studied invest heavily in ongoing training programmes to ensure that they possess leading edge skills and knowledge to defend their positions of competitive advantage.

The Evolution of Marketing – a Summary

The simple conclusion we reach is that marketing is still evolving and that it is, currently, in a growth cycle rather than in decline, as some commentators have suggested. The current criticism that marketing is attracting relates, we suggest, more to the poor functional marketing capabilities of many businesses, than to the failure of the philosophy or its uptake. The evidence from the companies that we have studied is that marketing is increasing in influence. Companies are moving away from applying marketing in a relatively tactical way. Marketing in leading companies is now truly becoming adopted as a philosophy for everyone in the organisation. The leading companies of the 1990s are likely to demonstrate the following characteristics. They will be market-led, responsive and flexible, organised around core processes that reflect the customers' preference, and with a high multi-skill base.

One consequence of this trend is that formal, traditional marketing departments are likely to shrink in size, as marketing escapes from the marketing department and permeates the whole organization. This is already happening in some of the companies that we have studied. In terms of the marketing lifecycle, we find that marketing is somewhere between childhood and adolescence.

The Growing Importance of Marketing

The prizes for those companies that successfully adopt a truly customer-facing orientation and are able to anticipate and meet the needs of their customers are likely to be immense. From our research, we are conscious that internationalization is the key change in the business environment that offers a major opportunity as well as a major threat. Leaders have the potential to become very large and will make the leap to global operating. AT&T Global Information Solutions and Rentokil, for example, have already made the leap.

Internationalisation of markets implies that national markets are becoming merely niches of global markets. In our view, companies that are not able to make the leap to global status will find themselves increasingly on the sidelines and targets for acquisition by the global giants. This picture of a few winners, and the potential to find oneself sidelined, explains why internationalisation is so important to the companies we studied. The trend itself is irreversible; companies say that it is often their customers who are leading the way to international markets. When they become global players themselves, they expect their suppliers to be able to supply them on a global basis. We anticipate an increased polarity between four types of market-positioning strategies. Their relative positions in terms of the key dimensions of differentiation and cost-effectiveness are shown in Figure 1.3.

The Emergent Marketing Orientation

Finally, our research suggests that there are certain key aspects to achieving a true marketing orientation. Some of these, such as leadership, reorganisation and the move to process thinking, have already been mentioned.

The keys to managing the change process to make an organization truly marketing and customer-orientated seem to be leadership, flexibility and empowerment.

Leadership refers to the change driver in the organization and its visible commitment to the new philosophy, which must be at the very highest levels of the organization.

Flexibility means being prepared to accept change, not just as a one-off, but constantly. Given that the needs and wants of customers and consumers are

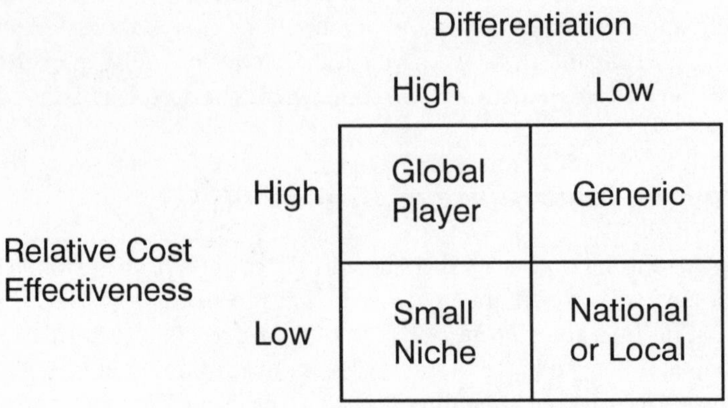

| | | Differentiation | |
		High	Low
Relative Cost Effectiveness	High	Global Player	Generic
	Low	Small Niche	National or Local

Figure 1.3 Four market positioning strategies in global markets

constantly changing, truly marketing-led organisations cannot expect to change once and then to stay still. Flexibility must be built into the organisation by methods such as cross-functional working, so that customer wants can be anticipated.

Empowerment has two meanings for the market-led company, one internal and one external. Internally, it means encouraging the customer-facing teams to feed information back to the organisation, particularly for the purpose of strategy development. Externally, it means allowing the customer-facing teams latitude to implement the strategy in the way that they believe will truly delight the customer. In order to do this, they will need not just to be empowered, but also to be equipped with the necessary marketing skills.

In essence, the emergent marketing orientation combines company-wide embracement of the marketing philosophy with the necessary functional skills to deliver the needs of customers.

Figure 1.4 shows a matrix of marketing philosophy, on which is plotted, in diagrammatic form, the relationship between the adoption of marketing as a philosophy with the levels of marketing skills within the organisation. Box 4 represents all that is worst in industry – ie, a low marketing skills base and weak customer orientation.

Box 3 represents organisations that have recruited managers with excellent marketing skills, but which do not have an overarching marketing philosophy. In these organisations, marketing is likely to be tactical rather than strategic. In box 2 we find organisations that have recognized the need to be market-led, but which do not yet have the marketing skills fully to achieve this.

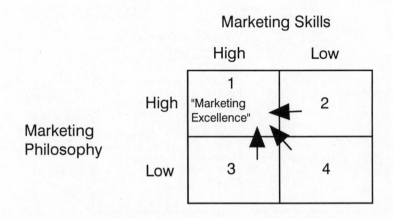

Figure 1.4 The new marketing orientation

It is organisations in boxes 2, 3 and 4 that have led to the criticisms levelled against marketing in the past. In contrast, the excellent companies in our study were either in box 1, or moving rapidly towards it. For organisations in box 1, marketing has a major contribution to make to business success in the 1990s.

In conclusion, it is clear that marketing, both as a philosophy and as a function, is still in its infancy. In part, difficulties in implementing 'marketing' in British industry have stifled its growth. However, this chapter highlights the steps that leading companies are now taking in order to implement marketing practice and the success they are achieving. It provides a route plan for others to follow. In excellent companies, marketing is now rapidly evolving into manhood and will clearly be a major driving force in the late 1990s, for those companies that embrace it in the manner shown in Figures 1.5 and 1.6.

For further details of the full, 120 page report, please contact the Chartered Institute of Marketing, Moor Hall, Cookham, Berkshire SL6 6QH. The report is entitled *Marketing – The Challenge of Change*.

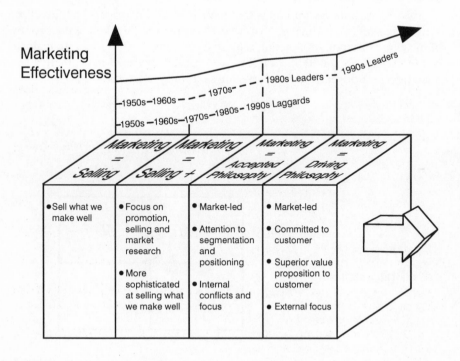

Figure 1.5 The evolution of marketing in industrial and service companies

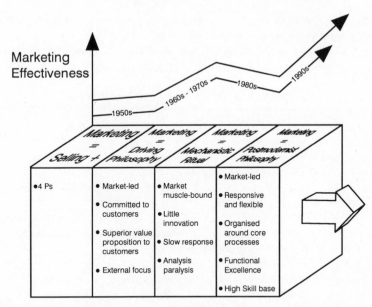

Figure 1.6 The evolution of marketing in fast-moving consumer goods companies

References

Avlonitis, GJ, Kouremenos, A and Gounaris, SP (1992) 'Company performance: does marketing orientation matter?', *European Marketing Academy Conference Proceedings*, Aarhus, pp 83–94.

Baker, MJ, Hart, SJ, Black, CD and Abdel-Mohsen, T (1986) 'The contribution of marketing to competitive success; a literature review', *Journal of Marketing Management*, Vol 2, No 1, pp 39–61.

Barksdale, HC and Darden, B (1971) 'Marketers' attitudes towards the marketing concept', *Journal of Marketing*, Vol 35, No 4, pp 29–36.

Brady, J and Davis, I (1993) 'Marketing in transition: marketing's mid-life crisis', *The McKinsey Quarterly*, No 2, pp 17–28.

Doyle, P (1987) 'Marketing and the British chief executive', *Journal of Marketing Management*, Vol 3, No 2, pp 121–32.

Doyle, P (1992) 'What are excellent companies?', *Journal of Marketing Management*, Vol 8, No 2, pp 101–16.

Doyle, P, Saunders, J and Wright, L (1988) 'A comparative investigation of US and Japanese marketing strategies in the British market', *International Journal of Research and Marketing*, Vol 5, No 3, pp 171–84.

Garda, RA (1988) 'Comment by RA Garda on the AMA Task Force study', *Journal of Marketing*, Vol 52, No 4, October, pp 32–41.

Griffin, T (1982) 'Linking the use of modern marketing methods to company success', *Columbia Journal of World Business*, Vol 17, No 3, Autumn, pp 52–61.

Hammer, M (1990) 'Re-engineering work: don't automate, obliterate', *Harvard Business Review*, July–August, pp 104–12.

Hansen, F, Gronhaug, K and Warneryd, K (eds) (1990) 'Excellent marketing, the concept, its measurement and implications', *Marketing & Research Today*, Vol 18, No 2, pp 98–106.

Hise, RT (1965) 'Have manufacturing firms adopted the marketing concept?', *Journal of Marketing*, July, pp 9–12.

Hooley, GJ, West, CJ and Lynch, JE (1984) *Marketing in the UK: A Survey of Current Practice and Performance*, Institute of Marketing.

Jaworski, BJ and Kohli, AK (1993) 'Market orientation: antecedents and consequences', *Journal of Marketing*, Vol 57, July, pp 53–70.

Lazer, W (1993) 'Changing dimensions of marketing management – the new realities', *Journal of International Marketing*, Vol 1, No 3, pp 93–103.

Liu, H, and Wensley, R (1991) 'Markets, marketing and marketing behaviour – an empirical examination in Britain and China', *European Marketing Academy Conference Proceedings*, University College Dublin, pp 844–63.

Liu, H, Wensley, R and Whittington, R (1991) 'Market effect, control effect, and market orientation', *Marketing Education Group Proceedings*, Cardiff Business School, pp 626–35.

Lusch, RL, Udell, JG and Laczniak, GR (1976) 'The future of marketing strategy', *Business Horizons*, Vol 19, No 6, December, pp 65–74.

Lynch, JG, Hooley, GJ and Shepherd, J (1990) 'The marketing concept: putting the theory into practice', *European Journal of Marketing*, Vol 24, No 9, pp 7–23.

McDaniel, SW and Hise, RT (1983) 'Have CEOs adopted the marketing concept?', in Varadarajan, P (ed) *The Marketing Concept: Perspectives and Viewpoints*, Texas A & M University, Texas.

McGee, LW and Spiro, RL (1988) 'The marketing concept in perspective', *Business Horizons*, Vol 31, No 3, May–June, pp 40–5.

McKenna, R (1991) 'Marketing is everything', *Harvard Business Review*, Vol 69, No 1, January–February, pp 65–79.

McNamara, CP (1972). 'The present status of the marketing concept', *Journal of Marketing*, Vol 36, No 1, pp 50–7.

Mueller-Heumann, G (1993) 'CEOs perceptions of marketing', *Marketing Education Group Proceedings*, Loughborough University Business School, pp 702–11.

Narver, JC and Slater, SF (1990) 'The effect of a market orientation on business profitability', *Journal of Marketing*, Vol 54, No 4, October, pp 20–35.

Norbet, D, Birley, S and Dunn, M (1988) 'Strategic marketing effectiveness and its relationship to corporate culture and beliefs: A cross-nation study', *International Studies of Management & Organization*, Vol 18, No 2, pp 83–100.

Pallister, J, Jones, W and Higgins, L (1993) 'Marketing's role in business process redesign', *MEG Proceedings*, Loughborough University Business School, pp 765–74.

Piercy, N (1985) 'The corporate environment for marketing management', *Marketing Intelligence and Planning*, Vol 3, No 1, pp 23–40.

Schon, DA (1983) 'The reflective practitioner – how professionals think in action', Basic Books, New York, NY.

Shaw, V and Doyle, P, (1991) 'Marketing strategies and organizational characteristics of British and German companies – preliminary findings of a study of the machine tool industry', *Marketing Education Group Proceedings*, Cardiff Business School, pp 1011–30.

Varadarajan, P (1983) (ed) *The Marketing Concept. Perspectives and Viewpoints.* Proceedings of Workshop, Texas A & M University, Texas.

Whittington, R and Whipp, R (1992) 'Professional ideology and marketing implementation', *European Journal of Marketing*, Vol 26, No 1, pp 52–63.

Wink, N (1992) 'Historical perspective in marketing management explicating experience', *Journal of Marketing Management*, Vol 8, No 3, pp 219–37.

Wong, V, Saunders, J and Doyle, P (1989) 'The barriers to achieving stronger marketing orientation in British companies: an exploratory study', *Marketing Education Group Proceedings*, Glasgow Business School, pp 34–64.

Appendix list of respondents

Academics

Professor Patrick Barwise	London Business School
Professor Martin Christopher	Cranfield School of Management
Dr Gordon Greenley	University of Birmingham
Professor Graham Hooley	Aston University
Professor Gerry Johnson	Cranfield School of Management
Dr Simon Knox	Cranfield School of Management
Visiting Professor Simon Majaro	Cranfield School of Management
Professor Malcolm McDonald	Cranfield School of Management
Professor Stephen Parkinson	University of Bradford
Professor Adrian Payne	Cranfield School of Management
Professor Nigel Piercy	Cardiff Business School
Professor John Saunders	Loughborough University Business School
Professor Peter Turnbull	UMIST
Professor Robin Wensley	Warwick Business School

Consultants

Tom Brannan	Primary Contact
John Brady	McKinsey & Co
Mike Wilson	Marketing Improvements

'Marketing excellent' companies

- *Service sector*
  Allied Dunbar
  British Airways
  British Telecom
  Rentokil
  Standard Life

- *Consumer manufacturing*
  Black & Decker
  Boots Healthcare International
  Johnson & Johnson
  Land Rover
  SmithKline Beecham
  Sony (UK)

- *Industrial manufacturing and distribution*
  AT&T Global Information Solutions
  Electrospeed
  Renishaw
  Rolls-Royce Aero Engines

2

STRATEGIC MARKETING PLANNING: THEORY, PRACTICE AND RESEARCH AGENDAS*

Malcolm McDonald

OVERVIEW

This chapter reviews the development of strategic marketing planning from the early 1960s to 1995. While it focuses on the scientific planning model, which dominates research and teaching during this period, it also briefly reviews other planning models.

In evaluating the legitimacy of the universal belief in the efficacy of marketing planning, a number of contradictions are apparent, which surface in studies of marketing planning failures. The reasons for these failures, however, are not linked to any general 'theory', but seem to cluster around the cultural and cognitive dimensions of planning. These dimensions are explored in detail and an agenda for future research is suggested.

*This paper was first published in the *Journal of Marketing Management*, 12, 1996, pp5–27 and is reproduced with the kind permission of The Dryden Press.

MODES OF STRATEGIC DECISION-MAKING

As some organisations incorporate plans for their markets into their corporate plans (McDonald, 1982), it is impossible to address the topic of strategic marketing planning without reference to the substantial body of literature on strategic planning, which is, once again, high on the academic agenda following a flurry of publications from Mintzberg (1994). In particular, his book, *The Rise and Fall of Strategic Planning*, sets out to attack the very basis of strategic planning, but offers no concrete advice on how to create some sort of order out of the organisational chaos of trying to run a global, multicultural, multidivisional, multiproduct, multimarket, multinational, multifunctional operation – ie, the milieu which strategic planning seeks to address.

In repost, Ansoff (1994), among others from the academic community, accuses Mintzberg of having his understanding of strategic planning frozen in the 1960s and of conveniently ignoring the fact that strategic planning did not die, it was simply transmitted into several different forms to take account of the changing environmental challenges of the past three decades.

The key point, made by Ansoff, however, that guides the debate forward as the starting point for this chapter, is his restatement that the different environmental challenges of the 1990s require different strategic responses and, as a consequence, different planning approaches. Even in that subset of strategic planning that concerns the product/market dimensions, this has always been true.

Strategic decisions are concerned with:

- The long-term direction of the organisation, as opposed to day-to-day management issues.
- Defining the scope of the organisation's activities in terms of what it will and will not do.
- Matching the activities of the organisation to the environment in which it operates, so that it optimises opportunities and minimises threats.
- Matching the organisation's activities to its resource capacity, be it finance, manpower, technology or skill levels.

Strategic management is characteristically dealing with an uncertain future and new initiatives. As a result of this, it is often the harbinger of change. Organisations build their business strategies in a number of different ways. There are six accepted strategy-forming models (Bailey and Johnson, 1994).

A *Planning Model*

Strategic decisions are reached by use of a sequential, planned search for optimum solutions to defined problems. This process is highly rational and is fuelled by concrete data.

An Interpretative Model

The organisation is regarded as a collection of associations, sharing similar values, beliefs and perceptions. These 'frames of reference' enable the stakeholders to interpret the organisation and the environment in which it operates, cultivating the emergence of an organisational culture particular to that company. Strategy thus becomes the product, not of defined aims and objectives, but of the prevailing values, attitudes and ideas in the organisation.

A Political Model

Strategy is not chosen directly, but emerges through compromise, conflict and consensus seeking among interested stakeholders. Since the strategy is the outcome of negotiation, bargaining and confrontation, those with the most power have the greatest influence.

A Logical Incremental Model

Strategies emerge from 'strategic subsystems', each concerned with a different type of strategic issue. Strategic goals are based on an awareness of needs, rather than the highly structured analytical process of the planning model. Often, owing to a lack of necessary information, such goals can be vague, general and non-rigid in nature until such a time when events unfold and more information becomes known.

An Ecological Model

In this perspective, the environment impinges on the organisation in such a way that strategies are virtually prescribed and there is little or no free choice. In this model, the organisation which adapts most successfully to its environment will survive in a way which mirrors Darwin's natural selection.

A Visionary Leadership Model

Strategy emerges as the result of the leader's vision, enforced by his/her commitment to it, his/her personal credibility, and how he/she articulates it to others.

It is unlikely that an organisation will use a pure vision of any of these models. In all probability, its strategic decision-making model will be a hybrid of some of them. However, it is possible that one or two of these will predominate and thereby give strategic decision-making a distinct 'flavour'.

While these various models help to explain the different flavours of strategic decision-making, at first sight they appear to have little in common. Closer

examination shows that this is not the case. All of them see the organisation and the environment as inseparable, even though the point at which the balance is struck varies from model to model. For instance, in the ecological model, the environment looms large, whereas in the incremental model, the organisation appears to receive most consideration.

Another common theme is that strategies are perceived as necessary to help the organisation to cope with changes in the environment. Again, the various models infer and accept different degrees of uncertainty in the environment. Thus, the ensuing strategies exhibit different degrees of flexibility. For example, the planning model assumes that the environment is more or less stable over the strategic time frame, or that any changes can be anticipated with some certainty. In contrast with this, the logical incremental model tests the environment continually and is prepared to revise strategies if they are seen to be unsuitable.

While academics cannot seem to agree on a single, best approach, company executives have to get on with strategy formulation as best they can, using a combination of experience, intuition and hope. One of the earliest PhDs in the domain of marketing planning (McDonald, 1982) came to the conclusion that the process they go through is some sort of a logical sequence leading to the setting of objectives and the formulation of strategies and tactics for achieving them, together with the associated financial consequences. The formality of this process will be a function of the degree of product/market complexity, organisational size and the degree of environmental turbulence. In other words, the degree of formality will be driven in part by the dominant decision-making model in the organisation.

Strategic marketing planning obviously cannot be discussed in isolation from the above strategic planning modes, and it is likely that the way in which an organisation's marketing planning is carried out will be a microcosm of the principal mode of the total process.

The next section of the chapter will briefly review the history of marketing planning in the context of strategic decision-making.

THE EVOLUTION OF MARKETING PLANNING

The theories and principles of marketing which have evolved over the past four decades do not include much work of substance in the domain of marketing planning.

Wilson's (1965) intensive examination of marketing literature failed to produce any detailed study of the process of marketing planning. He found that there was no accessible body of knowledge on this topic on which writers could build. His conclusion was endorsed by Winkler (1972), who wrote:

> Strange as it may seem, there are not many books about marketing planning specifically; most books on marketing include only a chapter or so about the planning function, but since planning is the name of the marketing game, that hardly seems to do it justice.

While research into the domain improved in the early 1980s, it will be shown that there remains much work to be done. Very little has been written specifically about the background and history of marketing planning. To address this, we need to take a broader perspective in our literature review and look at the origins and basis for planning in business management.

The principal landmark in the history of the generic nature of planning as a formal business activity is seen to be the Second World War and the military influences that resulted.

Since the early 1960s, planning has consistently been seen by academic commentators to be of increasing relevance as a means of coping with the growing turbulence of the business environment and the increasing complexity of the marketing task in all kinds of enterprises. It was writers such as Ansoff (1965) and the corporate planning books of the 1970s, that guided thinking in the area, which expressed the dominant view that strategies are developed through a logical and analytical process.

Ansoff (1977) and Ringbakk (1971) postulated that planning systems evolved from the static systems embodied in organisational structures during the 1950s and 1960s. Gradually developing out of organisational structures during the same period were dynamic systems concerned with information and decision-making flows, in response to an environment which was gradually ceasing to be only mildly competitive and unstable. Examples of dynamic systems are financial control, budgeting, management by objectives and project planning.

One such system which emerged was long-range planning, the first 'total system' geared to preparing an organisation for its future. Its weakness was that it was extrapolative, assuming smooth projections of demand, prices, economic climate, and so on.

Strategic planning, with its systematic analysis of alternative possible futures, developed out of this, but eventually the growing need for a tighter fit between long-range strategic planning and action plans led to the development of planning, programming, and budgeting systems, which were centred around product/market missions as opposed to organisational convenience. This in turn led to the development of the 'strategic business unit' and eventually into strategic portfolio management and the planning systems of today.

Typically, however, there would be systematic consideration given to the broad environment in which the firm operates and to the way in which it relates to its own internal strengths and weaknesses. A forecast of discontinuities in the environment may well thus result in a shift of emphasis in the objectives of the firm.

The early systems lacked most of this, usually resulting in only budgets, forecasts and goals, which tended to be extrapolations of the past.

From this brief review of the evolution of planning systems, it can be concluded that organisational issues are intricately involved with planning system effectiveness, and that planning systems evolved gradually and grew in sophistication in response to pressures brought to bear on the firm by environmental conditions. But, while the most intricate and advanced systems appear to have been developed by firms operating in a complex and increasingly hostile environment, there is much evidence to show that there is almost universal belief among academics in the efficacy of formalised marketing planning in any circumstances.

UNIVERSAL BELIEF IN THE NEED FOR MARKETING PLANNING

The literature is replete with papers and books universally commending marketing planning as a process. A substantial body of what literature there is on marketing planning deals in an assertive way with the need for marketing planning. Up to about 1980, little empirical evidence was provided to substantiate these views. Writers such as Davidson (1972), Dodge (1970), Winkler (*op cit*) and Tilles (1969) are fairly representative of writers who exalted marketing planning as a panacea for commercial problems, with little evidence for their views.

Those who wrote about marketing planning internationally, such as Pryor (1965), Scholhammer (1971) and Yoshino (1965), followed the same line of argument, except that they believed it was even more vital when operating in international markets.

Another substantial part of the literature, represented by writers such as Miracle and Albaum (1970), Cateora and Hess (1971), and Fisher (1970), made reference to the problems which would result inevitably from a lack of marketing planning.

While such views were intellectually appealing at the time, it must be seriously questioned with hindsight whether the facts actually justified them. There were many examples of 'successful' international companies that did not 'systematically plan' their overseas operations.

There were, however, some attempts in the literature – eg, Thompson (1962) and Kollatt *et al* (1972) – to justify their views empirically. Thompson, for example, carried out a three-year study on the planning practices of 20 large American companies. The overwhelming view which emerged from this study was that those companies which prepared plans for known needs, probable developments and even uncertain eventualities, fared better than those which let themselves get caught unawares by changes in markets, products and methods.

Notwithstanding the paucity of empirical evidence, however, the over-whelming body of literature asserts that marketing planning is 'a good thing'. Indeed, a number of benefits are promised to those who invest in this process. Thompson's conclusion (1962) was that marketing planners 'will always out-perform those who do not plan'. Pearson (1973), Boyd and Massey (1972) and Terpstra (1972) confirmed the following as being the principal benefits result-ing from marketing planning: the better co-ordination of many individuals whose actions are inter-related over time; an increased likelihood of identify-ing expected developments; greater preparedness to meet change; a minimali-sation of non-rational responses to the unexpected; better communications among executives; a reduction in conflicts between individuals; systematic thinking ahead; more effective allocation of corporate resources against mar-ket opportunities; and the provision of a framework for a continuing review of operations.

There is also some evidence of a relationship between marketing planning and financial success.

A study of Leighton (1966) of the 400 leading US corporations showed a high correlation between those companies that showed the highest growth rate and those that used systematic planning procedures. The emphasis in suc-cessful companies was found to be on written plans and systematic procedures for their preparation, implementation and review.

Ansoff *et al* (1970), and Thune and House (1970) used standard financial measures such as debt/equity to determine the performance benefits of mar-keting planning. They found there was 'conclusive and significant' evidence that planners outperform non-planners:

> In this study, companies that engage in formal long range planning, when consid-ered as a group, have historically outperformed a comparable group of non-plan-ners. (Thune and House, 1970)

Schoeffler (1974), writing about the influential PIMS study of the Marketing Science Institute, also concluded that a systematic planned approach to strate-gy formulation leads to a higher return on investment.

A seminal paper by Denison and McDonald (1995) on the role of marketing past, present and future, based on research into marketing in excellence con-ducted for the Chartered Institute of Marketing, showed that, for excellent companies, marketing exists at three levels – the corporate level, the strategic or SBU level, and the functional/operating level. This results in three difference dimensions: marketing as a culture (values and benefits), as strategy (segmen-tation, positioning, branding, information, etc) and as tactics (the four Ps). The excellent companies in the sample all had marketing planning systems which coped appropriately with each of these levels, and, notwithstanding the differ-ent organisational forms adopted by the respondent companies, there was nothing whatsoever to indicate that the process of marketing planning as described in the literature was in any way incorrect. Also, the distinction between strategic business planning and strategic marketing planning disappears, as strategic business planning is simply the strategic marketing plan taken to its logical conclusion, representing the major input to total customer satisfaction by all functions and processes. The tactical marketing plan is simply the scheduling and costing out of the first year's actions at the operational level.

The definitions, concepts and practicalities of strategic and tactical marketing planning and their relationship to strategic planning are dealt with comprehensively by writers such as Abell and Hamond (1979), Day (1984), McDonald (1982), Brownlie (1985), and Greenley (1986), and there is wide agreement about the process and contents of strategic marketing plans.

Denison and McDonald's paper (1995) confirms that, in general, much of the theory of strategic marketing planning can be substantiated by studying excellent companies.

The major criticisms of most of these studies, however, is that there was an inherent assumption that there is a causal relationship between commercial success and formalised marketing planning. There was no exploration of, or attempt to explain, the reasons for the commercial success of those companies that did not engage in formal marketing planning. Nor was there any exploration of the circumstances of those commercially unsuccessful companies that also had formalised marketing planning systems, and it must be concluded that such studies left a number of vital questions unanswered.

Nevertheless, it would be foolish, in the face of the evidence, not to assume that there appears to be some kind of relationship between formalised marketing planning and commercial success in certain circumstances. It would be equally foolish, however, to use such evidence to prove that commercial success will automatically accrue to companies that adopt formalised marketing planning procedures. Indeed, a study by Martin (1979) showed that of 100 *Times* top 1000 companies, all claimed to be planning, but only 10 per cent engaged in 'comprehensive planning', according to Martin's definition. The remaining 90 per cent engaged only in various forms of forecasting and budgeting. Studies by Hopkins (1981), Greenley (1982), Cosse and Swan (1983), Hooley *et al* (1984), McDonald (1982), and Leppard (1987), showed that most companies do not follow the prescription for planning. They also showed that, although 70 per cent of companies produce marketing plans, only 10–14 per cent are adequate when judged even in the most lenient terms against established theory.

Surely, therefore, given the apparent gap between theory and practice, academics have, in general, been guilty of a gross over-simplification of a subject which has an infinite number of contextual ramifications.

To summarise, this brief review of the literature on marketing planning points to the view that companies with complete marketing planning systems will be more successful than those without, in environmental and competitive circumstances which are directly comparable. However, given the apparent gap between theory and practice, some obvious contradictions are apparent and it is clear that there are many barriers to the implementation of effective marketing planning.

BARRIERS TO EFFECTIVE MARKETING PLANNING

Notwithstanding the importance of marketing planning and its universal acceptance by scholars as being central to the profit-making process, little research has been carried out to find out why it appears to be poorly understood and badly executed by a large number of companies on both sides of the Atlantic.

A review of the early literature on marketing planning failures (Liander, 1967; Ames, 1978; Saddick, 1968; Ringbakk, 1971; Camillus, 1975; Weichmann and Pringle, 1979) reveals that recent studies are coming to conclusions similar to those carried out 25 years ago. Also, what research has been carried out describes planning difficulties quite well, but generally fails to link these difficulties back to any general 'theory'. These findings are summarised in Table 2.1.

There seems to be wide agreement in the literature that the two biggest barriers are:

1. Cultural/political, lack of a belief in marketing planning and/or the need to change.
2. Cognitive, lack of knowledge and skills.

More recently, much attention has been paid to these two factors as key determinants of strategic marketing planning success. The following sections will address each of these in turn.

THE CULTURAL DIMENSION

McDonald (1982) identified several factors which had a strong influence on a company's ability to introduce and develop a complete marketing planning process. These are discussed under the heading of culture.

Many writers have observed that as a company grows and learns to cope with new problems associated with its increased size and success, it also changes in character.

Lievegoed (1973) identifies three quite distinct phases of organisational life which he terms: pioneer, differentiated (or scientific), and integrated. Greiner (1972) has similar views, but suggests that there are a number of evolutionary growth periods in a company's life, each followed by a revolutionary crisis phase which signifies that the period of natural growth is over. These are illustrated in Figure 2.1.

Table 2.1 Marketing planning barriers

	Research studies										
Barriers	1	2	3	4	5	6	7	8	9	10	11
Roles people play											
B1 Lack of chief executive/senior management involvement	*	*	*	*	_	_	*	*	*	_	_
B2 Lack of cross-functional involvement	*	*	*	*	_	_	*	*	*	*	_
B3 Lack of top management support	*	*	_	_	_	_	*	*	*	_	_
Cognitive											
B4 Knowledge and skills	*	_	_	_	_	*	*	_	_	_	_
B5 Lack of innovation/non-recognition of alternatives	_	*	*	_	_	_	*	_	_	*	_
Systems and procedures											
B6 Lack of care in marketing planning introduction	*	_	_	_	*	_	_	_	_	*	_
B7 Forecasts without documentation of intervention	*	_	*	_	_	_	*	_	_	_	_
B8 Inflexible application of textbook process	*	_	*	_	_	*	_	_	_	*	_
B9 Lack of follow-through to tactics	*	_	*	_	_	_	_	_	_	_	_
B10 Too much detail	*	_	*	_	_	_	*	_	*	_	_
Resources											
B11 Lack of time (elapsed and/or effort)	*	*	_	_	_	_	_	_	*	*	_
B12 Lack of money (for market research etc)	*	_	_	_	_	_	_	_	_	*	_
Organisational environment/culture											
B13 Organisational structure inappropriate	*	_	*	_	_	*	*	*	_	_	_
B14 Stage of organisational development	_	_	_	_	*	_	_	_	_	_	_
B15 Corporate politics	_	*	*	_	_	_	*	*	_	_	_
B16 Short-term oriented reward systems	*	_	_	_	_	_	_	_	_	_	_
B17 Culture stifling idea generation/openness	_	_	*	*	*	_	_	_	_	*	_
Data											
B18 Lack of information	*	*	*	*	_	*	_	_	*	_	_
Environmental											
B19 Difficulty of forecasting in times of turbulence and inflation	_	*	_	_	_	_	_	_	_	_	_

Key to studies: 1. McDonald (1982); 2. Hopkins (1981); 3. Ames (1968); 4. Stasch and Lanktree (1980); 5. Leppard (1987); 6. Hooley *et al* (1984); 7. Liander (1967); 8. Saddick (1966); 9. Ringbakk (1971); 10. Camillus (1975); 11. Weichmann and Pringle (1979).
* The study explicitly claims to have derived the barrier from empirical data with a clearly described and plausible research method.

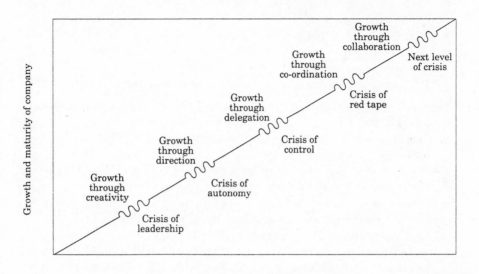

Figure 2.1 Organisational cultures over time

Normann (1977) and Bhattachary (1981) view company size in a different way and see growth as being a reflection of the stage of development along a life-cycle curve. For Normann, the subject for the life cycle is the business idea itself and clearly this is capable of being modified and adapted in the light of experience. Bhattachary, on the other hand, claims that the company overall has a life cycle and has the capability of passing through a period of early struggle, to one of motivation, to one of complacency and ultimately decline. In his terms, organisational renewal is not an easy option.

A number of works were studied and the following overall conclusions can be drawn:

- A company's history has a significant impact on its culture and because of this influences many of the decisions which are made.
- A company's learning is inextricably tied up with its history, as a result of things that have worked, or problems that have been overcome, in the past.
- Senior executives are the 'culture carriers' and as such can either reinforce or work to change the existing culture.
- Organisational myths and heroes sustain the culture and with it the existing political power structure.
- A shared values system can be a source of strength and commitment to the company.

- The more explicit the values system and organisational vision, the more committed are the staff.
- Culture only has to be 'sensible' to those who operate within the company. It doesn't necessarily have to be rational or congruent with the current business environment.
- The more deeply a culture is embedded, the more difficult it is to change.

Thus, corporate cultures can be anti-developmental since they are backward-looking. Equally, it takes a senior executive with vision and high commitment to overthrow an out-of-date culture and replace it with a new set of more appropriate norms of behaviour.

Schein (1985) claims that there are a number of different ways of intervening in a company in order to bring about a change in corporate culture. By and large, these intervention techniques need to be matched to the company's stage of development and are required to be more and more coercive, the stronger the existing culture is embedded.

Schein's study of culture carriers identified five main observable actions that leaders take, either consciously or subconsciously, which transmit and embed culture. These primary mechanisms are:

- How the leader reacts to crises or critical incidents.
- The criteria they establish for allocating rewards and status.
- The areas to which the leader pays attention, measures and controls.
- The criteria they establish for recruitment, selection, promotion, retirement and dismissing staff.
- The role model the leader promotes either by their own behaviour, or by coaching and teaching others.

Schein also identified a second tier of cultural transmitters, which are:

- Organisational systems and procedures.
- Organisational design and structure.
- Design of physical space, façades and buildings.
- Formal statements about organisational philosophy, creeds and charters.
- Stories, legends, myths and parables about important people and events in the company's life.

From the literature review, it seems that there are two main determinants of corporate culture:

- The culture that has evolved as the company developed and which is related to its maturity or stage of development.
- The 'culture' promoted by the senior executive or an equally powerful culture carrier or group.

It appears that the most potent of these two forces is the former.

As the literature has shown, organisations have their own 'built in' mechanisms for dealing with change. Often the culture carrier is not an agent for development, but merely an upholder of past tradition.

As was pointed out at the start of this chapter, formal planning is only one approach that organisations may select to determine their business strategy. From the literature, it is quite apparent that the adoption of formalised planning will not automatically result in a successful strategy. The business culture must be appropriate.

A complete marketing planning process is not simply a series of action steps. It also embodies a set of values and assumptions which, while not being explicit, are nevertheless an integral part of the whole process. Similarly, an organisation is not just a conglomeration of people and resources. It, too, embodies particular values and assumptions which give rise to its distinctive corporate climate and culture. Moreover, its culture would appear to be influenced to some degree by its level of learning or maturity. If the underlying values of a complete marketing planning process are more or less consistent with those of the organisation, there is a high probability that the planning process would be adopted. If there is a conflict of values between those underlying the marketing planning process and those of the organisation, it could be expected that the planning process would be rejected. An organization will not change its values system or culture unless something very significant take place to make such a change seem worthwhile.

Although the marketing planning process can be represented diagrammatically, as in Figure 2.2, it is not necessarily the straightforward, linear sequential operation the diagram suggests. Clearly, marketing planning has to be tailored to suit the culture of the company, while steering a course between the Scylla of good intentions and the Charybdis of bureaucracy.

However, agreeing a suitable definition of corporate culture is quite difficult. Depending on which researcher's work one studies, culture can be ... 'observable behaviour regularities', 'language', 'a philosophy', 'rules of a game for getting accepted', 'physical layout' or 'ways by which the organisation relates with outsiders', and so on.

A definition by Schein (1983) seems to encapsulate most of the elements of culture:

> A pattern of basic assumptions that a given group has invented or developed in learning to cope with its problems of external adaptation and internal integration, and that have worked well enough to be considered valid, and therefore, to be taught to new members as the correct way to perceive, think and feel in relation to these problems.

This definition underlines the complexity and breadth of the concept of corporate culture. Also, by implication, it suggests that cultures are, by and large,

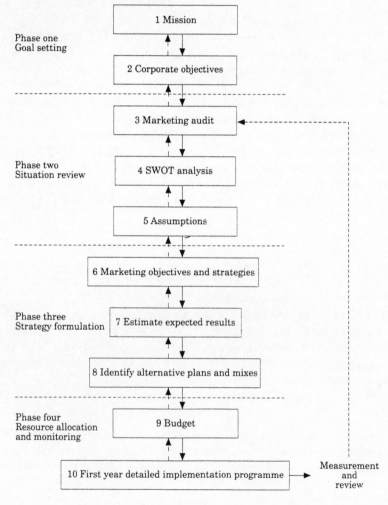

The strategic plan
(output of the planning process)

Mission statement
Financial summary
Market overview
SWOT analyses
Portfolio summary
Assumptions
Marketing objectives and strategies
3-year forecasts and budgets

1 Mission

Phase one
Goal setting

2 Corporate objectives

3 Marketing audit

Phase two
Situation review

4 SWOT analysis

5 Assumptions

6 Marketing objectives and strategies

Phase three
Strategy formulation

7 Estimate expected results

8 Identify alternative plans and mixes

Phase four
Resource allocation
and monitoring

9 Budget

10 First year detailed implementation programme

Measurement
and
review

Figure 2.2 The marketing planning process
Source: McDonald (1995)

backward-looking and conservative, in the sense that they are based on successful coping strategies which worked in the past.

Already an interesting scenario can be developed from these two crucial definitions. Marketing planning is a forward-looking process, whereas corporate culture seems to have its origins in the past. Therefore, it would be useful to analyse each step of the marketing planning process with this apparent contradiction in mind in order to understand the implications.

An example of analysis applied to the first two stages of the planning process is given in Table 2.2.

The total analysis of the marketing planning process enables a number of hypotheses to be made.

Leppard (1987), researching corporate culture and marketing planning, used 34 case studies to test five hypotheses, which were:

1. *A complete marketing planning process is not simply a series of action steps. It also embodies a set of values and assumptions which, while not being explicit, are nevertheless an integral part of the whole process.*

This was shown to be true. Furthermore, there were some strong clues from the analysis of the complete marketing planning process that companies best equipped to make the process work would be:

> largely run on democratic principles, not be too hierarchical, be flexible rather than bureaucratic, use motivational mechanisms which promote openness and commitment to the organisation, have a collaborative climate which favours team-work, be interested in finding quality solutions when faced with problems, and have a genuine concern for providing customer satisfactions.

Clearly, such companies are relatively sophisticated and mature, when compared with a typical cross-section of their contemporaries. It also follows that by analysing the assumptions behind any company's marketing planning process, it ought to be possible to get closer to understanding its underlying beliefs and values.

2. *An organisation is not simply a conglomeration of people and resources. It embodies a set of values and assumptions which give rise to its distinctive corporate climate and culture. Moreover its culture would appear to be influenced to some degree by its level of learning or maturity.*

Again, this hypothesis was shown to be true. Organisations, no matter how they are structured, never become inanimate machines. The people involved, their experience of the company's history, their own beliefs and values, all contribute to organisational life.

Leppard's research showed that as an organisation learns and moves along its biographical lifeline, different issues can exercise it at different life phases. In overcoming these issues, it in turn becomes more 'mature'.

Table 2.2 Example of an analysis of the marketing planning process

Process step	Knowledge	Skill	Underlying assumptions
1. Set corporate objectives	Knowledge about: a) corporate planning b) setting objectives	Ability to: a) produce a corporate plan b) set corporate objectives	a) The organisation possesses the required knowledge and skills b) It sees a need for a corporate plan c) The corporate plan is used to 'direct' sub-objectives d) The corporate plan specifies corporate objectives in five areas: marketing, production, finance, distribution, personnel e) The corporate plan is authoritative enough to be believed f) There are adequate resources allocated to planning
2. Conduct marketing audit	Knowledge about: a) marketing systems b) audit theory c) sources of information d) product life cycle analysis e) various analytical 'tools' e.g. customer segmentation benefit analysis, gap analysis, Boston Consulting Group Matrix, etc.	The ability to: a) critically appraise all steps of the marketing system b) separate fact from opinion c) use analytical tools in a workmanlike manner	a) That required knowledge and skills exist b) There is a willingness to appraise the marketing operation c) Data exists which makes this possible d) Somebody (or group) has the responsibility to conduct the audit e) Time is made available for the audit to be conducted f) It is a critical process which genuinely strives for improvement rather than for maintaining the *status quo*

Equally, 'culture carriers' can be a power for change or stability, depending upon the values they make explicit by their behaviour (as opposed to those to which they publicly subscribe).

3. *If the underlying values of a complete marketing planning process are*

*more or less consistent with those of the organisation, then there is a high
probability that the planning process will be adopted.*

It was found that the 'mature' company, described under hypothesis 1 above,
had an uncanny resemblance to the integrated organisation described by
Lievegoed (1973) and those at the more advanced stages of development put
forward by Greiner (1972) and many others.

The research conducted confirmed that planners were further along the
development path than other companies. Other factors, such as company size,
nature of business, growth rate, and so on, were checked in case they were
hidden influences. However, within the bounds of this study, the original
results held true.

All this suggested that hypothesis 3 is correct.

4. *If there is a conflict of values between those underlying the complete marketing planning process and those of the organisation, then it could be
expected that the planning process would be rejected.*

From this research, there were found to be a number of barriers to marketing
planning, namely, cognitive, information, resource, behavioural and cultural.
Therefore, a rejection of marketing planning could not be attributed to an
organisation's cultural value system alone.

However, if an organisation made a genuine and determined attempt to
introduce marketing planning, most of the above barriers would not prove to
be insurmountable obstacles. What the organisation would require, however,
would be a level of maturity that doesn't come readily to all companies.

5. *An organisation will not change its values system or culture, unless something very significant takes place to make such a change seem worthwhile.*

All the works about change studied in the literature review confirmed this
hypothesis. Schein (1985) went as far as saying that corporate culture itself is
the rock upon which change founders.

What might be termed significant will vary from organisation to organisation,
but it will probably have to be something which is either unplanned or discon-
tinuous, otherwise incrementalism will strive to neutralise its impact.

Thus, intellectual curiosity on the part of the company would not appear to
be a sufficient stimulus for introducing marketing planning, whereas falling
sales or dwindling market share would be a different story.

Equally, a new culture carrier championing marketing planning might prove
to be the discontinuity to bring about change. However, as we have seen, the
old culture would strive to maintain the *status quo* or to marginalise the
change.

The question of change raises another interesting issue. Can the old culture
carriers stay in command and introduce a new culture? Evidence for this is very

mixed. Perhaps a new organisational broom can sweep cleaner. The political nature of change ensures that there are no easy answers to the dilemma.

As we have seen, marketing planning is not a neatly packaged cognitive process. It is much more than this, and it brings the marketing adviser face to face with the political realities of corporate life.

For their part, chief executives will have to recognise that to introduce marketing planning successfully, many things will have to change within the organisation, not least, the way they behave and the role model they set for others.

The second key determinant of marketing planning success will now be explored.

THE COGNITIVE DIMENSION

Intellectually, it seems reasonable to assume that cognition will be central to marketing planning success, for without this anchor, all other domains would have nothing to hold them in place.

Greenley's (1994) paper outlining research into marketing planning practices in UK and US companies set out to validate a theoretical model proposed by Piercy and Morgan (1990) for investigating marketing planning as a multi-dimensional process.

This process incorporates the following dimensions:

Analytical	– Techniques
	– Procedures
	– Systems
Behavioural	– Managerial perception
	– Participation
	– Motivation
	– Commitment
	– Ownership
Organisational	– Information
	– Structural
	– Culture
	– Managerial signals

While Greenley's results were consistent with earlier research into behavioural and organisational barriers to marketing planning, another conclusion reached, and the one which is the focus of this section of this chapter, was that only 13 per cent of the population studied could be described as sophisticated marketing planning decision-makers and that, apart from this small group, few companies use the analytical techniques that are advocated in prescriptive literature. He also postulated adverse attitudes towards the techniques, procedures and information inputs of the marketing planning process.

The conclusion adds yet further weight to earlier research into the usage levels of the more popular analytical tools and techniques of marketing. Greenley's summary of this research is reproduced as Table 2.3 and clearly shows a relative low level of utilisation.

To this list can be added the comments of McBurnie (1989): 'Some two thirds of British companies ... do not use basic marketing disciplines'. Burke *et al* (1988) concluded that, although companies would actually like to make use of existing marketing techniques, few did.

Although there was much variation in the investigative methods used across all of these studies, none attempt to explain this low level of utilisation and, as such, they represent very little advance in knowledge.

Table 2.3 Outline of previous research

Study	Country	Focus	Outline of results
Buzzell and Wiersema (1981)	USA	SP	Limited use of formal planning methods
McColl-Kennedy *et al* (1989)	Australia	MP	Awareness and usage of methods – low
Greenley (1985)	UK	MP	Only 24% use portfolio analysis; half use PLC analysis
Haspeslagn (1982)	USA	SP	Only 45% use portfolio analysis regularly
Hopkins (1981)	USA	MP	A quarter use portfolio analysis; only 13% use PLC analysis
Hooley *et al* (1984)	UK	MP	Half use SWOT analysis, one-third use PLC; only a few use portfolio, PIMS, perceptual mapping and conjoint analysis
Reid and Hinkley (1989)	UK/Hong Kong	SP	Little awareness of portfolio and PLC analysis, and PIMS
Ross and Silverplatt (1987)	USA	SP	Half use portfolio analysis regularly, and a quarter use PIMS regularly
Verhage and Waarts (1988)	Netherlands	MP	15% use portfolio analysis, 27% use PLC with 62% using SWOT
Wittink and Cattin (1989)	USA	MP	Limited use of conjoint analysis by MR consultants
Wood and LaForge (1986)	USA	SP	Portfolio analysis used by 67% of sample

MP: marketing planning; SP: strategic planning.
Source: Greenley (1994)

None of the studies listed in Table 2.1 attempted to investigate the quality of the outputs resulting from utilisation of the techniques, so to take the quantitative evidence at face value would seem to be extremely dangerous, especially when much of the data was collected by means of mail questionnaires. Marketing terms are interpreted in different ways by different managers and questionnaire approaches may not be the most appropriate investigative tools for subjects like this (McDonald, 1985). There is some evidence for taking such a sceptical view. Piercy and Giles (1990) shows that, while most organisations claim to be doing SWOT analyses, few used the technique correctly or in an effective way. Likewise, McDonald (1982) showed that most organisations claimed to be doing marketing planning, but fewer than 15 per cent got beyond crude fiscally-driven forecasts and budgets.

John Hughes (1988), in his wide-ranging review of the teaching of management, concluded:

> The mistake we have made in teaching during the past 40 years has been to follow the logic approach in teaching theory first, followed by an assumed application in practice.

Marketing Techniques/Structures/Frameworks

Most foundation courses in marketing cover at least the following basic frameworks:

- The Ansoff matrix.
- Market segmentation.
- Product life-cycle analysis.
- Portfolio management (Boston box and the directional policy matrix).
- Marketing research and marketing information systems.

Additionally, a host of techniques revolve around the four basic elements of the marketing mix: Product, Price, Promotion and Place. Even a cursory glance through Philip Kotler's standard marketing management text reveals a vast and complex armoury of tools and techniques that can be used by marketing practitioners to gain a sustainable competitive advantage for their product or service (Kotler, 1988).

During the past three decades, each one has been the focus of numerous academic and practitioner papers which have sought to explain their complexities and to persuade managers to adopt them as part of the process of marketing management. There are, however, a number of issues that revolve firstly around methodological problems associated with the actual tools and techniques themselves, and secondly with the complexity of trying to link a number of them together.

Problems of Understanding

If we take a look at some of the more important structures and frameworks used in marketing management, we will observe a number of issues of varying degrees of difficulty in understanding, hence in application.

Doyle's paper (1989) dealt with the difference between a product life-cycle and a brand life-cycle. Failure to understand basic points such as these and others has destined product life-cycle analysis to be a topic of interest solely to academics. In the world of business, it lies largely dormant.

Another well-known, under-utilised and misunderstood tool taught by marketing academics is the *directional policy matrix* (McDonald, 1990). Even Michael Porter's apparently more easily assimilated matrix describing the relationship between costs and degree of marketing differentiation has become the latest victim of misunderstanding and abuse through ignorance (Speed, 1989).

Reid and Hinkley (1989) drew the following conclusion from their own study:

> It reflects a failure of business schools to disseminate knowledge of strategic methodologies.

The main problem, however, is not just that virtually every tool and technique for marketing is open to serious misunderstanding and abuse, but that no one method by itself can deliver the kinds of benefits demanded by practising managers. Most academics would readily acknowledge the singular contribution to diagnosis that can be made by each device, irrespective of whether it is from the school of life or from the more rigorous academic school. For example, while it is easy (and tempting) to dismiss most of what Peters and Waterman (1982) had to say (largely because of its lack of rigour), few would deny their contribution to marketing by dint of the attention focused on the need to service the needs of customers effectively. Yet subsequent events have clearly indicated the inadequacy of Peters and Waterman's views when used in isolation. Likewise, anyone who tries to run their company just on the basis of what Michael Porter says, soon discovers the inherent inadequacies of the nostrum, just as those did who worshipped at the altar of Bruce Henderson and the Boston Consulting Group in the late 1960s and the early 1970s. Yet few would deny the abiding relevance to business in the 1990s of what all these great writers, researchers and teachers had to offer.

To summarise, not only are most of the tools and techniques themselves inherently complex (and therefore misunderstood and misused), but no one tool on its own is adequate in dealing with the complexity of marketing.

There is, then, clearly a need to be able to use a number of these tools and techniques in problem-solving, especially when a process as complex as strategic marketing planning is concerned. This raises an additional dimension of complexity for both academics and practising managers, for it then becomes necessary to understand not only the techniques themselves, but the nature of the interrelationships between them, how inputs for one model can also be used for another, and how outputs from some models can also be used as inputs to others.

The author's work during the past five years at the cutting edge of marketing planning with some of the world's leading companies has thrown into sharp relief the uselessness of many of the core techniques of marketing when they are incorrectly used. The list includes 23 companies which are in the world's top 500. Many of these organisations are industrial companies, some are service and others are essentially consumer, but very little difference has been observed in techniques applications. What has thrown this subject into sharp relief is that most of them have been forced by circumstances to look more carefully at how to develop differential advantage, given the level playing-field on which many of them now compete. This, in turn, has shown the inadequacy of their erstwhile largely financially driven, extrapolative approaches.

In order to develop a clearer picture of the blockages to the effective use of marketing techniques, a case-study approach was adopted. The case study approach permits actual examples to be studied in detail, so throwing light on the nature of some of the problems of applying theory in practice, and while there is no claim to statistical validity from the four case histories studied, the author is encouraged to believe that these are not untypical, as a more quantitative log-book is being kept and monitored of all techniques applications and blockages to understanding.

Preliminary findings indicate inadequate understanding and inappropriate use of SWOT analyses, the directional policy matrix, market segmentation, and objective and strategy setting.

Discussion and Research Agendas

The three companies included in the four case histories referred to above had highly qualified graduates in their teams. The facts are as shown in Table 2.4. From this, it can be seen that 84 per cent of the marketing managers involved had either a professional marketing qualification or a business degree. While this may not be typical of marketing departments, it is likely that the number of qualified people will increase rapidly during the new few years. It must obviously be of some concern to academics that people as well qualified as this seemed unable to use the analytical tools appropriately to help them to develop competitive advantage.

At this stage, our hypothesis that marketing techniques, when used, are used incorrectly and are, therefore, largely ineffective, is largely exploratory and we have not dignified it with formalised research. The evidence, however, would seem to indicate a need to carry out more formal research to establish exactly what the most common blockages are to effective marketing techniques

Table 2.4 Degree of professionalism

	Number of managers at the in-company workshop	Number holding MBA or marketing degrees	Number holding marketing diplomas
Company 1	15	10	2
Company 2	10	5	2
Company 3	13	13	1
	38 (total)	71%	13%

utilisation. The ultimate deliverable, we hope, would be an improvement in the professionalism of marketing at the practitioner level. Also, if our hypothesis is true, it will go some way towards explaining the low level of practitioner professionalism in marketing and why marketing is generally held in such low regard (Chartered Institute of Marketing, 1994).

Greenley (1994) recommended more research to discover more about the extent of the utilisation of analytical techniques. However, it will be appreciated why we do not believe more quantitative research into techniques usage will further the interests of marketing.

Following publication of Leppard's research (1987), Saker and Speed (1992) commented on the danger of confusing a non-planning culture with an inefficient culture. Indeed, it is clear that non-planning company cultures are not necessarily inefficient. Some of the most profitable companies have been non-planning, pioneering organizations in their creative evolutionary phase.

Like a stream, as organisations become bigger, wider or deeper they become quite different in nature. What sustained company life and made it successful at one stage will certainly be out-grown as it matures.

Leppard's research set out to throw some further light on why marketing planning was adopted by such a relatively small number of UK companies. How he chose to define marketing planning was more or less a consensus view of those who have worked in this area. However, because this planning process embraces a number of implied assumptions and normative values, he found that an organisation had to be reasonably sophisticated and mature if it was to use the process to its advantage.

However, it is important to point out that there were two things Leppard *did not* set out to do:

1. Advocate that all organisations should use marketing planning and strive to change their culture.
2. Investigate non-profit making organisations.

It is recognised that there are other models that planners might use, as is illustrated in the tentative 'model' in Figure 2.3.

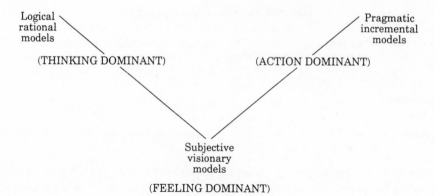

(FEELING DOMINANT)

Figure 2.3 Alternative planning models

It can be hypothesised that in a manner similar to that in which the three primary colours can combine, in various proportions to form all other colours, so might all shades and hues of planning approaches be possible according to the proportions of the components of Figure 2.3. Leppard's (1987) intention was to explore the logical/rational 'territory' in this triangle of possibilities, for that is where marketing planning (as most have defined it) sits.

By making their observations about Leppard's (1987) paper, Saker and Speed (1992) confirmed that the more we believe we know about marketing planning, the more we discover there is to learn. Their comments and the 'model' shown in Figure 2.3 ought to provide a stimulus for some inquisitive researchers to take matters further.

References

Abell, DF and Hammond JS (1979) *Strategic Marketing Planning*, Prentice Hall, Englewood Cliffs.

Ames, BC (1968) 'Marketing Planning for Industrial Products', *Harvard Business Review*, Vol 46, September–October, pp 100–112.

Ansoff, HI (1965) *Corporate Strategy*, McGraw Hill, New York.

Ansoff, HI (1977) 'The State of Practice of Planning Systems', *Sloan Management Review*, Vol 18, No. 2, pp 1–24.

Ansoff, HI (1994) 'Comment on Henry Mintzberg's Rethinking Strategic Planning', *Long Range Planning*, Vol 27, pp 31–32.

Ansoff, HI, Arner, J, Brandenberg, R, Portner, F and Rusoderich, R (1970) 'Does Planning Pay? The Effect of Planning on the Success of American Firms', *Long Range Planning*, Vol 3, December, pp 2–7.

Bailey, A and Johnson, G (1994) 'The Process of Strategy Development', *Cranfield School of Management Research Paper* (unpublished).

Bhattachary, K (1981) Article in *Financial Times*, 27 November.

Boyd, H and Massey, W (1972) *Marketing Management*, McGraw Hill, New York.

Brownlie, D (1985) 'The Anatomy of Strategic Marketing Planning', *Journal of Marketing Management*, Vol 1, pp 35–63.

Burke, R, Rangaswany, A, Wind J and Eliashberg, J (1988). 'Expert Systems for Marketing', *Marketing Science Institute Working Paper*, Report Nos 87–107.

Buzzell, RD and Wiersema, FD (1981) 'Successful Share-Branding Strategies', *Harvard Business Review*, Vol 59, pp 135–144.

Camillus, JC (1975) 'Evaluating the Benefits of Formal Planning Systems', *Long Range Planning*, Vol 8, No 3, June, pp 33–40.

Cateora, PR and Hess, JM (1971) *International Marketing*, Homewood, Illinois, Irwin.

Chartered Institute of Marketing (1994), *The Challenge of Change*.

Cosse, TJ and Swan, JE (1983) 'Strategic Marketing Planning by Product Managers', *Journal of Marketing*, Vol 47, No 3, pp 92–102.

Davidson, JH (1972) 'Offensive Marketing – How to Make Your Competitors Followers', Cassell, London.

Day, GS (1984) *Strategic Marketing Planning: The Pursuit of Competitive Advantage*, West Publishing, St Paul.

Denison, T and McDonald, MHB (1995) 'The Role of Marketing Past, Present and Future', *Journal of Marketing Practice*, Vol 1, No 1, Spring, pp 54–76.

Dodge, HR (1970) *Industrial Marketing*, McGraw Hill, London.

Doyle, P (1989) 'Building Successful Brands: The Strategic Options', *Journal of Marketing Management*, Vol 5, No 1, pp 77–95.

Fisher, L (1970) *Industrial Marketings: An Analytical Approach to Planning and Execution*, Brandon Press, Princeton.

Greenley, GE (1986) *The Strategic and Operational Planning of Marketing*, McGraw Hill, London.

Greenley, GE (1982), 'An Overview of Marketing Planning in UK Manufacturing Companies', *European Journal of Marketing*, Vol 16, No 7, pp 3–15.

Greenley, GE (1985) 'An Investigation of Company Product Decision Making', *Omega, International Journal of Management Science*, Vol 13, No 3, pp 175–180.

Greenley, GE (1994) 'Marketing Planning Processes in UK and US Companies', *Journal of Strategic Marketing*, Vol 2, No 2, pp 140–154.

Greiner, LE (1972) 'Evolution and Revolution as Organisations Grow', *Harvard Business Review*, July–August, pp 37–46.

Haspeslagh, P (1982) 'Portfolio Planning: Uses and Limits', *Harvard Business Review*, Vol 60, January–February, pp 58–73.

Hooley, GJ, West, CJ and Lynch, JE (1984) *Marketing in the UK: A Survey of Current Practice and Performance*, Institute of Marketing, UK.

Hopkins, DS (1981) 'The Marketing Plan', *Research Report No 801*, The Conference Board, New York.

Hughes, J (1988) 'The Body of Knowledge in Management Education', *Management Education and Development*, Vol 19, No 4, pp 301–310.

Kollatt, DT, Blackwell, RD and Robeson, JF (1972) *Strategic Marketing*, Holt, Reinhart and Winston Inc.

Kotler, P (1988) *Marketing Management*, Prentice-Hall, New York.

Leighton, DSR (1966) *International Marketing: Text and Cases*, McGraw Hill, New York.

Leppard, JW (1987) 'Marketing Planning and Corporate Culture: A Conceptual Framework Which Examines Management Attitudes in the Context of Marketing Planning', MPhil thesis, Cranfield Institute of Technology.

Leppard, J and McDonald, MHB (1987), 'A Reappraisal of the Role of Marketing Planning', *The Quarterly Review of Marketing*, **13**, Autumn, pp 1–7.

Liander, B (1967) *Comparative Analysis for International Marketing*, Allyn and Bacon, Boston, Massachusetts.

Lievegoed, BJC (1973) *The Developing Organisation*, Tavistock, London.

Martin, J (1979) 'Business Planning: The Gap Between Theory and Practice', *Long Range Planning*, Vol **12**, December, pp 2–10.

McBurnie, A (1989) 'The Need for a New Marketing Perspective', *MBA Review*, Vol 1, No **1**, pp 10–11.

McColl-Kennedy, JR, Uau, OHM and Kiel, CC (1989), 'Marketing Planning Practices in Australia: A Comparison Across Company Types', Graduate School of Management, *University of Queensland Research Paper*.

McDonald, MHB (1982) 'The Theory and Practice of Marketing Planning for Industrial Goods in International Markets', PhD thesis *Cranfield Institute of Technology*, UK.

McDonald, MHB (1985) 'Methodological Problems Associated with Qualitative Research', *International Studies of Management & Organisation*, Vol **XV**, No 2, pp 19–40.

McDonald, MHB (1990) 'Some Methodological Comments on the Directional Policy Matrix', *Journal of Marketing Management*, Vol 6, No 1, pp 59–68.

McDonald, MHB (1990) 'Technique Interrelationships and the Pursuit of Relevance in Marketing Theory', *QRM*, Vol **15**, No 4, pp 1–11.

McDonald, MHB (1995) *Marketing Plans: How to Prepare Them; How to Use Them* (3rd edition) Butterworth-Heinemann, Oxford.

Mintzberg, H. (1994) 'Rethinking Strategic Planning, Part 1, Pitfalls and Fallacies, Part 2, New Roles for Planners', *Long Range Planning*, Vol **27**, No 3, pp 12–21, 22–30.

Mintzberg, H (1994) *The Rise and Fall of Strategic Planning*, Prentice Hall, Hemel Hempstead.

Miracle, GE and Albaum, GS (1970) *International Marketing Management*, Irwin, Home-wood, Illinois.

Normann, R (1977) *Managing for Growth* John Wiley, London.

Pearson, EA (1973) '*Developing Short Range Marketing Plans*', *The McKinsey Quarterly*, Winter, pp 35–46.

Peters, TJ and Waterman, RH (1982) *In Search of Excellence*, Harper and Row, New York.

Piercy, N and Giles, W (1990) 'Revitalising and Operationalising the SWOT Model in Strategic Planning', *University of Wales Business and Economic Review*, No 5, pp 3–10.

Piercy, N and Morgan, N (1994) 'The Marketing Planning Process: Behavioural Problems Compared to Analytical Techniques in Explaining Marketing Planning Credibility', *Journal of Business Research*, Vol **29**, No 3, pp 167–178.

Piercy, NF and Morgan, NA (1990) 'Organisational Context and Behavioural Problems as Determinants of the Effectiveness of the Strategic Marketing Planning Process', *Journal of Marketing Management*, Vol 6, pp 127–144.

Pryor, MH (1965) 'Planning in a Worldwide Business', *Harvard Business Review*, January–February, pp 130–139.

Reid, DM and Hinkey, LC (1989) 'Strategic Planning: The Cultural Impact', *Marketing Intelligence and Planning*, Vol 7, Nos 11–12, pp 4–12.

Ringbakk, KA (1971) 'Why Planning Fails', *European Business*, Vol 29, Spring, pp 15–26.

Ross, JE and Silverblatt R (1987) 'Developing the Strategic Plan', *Industrial Marketing Management*, Vol 16, pp 103–108.

Saddick, SMA (1968) 'Marketing in the Wood, Textile, Machinery and Clothing Industry', PhD Thesis. University of Bradford.

Saker, J and Speed, R (1992) 'Comment – Corporate Culture: Is it Really a Barrier to Marketing Planning?' *Journal of Marketing Management*, Vol 8, pp 177–181.

Schein, EH (1983) 'The Role of the Founder in Creating Organisational Climate', *Organisational Dynamics*, Vol 12, No 1, Summer, pp 13–28.

Schein, EH (1985) *Organisational Culture and Leadership*, Jossey-Bass, San Francisco.

Schoeffler, M (1974) 'Impact of Strategic Planning on Profit Performance', *Harvard Business Review*, March–April, pp 137–145.

Scholhammer, H (1971) 'Company Planning in Multinational Firms', *Columbia Journal of World Business*, September–October, pp 70–90.

Shinmer, DV (1988) 'Marketing's Role in Strategic and Tactical Planning', *European Journal of Marketing*, Vol 22, No 5, pp 23–31.

Speed, RJ (1989) 'Oh Mr Porter! A Reappraisal of Competitive Strategy', *Marketing Intelligence and Planning*, Vol 7, Nos 5–6, pp 8–11.

Stasch, SF and Lanktree (1980) 'Can Your Marketing Planning Procedures be Improved?' *Journal of Marketing*, Vol 4, No 3, pp 79–90.

Terpstra, V (1972) *International Marketing*, Dryden Press, Hinsdale, Illinois.

Thompson, S (1962) 'How Companies Plan', *AMA Research Study*, No 54, AMA.

Thune, S and House, R (1970) 'Where Long Range Planning Pays Off', *Business Horizons*, Vol 13, No 4, pp 81–87.

Tilles, S (1969) *Making Strategy Explicit* in *Business Strategy* (ed) Ansoff, HI, Penguin, London.

Verhage, BJ and Waarts, E (1988) 'Marketing Planning for Improved Performance: A Comparative Analysis', *International Marketing Review*, Vol 5, No 2, pp 20–30.

Weichmann, UE and Pringle, LE (1979) 'Problems that Plague Multinational Marketers', *Harvard Business Review*, July–August, pp 118–124.

Wilson, A (1965) *The Marketing of Industrial Products*, Hutchinson, London.

Winkler, J (1972) *Winkler on Marketing Planning*, Cassell Association Business Programme, London.

Wittink, DR and Cattin, P (1989) 'Commercial Use of Conjoint Analysis: An Update', *Journal of Marketing*, Vol 53, No 3, pp 91–96.

Wood, DR and LaForge, RL (1986) 'Lessons from Strategic Portfolio Planning in Large US Banks', *SAM Advanced Management Journal*, Vol 51, No 1, pp 25–31.

Yoshino, MY (1965) 'Marketing Orientation in International Business', *Business Topics*, Vol 13, Summer, pp 7–13.

3

COMPETITIVE MARKETING STRATEGY: CONCEPTS AND APPLICATION*

Malcolm McDonald and Linden Brown

This chapter is about competitive advantage – establishing, building, defending and maintaining it – and the strategies required to do that in a competitive environment. What those strategies should be will depend upon an organisation's existing competitive position, where it wants to be in the future, its capabilities and the competitive market environment it faces. The pertinent concepts are explored and their application examined in the European context by example, illustration and case study.

THE TASK OF COMPETITIVE MARKETING STRATEGY

Effective action is preceded by four interrelated steps: audit, objectives, strategies and plans for implementation. Following a situation review, objectives specify what is to be achieved, usually in terms of revenue, profit and market

*This chapter brings up to date an earlier version of this paper which appears in Dr Linden Brown's book *Competitive Marketing Strategy: developing, maintaining and defending competitive position*, published by Thomas Nelson, Australia, 1990, and is reproduced with his kind permission.

share. Strategies set out the route that has been chosen – the means for achieving the objectives. Plans for implementation provide the vehicle for getting to the destination along the chosen route.

In a competitive environment, the starting point is to identify the competitive position, set business objectives, which will comprise revenue, market share and profit requirements, then formulate the strategies necessary to achieve the new position. Under these conditions, marketing strategies are the centrepiece.

The task of competitive marketing strategy is to move a business from its present position to a stronger competitive one. This must be done by adapting and responding to external trends and forces such as competition, market changes and technology, and developing and matching corporate resources and capabilities with the firm's opportunities (see Figure 3.1). Recognition of the complexity of this task, especially for large diversified companies, has led to the development of theories, concepts and techniques that prescribe the process of strategy formulation in a systematic manner. This has become known as the strategic planning process.

THE STRATEGIC PLANNING PROCESS

Strategic planning is the process of formulating longer-term objectives and strategies for the entire business or business unit by matching its resources with its opportunities. Its purpose is to help a business to set and reach realistic objectives and achieve a desired competitive position within a defined time.

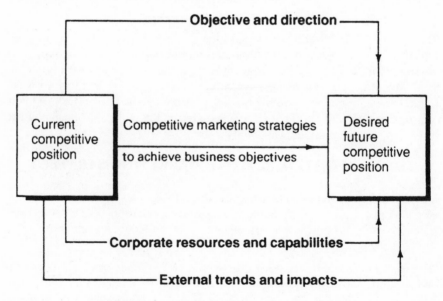

Figure 3.1 Strategies to achieve future position

It aims to reduce the risk of error and place the business in a situation in which it can anticipate change, respond to it, and even create change to its advantage.

Evolution of the Process

In the 1960s, strategic planning (known then as corporate planning) was essentially a financial plan of the business extrapolated from a base year. It worked well as a planning tool when demand exceeded supply, markets were growing and external change was minimal. When major external changes hit companies and industries in the late-1960s and the 1970s, however, this type of planning was no longer adequate. The successful challenge to retail price maintenance, for example, changed the nature of the food manufacturing industry, and the lowering of tariffs and provision of import quotas on many categories of goods changed local industries.

Increasing competition, more demanding customers and changing markets have forced more commitment to marketing to enable firms to capitalise on competitive advantages. Some companies now manage resources, markets and competition through a multi-level system of objectives and strategies.

Aaker (1984, p 11) depicts the evolution of management systems. The final stage is a strategic market management approach in which the firm adopts a planning and review process that aims to cope with strategic surprises and fast-developing threats and opportunities. This is shown in Table 3.1.

Table 3.1 Evolution of management systems

	Budgeting/ control	Long-range planning	Strategic planning	Strategic market management
Management emphasis	Control deviations and manage complexity	Anticipate growth and manage complexity	Change strategic thrust and capability	Cope with strategic surprises and fast-developing threats/ opportunities
Assumptions	The past repeats	Past trends will continue	New trends and discontinuities are predictable	Planning cycles inadequate to deal with rapid changes
The Process	← ————————	— Periodic —	———————— →	Real Time
Time period associated with system	From 1990s	From 1950s	From 1960s	From mid-1970s

Source: Aaker, DA (1984) p 11.

75

In response to changing external factors such as technology and market maturity, firms changed their products and markets, sold and acquired businesses and reorganised. This required them to redefine their business scope because of the need to commit resources to new businesses and market development. Courtaulds, for example, originally in textiles, is now in paints and industrial plastics, and ICI, originally in bulk chemicals, is in pharmaceuticals, and the banks are in insurance and financial services. Allied Breweries is in hotels and leisure centres and WH Smith is in DIY.

Steps in the Process

In reality, firms adopt a hybrid of management systems depending upon their size, diversity, position in the market, rate and type of external change, resource commitments and management attitudes to planning.

What is important, however, is to recognise that a series of systematic steps can be useful in formulating strategies when the stakes are high and the resource commitment is significant to the firm. It reduces the risk of leaving out key issues, and it highlights the assumptions on which strategies are based and resources committed. A series of interrelated steps are involved in formulating strategies. Day (1984, p 49) shows a typical strategy formulation process in Figure 3.2.

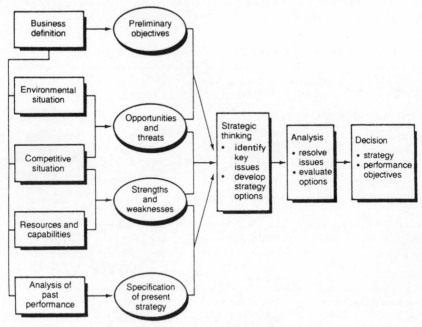

Figure 3.2 Strategy formulation process
Source: Day (1984), p 49

The basic steps are:

- Business definition – scope of planning activities.
- Situation assessment – analysis of internal and environmental factors.
- Preliminary performance objectives – based on past performance and initial corporate expectations, constrained by achievement reality.
- Strategic development – identification and evaluation of strategic options and choice of an option.
- Implementation – includes action programmes, functional budgets and timetables.
- Monitoring of performance against objectives.

In essence, an analysis of internal and external factors helps to develop the business definition, relative competitive advantage and broad objectives. The central issues must be identified, the strategy options set out and evaluated. Strategic decisions are taken by selecting the strategy and relevant performance objectives. Aaker (1984, p 22) expands some of the elements in this process.

The analyses by Day and Aaker relate primarily to strategy development for the strategic business unit (SBU). McDonald (1989) looks at planning from a more highly focused marketing perspective and views the marketing planning process within a corporate framework. They see the steps as:

- Corporate (business) objectives.
- Marketing audit – analyses of external environment and internal elements, including the marketing mix.
- SWOT analysis (ie, of strengths, weaknesses, opportunities and threats) and planning assumptions, including key determinants of marketing success or failure.
- Marketing objectives and strategies, including objectives for products, and markets and strategies for each part of the marketing mix.
- Programmes containing details of timing, responsibilities and costs, with sales forecasts and budget.
- Measurement and review.

The development of competitive marketing strategies needs to draw from both perspectives. The SBU level provides tools of strategic analysis that are applicable to the development of marketing strategies and cut across the whole business. The functional marketing level helps to define the elements that make up a marketing strategy for each of the product lines and market segments. Specific brand positioning and marketing mix decisions become more narrowly defined at the product market level of analysis. The SBU level provides tools of strategic marketing analysis, while the functional marketing level helps to define the elements that make up a marketing strategy.

The Planning Process and Conceptual Analysis

There is a considerable number of strategic analysis concepts, methods and techniques from which to draw guidelines for competitive marketing strategies. The problem is to determine which are the most useful and relevant. It is important to recognise that each concept or technique provides only part of the picture and should not be relied upon as the only guide to strategy formulation. These concepts have evolved from the field of marketing and, in recent years, the area of strategic planning.

Much of the literature (eg, Porter, 1980) focuses on competitive analyses as the key to identifying competitive advantages, and on the need to develop global strategies such as those that have been successfully implemented by Japanese corporations (Kotler *et al*, 1986). Many attempt to provide guidelines and general principles for the selection of strategies under different conditions. Indeed, the links between strategy and performance have been the subject of detailed statistical analysis by the Strategic Planning Institute (Buzzell and Gale, 1987, pp 6–15, 30–35). The PIMS Project identified six major links from studies of more than 2600 businesses. From this analysis, principles have been derived for the selection of different strategies, depending upon industry type, market conditions and competitive position of the business.

A reaction against theoretical approaches to strategic planning has occurred in recent years, however, with particular focus on the limitations of portfolio planning (Andrews, 1984). Some writers argue that there are no valid generalisations about strategy and criticise strategy consultants, who, they claim, have misled managers by making recommendations based on excessively broad principles. Lubatkin and Pitts (1985, pp 85–92) compare a 'policy perspective' with the 'PIMS perspective'. They suggest that a policy perspective assumes that no two businesses are exactly alike and therefore that there are few specific formulae for achieving competitive advantage. They suggest that the PIMS perspective involves a mechanistic application of formulae to complex management problems, resulting in potentially misleading prescriptions for strategy.

What is agreed, however, is that strategic planning represents a useful process by which an organisation formulates its strategies, but it should be adapted to the organisation and its environments. The basic steps relevant to all business are:

- Analysis of external and internal trends.
- Strategic analysis.
- SWOT and issues analysis.
- Objective setting.
- Strategy selection.
- Action plans.
- Implementation.
- Performance review and evaluation of performance.

These steps are generally agreed to include the most prominent features of strategic planning. They include, in summary form, the steps proposed by Day (1984), McDonald (1989) and Aaker (1984). In practice, the weakest and often most difficult parts of this process are in strategic planning analysis and strategy selection.

STRATEGIC ANALYSIS CONCEPTS

The range of concepts relevant to analysis of competitive marketing strategy emanate from a number of disciplines, including marketing, sociology, economics, financial management and the new area of strategic management.

The Product Life-Cycle

One of the first attempts to form an analytical framework for determining marketing strategy was product life-cycle theory. The product life-cycle concept describes stages in the sales history of a product category or form. Most representations of the life cycle have the following characteristics:

- A product has a limited life.
- Its sales history follows an 'S'-curve until sales eventually decline.
- The inflection points in the sales history locate the stages known as introduction, growth, maturity and decline. Some representations show an additional stage of competitive turbulence or shakeout once the growth rate slows.
- The life of the product may be extended.
- The average profit per unit (of the industry) rises, then falls over the life cycle.

Figure 3.3 shows the idealised product life-cycle, which includes curve and unit profit trends (Day, 1986, p 60). It also shows market extension of the life cycle. Underlying the life cycle is the diffusion process and associated adopter categories which are classified according to their timing of entry on to the market. Figure 3.4 indicates the proportion of the total market of each category and the idealised diffusion pattern.

Innovators represent that 2.5 per cent of the market that will immediately accept the new product and try it. The early adopters are those who will 'make or break' the product, depending upon their experiences and opinions. If these are favourable, acceptance grows rapidly and most of the market enters quickly. The last group to accept the product, the laggards, buys for the first time, often when innovators and early adopters have moved to alternative products.

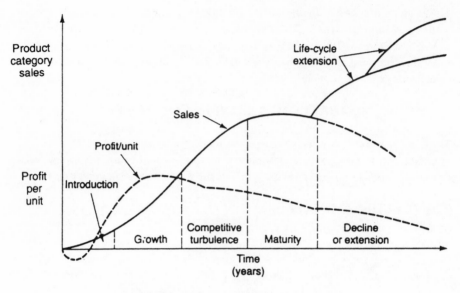

Figure 3.3 Life cycle of a typical product
Source: Day (1986), p 60

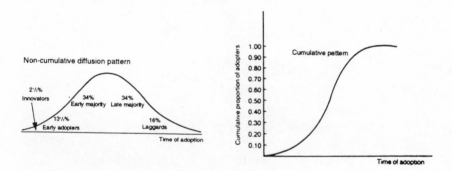

Figure 3.4 Diffusion pattern and adopter categories
Source: Windy (1982), p 28

Each stage of the life cycle represents different marketing challenges. At the introductory stage, the task is to create awareness and to achieve acceptance by opinion leaders within the early adopter group. During growth, the challenge is to maintain supply and quality consistency while establishing brand identification and market position. At the mature stage, the firm needs to maintain or improve its profit, defend its position and look for growth segments of the market. In decline, cost reduction, pricing and targeting are important to profitability, and planning is required to determine exit timing. Examples of products at different life-cycle stages in Europe in the early 1990s are shown in Table 3.2.

Table 3.2 Products at different life-cycle stages

Introduction	Growth	Maturity	Decline
Filmless cameras	Compact disc players	Microwave ovens	Draught ale
Computer scanners	Facsimile transmission	Washing machines	Typewriters
Stress wave sensing Expert systems	Lap-top computers	Brandy	

Strategic implications

The strategic implications of life-cycle theory are that each stage warrants different objectives, marketing mix, strategies and different management focus. Both Wasson (1974) and Day (1986, pp 91–92) have conducted comprehensive analyses of life-cycle management and propose marketing strategy guidelines for each stage. Each author adds an intermediate stage between growth and maturity, termed 'competitive turbulence', which recognises the implications of the effects of a slowdown in market growth and over-supply, brought on by the entry of new competitors and an increase in capacity by existing ones. Day (1986, p 90) and Wasson (1974, pp 247–248) provide a summary of the general strategic implications of life-cycle theory.

An example of this occurred in the British telex market. When it was introduced, telex offered an efficient, quick text transfer service as an alternative to the postal service. It rapidly became an essential business communication tool with maximum market penetration in the early 1980s. British Telecom implemented life-cycle extension strategies by adding features to telex terminals, enhancing user capabilities, allowing text transfer to computers and targeting non-user segments such as small businesses. The rapid growth of facsimile systems since the mid-1980s has brought about the decline of telex and a need for British Telecom to change its strategy to retain profitability and to plan for either product divestment or reformulation to enable future profit to be made on much lower telex volumes.

The introduction, growth and rationalisation of video hire shops is another example of predictable product market evolution. The rapid expansion of retail outlets resulted in over-supply, a shakeout of competitors, and now more stable competition.

Variations on a theme

Life-cycle patterns vary in practice. Some new products skip the introductory stage and grow rapidly from the outset. These are usually products that are readily understood by the market and for which a latent demand exists. Colour television and cellular mobile telephones are examples. New fads exhibit only rapid growth and rapid decline because of a novelty appeal, seasonality and associations with special events. Some products show a decline, then a regrowth pattern. Industrial and consumer durables, such as farm machinery and refrigerators, reveal this cyclical pattern. Other products fail and hardly register a blip on the life-cycle chart. A number of different variations to the life-cycle theme are depicted in Figures 3.5–3.8 (Meenaghan and Turnbull, 1981).

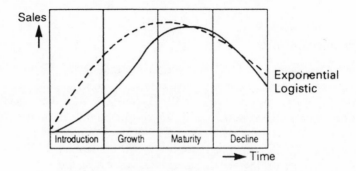

Figure 3.5 Basic product life-cycle stages
Source: Meenaghan and Turnbull (1981), p 2

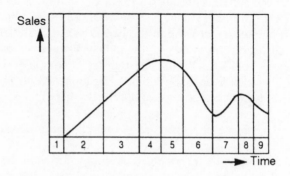

Figure 3.6 Alternative life-cycle shape and stages
Source: Meenaghan and Turnbull, (1981), p 2

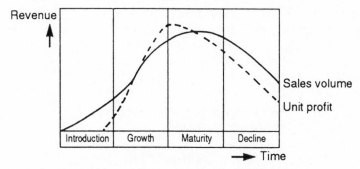

Figure 3.7 Profit-volume relationship over the life cycle
Source: Meenaghan and Turnbull (1981), p 5

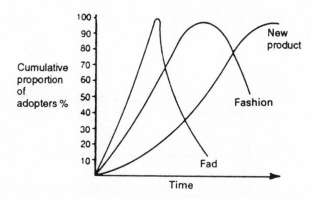

Figure 3.8 Generalised diffusion pattern for a fad, a fashion and a new product
Source: Meenaghan and Turnbull (1981), p 11

Limitations

The limitations of the concept for developing competitive marketing strategies depend on the variations of life cycles, problems defining the appropriate market and the focus on strategies that tend to be applicable to the dominant firm in the market and inapplicable to competitors holding different positions. Brownlie and Bart (1985, pp 25–26) highlight the issues:

- Clear definition of the market is necessary. This requires aggregation of product market segments, which can be misleading where market boundaries cannot be delineated accurately. In practice, it is more common for markets to be defined in terms of several competing brands within a product category. The key question, posed by Weitz and Wensley (1984, p 132) is: Which level of aggregation best captures the changing nature of the environment to which marketing strategy must respond?

- As a prescriptive tool, it is too general to enable the application of specific strategy guidelines to a given product or brand. It is difficult to predict when the turning points will occur, based purely on market analysis.
- The concept does not explicitly allow for the influence of uncontrollable external factors, such as technology, economic conditions, competitors' position and strategies, and the overall capacity of the industry in relation to demand. Conditions of short supply affect sales patterns and can reflect artificial turning points in the sales trends.
- It is not clear how far a firm can influence the shape of the life cycle by its marketing strategies and at which stages there is potential for the greatest influence. It is likely, however, that the pioneering firm and dominant players have a significant impact, particularly at the introduction, early growth and maturity stages.
- The length of stages varies within and between markets. Now, for most product types, duration of the entire life cycle is becoming shorter because of the increasing pace of technological innovations and introduction of new products.

Practical significance

The life-cycle concept brings into focus a number of market factors that are important for strategic planning:

- The notion of evolution of a market bringing changing market conditions represented by a variety of warning signs is a valuable contribution to marketing strategy formulation.
- Recognition of a finite limit to market potential for a product type sets the market size dimension. Penetration and usage levels at any point provide an indication of future potential.
- The distinction between market sales and a firm's product sales highlights the importance of market share trends and maintaining a focus on the total market. As the market matures, focus on sales trends and cycle stages of individual segments is useful.
- The dynamics of the diffusion process provide useful targeting insights. Target customer groups change over time. It is easier to obtain market share growth during the growth stage of the life-cycle as customers form opinions of brands and try alternatives. As the market matures, customers become more knowledgeable and their perceptions of the product type, and brands within it, change. Distinctions between brands are reduced and the product type becomes 'ordinary', having lost it newness and mystique. Customers progressively develop a 'commodity' view of the product. Figure 3.9 depicts the commodity slide which characterises the maturity of some markets, particularly those in which weaker competitors try to retain profit margins by withdrawing advertising support.

- Identification of products within a firm's range which are in markets at different life-cycle stages provides an indication of the balance of products according to their future growth prospects.
- Recognition of the changing pattern of competition and different types of competitive strategies that may evolve at each stage is a useful contribution to strategic thinking.

The Experience Curve

The concept

The results of the Boston Consulting Group's (BCG) studies of cost and price changes in relation to accumulated volume or experience across a variety of

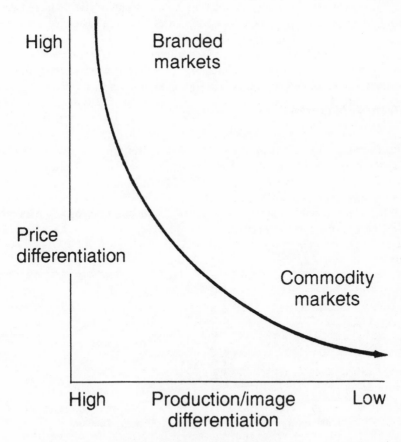

Figure 3.9 The commodity slide
Source: McDonald (1989)

industries, highlight cost dynamics and their impact on prices particularly in markets that are growing rapidly Boston Consulting Group, 1980; Day, 1986, 25–26). Change in market share can produce change in cost differentials between competitors, enabling a firm which is gaining market share to lower prices faster than its profit margin declines. The per unit cost experience curve, plotted over time in relation to accumulated volume, declines, owing to efficiencies from learning, technological improvements and economies of scale.

Figure 3.10 shows that cost declines with total accumulated volume – this takes the form of a curve on the linear scale. On a log-log scale, it shows a percentage change as a constant distance on the graph – i.e. a percentage change in one factor results in a corresponding percentage change in the other. In the case of cost-volume or price-volume slopes, the plotting of data about costs or prices and accumulated experience for a product on log-log paper in the BCG studies produces straight lines, reflecting a consistent relationship between experience and costs, and experience and prices. Across a variety of industries the BCG found that with each doubling of accumulated volume, costs dropped between 20 per cent and 40 per cent, depending upon the industry.

In response to industry cost declines, the BCG found varying price trends – some stable, others unstable. These are shown in Figures 3.11 and 3.12.

Strategic implications

Learning experience, and its impact on costs and price levels, has important implications for strategic planning. There is a minimum rate of cost decline required for survival by firms in an industry where learning experience affects costs and prices. This is reflected in Figure 3.13.

Pricing strategies of leading competitors in a market where learning experience affects costs will create a stable or unstable competitive environment. When a substantial gap develops between average unit price and average unit

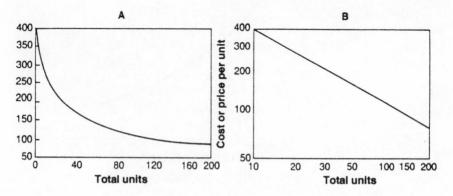

Figure 3.10 Experience cost relationships
Source: The Boston Consulting Group (1970), p 13

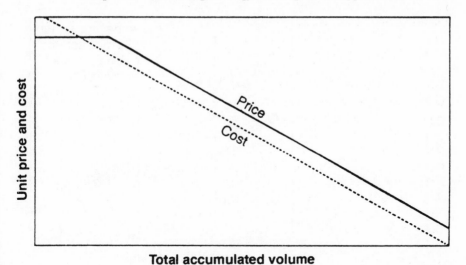

Figure 3.11 A typical stable pattern
Source: The Boston Consulting Group (1970), p 19

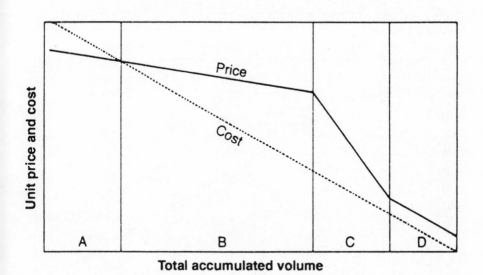

Figure 3.12 A characteristic unstable pattern after it has become stable
Source: The Boston Consulting Group (1970), p 21

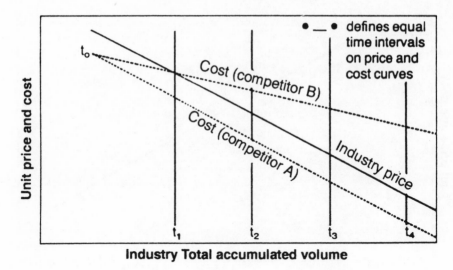

Figure 3.13 Competitor and industry price experience
Source: The Boston Consulting Group (1970), p 24

cost, opportunities exist for lowering prices and gaining more volume. This is usually done by smaller competitors. Figure 3.14 shows this pattern.

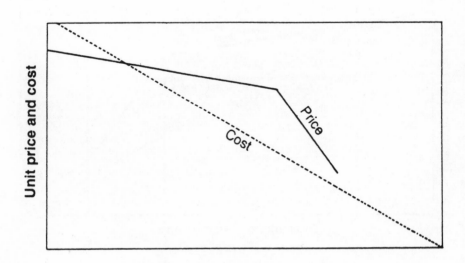

Figure 3.14 Unstable price gap
Source: The Boston Consulting Group (1970), p 20

The major strategic implication is that firms should seek market share dominance during the growth stage of the life cycle so that cost advantages can be reflected in price advantages, which, in turn, lead to market share increases. If this is done aggressively, using price penetration strategies, it is assumed that the firm will end up with the lowest unit costs, highest market share and an ability to lead the market during its mature phase. Texas Instruments adopted this strategy in the digital watch market, only to find that its prices ended at a point below its unit costs as the market matured and, despite its dominance, it was unable to make a profit. Clearly, this strategy requires confidence in the fact that volume growth is sufficient to achieve substantial cost reductions and that the firm can achieve, and can sustain, a lowest cost position in the industry.

Limitations of the concept

- The experience curve applies to broad categories of basic products such as television receivers, electric ranges or semi-conductors. When the definition is narrowed into subcategories of these groups, the relationship applies only to the value added component. At the individual product or brand level, this becomes difficult to apply because of the high proportion of joint costs involved.
- Variations in accounting practice can substantially distort reported costs as they affect experience curves and cost-volume analysis. Cost comparisons between competitors are difficult to make for both practical and accessibility reasons. Allocated costs can distort actual product costs. It is difficult, therefore, to gain consistent and reasonably accurate product cost trends.
- An appropriate inflation index is necessary to ensure that cost trends are measured in real terms. This is not always readily available for the product type under review.
- Experience can be readily transferred in ways other than accumulated volume. Hiring of experienced staff, licensing of technology, franchising arrangements and acquiring 'experienced' companies in the field of interest, enable firms with low-volume experience to operate on a low unit cost structure. Davidow (1986, p xvi) refers to 'toothpaste technology' in high-tech industries, where the demands of customers, governments and industry associations are forcing companies to base their products on identical technologies. More and more products are being built from identical 'product genes' which are now widely available technologies.
- Some markets do not respond to massive price cutting because of the nature of the industry. Insurance, furniture removals and medical services are based on trust, and low prices can be perceived in a negative light. Other markets respond to price reductions but, once set in motion, products become low margin commodities with very little profit. Some generic labels sold by supermarkets exhibit these characteristics, where constant price specials are necessary to generate sales.

Practical significance

Despite its appeal and empirical support, the experience curve applies only in certain situations. The earlier broad generalisations have been replaced with applications where the tool is recognised as one of a number of analytical methods. It does, however, focus on some key issues for strategic planning.

Costs require deliberate management to ensure competitiveness as industries, markets and cost structures change. British Leyland found in many of its manufacturing businesses, for example, that it could no longer remain cost competitive, and it divested many of its manufacturing companies during the 1980s.

The competitive marketing strategies adopted by firms in an industry have an impact on industry costs and cost trends. The experience curve concept focuses attention on cost/price/volume dynamics and indicates the importance of forecasting future costs, prices and profits in the industry.

The return on investment from improved market share can be high. The variables affecting profitability are profit margin, market share and market size. In a rapidly growing market, all three are more important in the future than in the present. The strategist needs to determine when to trade profit for future market share and when today's profit is better than more profit on a larger market share.

When experience effects do occur, competitors need to achieve an advantage on those cost elements that are important to particular market segments. These cost elements may differ significantly between segments, allowing specialists to dominate niches against broad-line competitors. Davidow (1986), in an account of marketing strategies relevant to high-technology industries, illustrates the importance of competitive cost differences and how costs and margin goals affect price. He demonstrates that small differences in costs and margin objectives yield significant differences in prices that can be charged by competitors.

The Growth-share Portfolio model*

The product portfolio concept has its origin in finance theory, where a variety of risk-return investments is balanced as a portfolio to provide the required return to the investor. Some investments are geared to immediate income at a low risk, some to capital growth with low immediate income, and others as higher risk ventures with potentially high future returns. In order to provide for both present and future cash flow, it is desirable to have a balanced portfolio.

When applied to marketing, this concept views products as investments that either require or yield cash according to their position in the portfolio. Some products, especially new ones, will have potentially high future cash flow but are high-risk investments. These may require substantial cash investment during development. Others may be declining and represent candidates for dele-

---

*Day (1986): Chapter 6 provides an extensive review of the growth-share matrix.

tion. Some products within the range may yield high cash flow, which is used to fund new developments.

Portfolio models, such as the Boston Consulting Group's growth-share matrix, have been almost synonymous with the development of strategic planning concepts. Frequently referred to as the BCG matrix, the growth-share portfolio model classifies each business or product by the rate of present market growth and by a measure of market share dominance. Market growth serves as a proxy for the need for cash, and relative market share is used to reflect profitability and cash generation. Relative market share is the ratio of the product's share to the share of its largest competitor in the same market.

The logic of this model is based on the dynamics of the product life-cycle (market growth rate) and the experience curve effect (the importance of relative market share and dominance). In its simplest form, the model depicts growth and relative share as either low or high. To reflect its future prospects and risks, each product classification is named – star, cash cow, dog and problem child/question mark. The model uses this matrix to suggest market share and investment objectives for each category:

- Stars: invest to hold or increase market share.
- Cash cows: maintain or milk to provide cash for problem child products and research and development.
- Dogs: reformulate to provide positive cash flow, reduce costs, or divest.
- Problem child/question mark: invest in share growth in those that show positive prospects; divest others.

Figure 3.15 indicates the cash flow position of each type and provides measures for placing products in the matrix. The market dominance axis measures the firm's market share relative to that of the largest competitor.

Strategic management guidelines

Brownlie and Bart (1985, p 14) in a review of the BCG model, provides a useful summary of strategic guidelines. The main guidelines are as follows:

- Star products require continued heavy investment during growth. Low margins may be essential to defer competition and consolidate competitive position.
- Cash cows are managed for cash, but some investment is required to reduce costs and maintain market dominance. Future market prospects will determine how long an investment in maintaining dominance is pursued and when the product is harvested to make the most profit.
- Problem children are managed to gain market share. Where star potential is not evident, divestment is recommended.
- Dogs have weak competitive positions in low growth and mature markets. Most have little potential for share growth and are unprofitable. Liquidation of dog products is usually recommended.

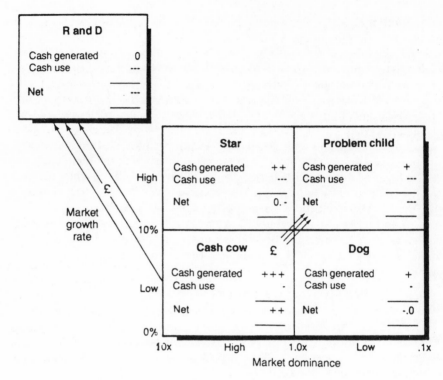

Figure 3.15 Portfolio positions and cash flows

The successful strategy sequence requires the development of a question mark product to a star, which in turn becomes a cash cow as the market matures. This may move towards dog status as it is milked for cash, but it should be withdrawn before negative cash flows occur.

An appropriate balance of cash cows, stars and question marks, enables the business to produce positive cash flows and profit, while continuing investment in future profitability.

Limitations

The major weakness of this model is its simplification of complex situations and the glib guidelines that flow from it. Measurement and definition problems must be overcome for it to be useful. Narrow definitions of the market are usually necessary to identify a useful portfolio of products. An analysis of Unilever's detergent products undertaken for the detergent market revealed that they were all dogs but, in effect, they were really golden retrievers, which returned large cash flows and profit. When the analysis was repeated at the market segment level, it showed that Unilever had a number of stars and cash cows.

Another limitation is the tendency of this type of analysis to limit vision and narrow the focus to a range of options that may be inappropriate. The notion, for example, that 'cows are for milking' does not distinguish between large share products in mature markets that have long-term profit and cash flow prospects, and require reinvestment and defence of share position and those that do not have future prospects, and should be harvested for maximum short-term profit and cash.

A further danger is that share may be seen as an end in itself, rather than as a means to achieving profitability. As Heinz discovered in the 1970s, a single-minded focus on dominating markes and maximising share does not necessarily bring with it long-term profitability.

Practical significance

The portfolio concept developed by the BCG does make a practical contribution to strategic planning, so long as its limitations are realised:

- It is a useful conceptual tool for understanding where products fit in relation to each other in a portfolio and identifying those that require significant investment to improve their market positions. It helps to focus attention on problem products for which management decisions are necessary.
- In common with the product life-cycle, it suggests a competitive evolution of a product from problem child to star to cash cow as the market matures, and it highlights the importance of building market share while the market is growing.
- By drawing attention to cash generation and cash use of products, it emphasises the desirability of a balanced portfolio, so that new initiatives can be funded and cash generators protected.

Attractiveness – Competitive Position Models

The problems posed by the simplified and generic structure of the BCG model are overcome by the development of models tailored to the conditions affecting the firm or industry. A number of large corporations use a nine-box matrix to identify the positions of their businesses according to market/industry attractiveness (of which market growth rate in the BCG model is one factor) and business strengths/competitiveness position (of which relative market share is one factor).

General Electric with McKinsey pioneered this model, making use of many variables to assess each dimension. The dimensions used for assessing position are believed to be representative of the significant elements of the internal and external environment from which strengths, weaknesses, opportunities and threats arise. However, the relative importance of these dimensions varies between firms and industries. GE's business assessment matrix, through qualitative analysis, assesses a business as being strong, medium or weak in terms of business strength, and assesses its industry attractiveness as high, medium or low. In common with the BCG model, general strategic guidelines are provided for investment, divestment or selective growth or harvesting strategies.

The Shell Chemical Company developed a similar portfolio model called the directional policy matrix, using as its two main assessment criteria competitive capabilities (similar to GE's business strengths) and prospects for sector profitability (analogous to GE's industry attractiveness).

More recently, a simpler four-box version of the directional policy matrix has been developed, together with computer software that enables practising managers to quantify the axes and include circles which accurately represent the relative importance of the contribution to the organisation of the products, services or markets represented on the matrix.

Strategic implications

These models have the advantage of taking account of specific factors relevant to the industry. Generic strategy guidelines, however, also emanate from them. Figure 3.16 shows a number of strategic options depending upon a business' position in terms of market attractiveness (high, medium or weak). Figure 3.17 indicates directions relevant to four different business positions, depending on objectives, resource availability and risk.

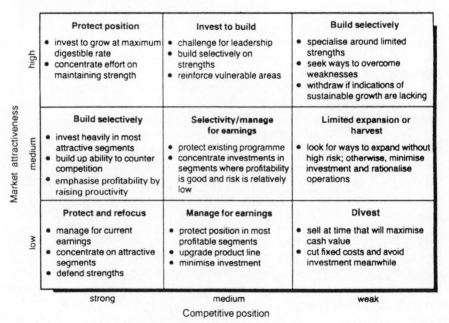

	strong	**medium**	**weak**
high	**Protect position** • invest to grow at maximum digestible rate • concentrate effort on maintaining strength	**Invest to build** • challenge for leadership • build selectively on strengths • reinforce vulnerable areas	**Build selectively** • specialise around limited strengths • seek ways to overcome weaknesses • withdraw if indications of sustainable growth are lacking
medium	**Build selectively** • invest heavily in most attractive segments • build up ability to counter competition • emphasise profitability by raising prouctivity	**Selectivity/manage for earnings** • protect existing programme • concentrate investments in segments where profitability is good and risk is relatively low	**Limited expansion or harvest** • look for ways to expand without high risk; otherwise, minimise investment and rationalise operations
low	**Protect and refocus** • manage for current earnings • concentrate on attractive segments • defend strengths	**Manage for earnings** • protect position in most profitable segments • upgrade product line • minimise investment	**Divest** • sell at time that will maximise cash value • cut fixed costs and avoid investment meanwhile

Market attractiveness

Competitive position

Figure 3.16 Generic strategy options
Source: Day (1986), p 204

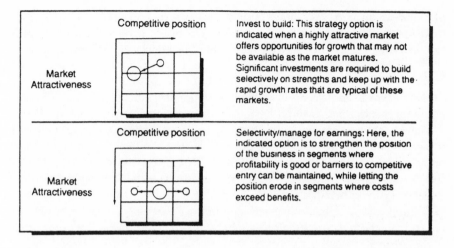

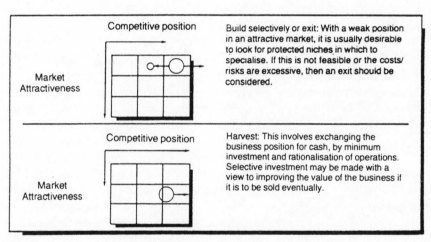

Figure 3.17 Strategy direction
Source: Day (1986), pp 174 and 205

Limitations

The main practical difficulty is the selection and weighting of relevant criteria for assessing a business' position on the matrix. Also, when assessing business-es in different industries, the success factors usually differ, and unless separate calculations are worked out for each, direct comparisons of different business-es on the same matrix may be inappropriate. There are often strategic reasons for staying in a business when the financial indications suggest divestment. For example, Hoover's assessment of the vacuum-cleaning market and its array of low-price international competitors, is that manufacturers are prepared to lose money long term in this market because it acts as an entry point to the household for a wide range of appliances and electronic products – the vacuum cleaner being one of the first products bought by new homemakers.

Practical significance

An important insight from these models is the strategic significance of competitive position as measured by relative business strengths, capabilities and market share. For instance, a market may be very attractive with rapid growth prospects and a wide range of opportunities, but the business' relative competitive position is weak, and competitive advantages are difficult to find and risky to implement. Alternatively, the business may have a strong competitive position in an unprofitable, declining market with poor long-term prospects. The implication is that the firm's competitive strength should be used to restructure the industry on a profitable basis or plan to divest from part or all of the business.

Ansoff's Product-market Growth Model

Igor Ansoff (1968; pp 127–131) a pioneer in strategic thinking, introduced the concept of the planning gap by first charting expected future sales or return on investment (ROI) based on no change to current strategies, then, charting potential sales or ROI based on market potential. In Figure 3.18, two gaps are identified between expected sales from present strategies and maximum sales growth potential – a competitive gap indicating sales potential from the existing business and a diversification gap suggesting sales potential from new businesses. Figure 3.19 modifies this concept to show the top-line sales trend to represent management objectives with the task of the marketer to develop strategies to close the gap.

Ansoff proposes options for closing the gap in this growth matrix based on a matching of present and new products with present and new markets, shown in Figure 3.20. A market penetration strategy using products in present markets involves increasing market share and consumption or use from existing customers. Market development requires the targeting of products into new market segments and converting non-users to customers.

Product development enables the firm to grow from new products offered to its existing markets. Diversification requires new products for new markets, which may be related or unrelated to the existing business. The strategic and relevant options will depend upon the size of the gap and the firm's competitive position in its markets. For instance, a high market share in existing markets, such as Asda's position in the North of England, suggests that growth will be sought from new markets such as the South and from new product ranges.

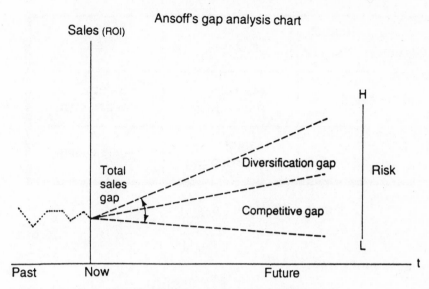

Figure 3.18 Product market directions

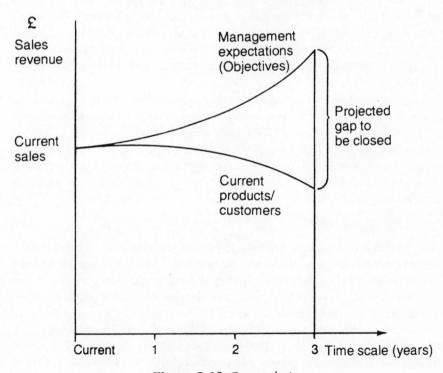

Figure 3.19 Gap analysis

Market \ Product	Present	New
Present	Market penetration	Product development
New	Market development	Diversification

Figure 3.20 Ansoff's growth vector matrix
Source: Brownlie and Bart (1985), p 29

Strategic implications

The product-market growth model has implications for objectives and strategies. Figure 3.21 indicates alternative directions for growth from the established business, where market penetration is the current strategy. Depending upon the firm and its environment, product development, market development or a higher risk move to diversification will be pursued. French and German supermarket groups have expanded into other EC markets as their position in their home markets became saturated. Coca-Cola, who for decades followed a policy of market extension, has recently moved along the product development route. British American Tobacco has diversified into a number of growth industries unrelated to the tobacco business.

Brownlie and Bart (1985, p 14) suggest that the sales or profit gap or both can be closed by one or a combination of three major strategies – sales growth, productivity improvement and redeployment of capital resources. Figure 3.22 depicts these options.

Practical application

Although a simplification of the issues involved, the planning gap and product-market growth concepts are a good starting point for identifying the strategic analysis task and providing broad indicators for strategic direction. It can indicate widely different growth or profit expectations from those that are realistic and therefore highlight problems to be addressed by management.

Sometimes, the gap analysis approach will show that the momentum of present strategies will take sales higher than is desirable, given the limited supply capabilities of the firm. In general, we find that companies have difficulty meeting demand during the rapid growth stage of the life cycle. The results of

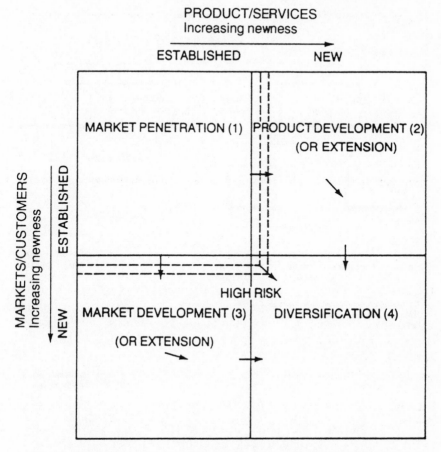

Figure 3.21 Using the Ansoff matrix in the objective setting process

customer complaints, poor service and decline in quality in an effort to meet demand, weaken the firm's competitive position.

The significance of these concepts is that market growth should be managed in line with capabilities to achieve realistic objectives. Strategic planning, therefore, should involve managing opportunities and capabilities to meet objectives. The setting of appropriate objectives is just as important as selecting appropriate strategies.

Strategy Experience Models – The PIMS Model

The basic premise underlying the pooling of business experience is that the conduct of a large series of strategy experiments on companies in a similar

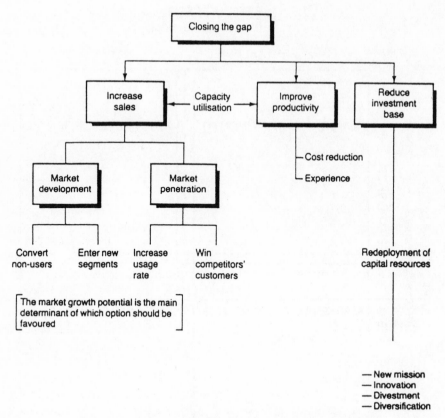

Figure 3.22 Strategy alternatives for closing the gap
Source: Brownlie and Bart (1985), p 14

competitive position will provide guidelines on successful and unsuccessful strategies that will be useful in evaluating options under review by a company. Also, the analysis of strategic experience of businesses under different market, competitive and operating conditions, helps to identify the strategic factors that primarily determine profitability. Statistical analysis and computer modelling of the data identify relationships between strategy and performance, and provide guidelines for strategic planning. This approach has been adopted by the Strategic Planning Institute in Boston with its PIMS programme, which was initiated in the early 1970s.

The PIMS approach seeks guidance from the collective experience of a diverse sample of successful and unsuccessful businesses. Since 1972 it has compiled a database from more than 450 corporations comprising analysis of over 2800 business units. Statistical analysis and computer modelling of the database provides member companies, which subscribe to and provide information for PIMS, with strategic guidelines based on pooled experience of many different strategic situations in a diverse range of industries. Two concepts are fundamental to the database:

1. The *business unit* – a division, product line or profit centre.
2. The *served market* – a portion of the total market in which the firm competes.

The PIMS analysis measures changes in the firm's competitive position, the strategies employed to achieve it, and the resulting profitability.

Analysis reveals that three sets of factors are persistently influential in affecting business profitability. One set describes competitive position, which includes market share and relative product quality. A second describes the production structure, including investment intensity and productivity of operations. The third reflects the relative attractiveness of the market growth rate and customer characteristics. Together, these variables account for 65 to 70 per cent of the variability in profitability in the sample. The purpose of the PIMS project is to apply this experience to specific strategic questions. These questions include:

- What rate of cash flow and profit is 'normal' for this type of business, given its market environment, competitive position and the strategy being pursued?
- If the business continues as at present, what market share and profitability performance could be expected in the future?
- How will this performance be affected by a change in the strategy?
- How have other firms in the same industry or in different industries facing the same conditions and similar competitive position performed, given different types of strategies employed?

Answers to these questions can help the strategist to evaluate alternative options under consideration.

The PIMS database is represented by many different industries, products, markets and geographic regions. Most of these are located in North America, although about 600 of the 2800 businesses are in the UK, Europe and a scattering of other countries.

PIMS findings

This analysis has resulted in observed links between strategy and performance. These general relationships can provide help for managers to understand and predict how strategic choices and market conditions will affect business performance. These are the most common links between strategy and performance:

- In the long run, the most important factor affecting a business unit's performance is the quality of its products and services, relative to those of competitors.

- Market share and profitability are strongly related.
- High investment intensity acts as a powerful drag on profitability.
- Many so-called dog and question mark businesses generate cash, while many cash cows are dry.
- Vertical integration is a profitable strategy for some kinds of businesses, but not for others. For small-share businesses, return on investment is highest when the degree of vertical integration is low. For businesses with above-average share positions, return on investment is highest when vertical integration is either low or high.
- Most of the strategic factors that boost return on investment also contribute to the long-term value of the business (Buzzell and Gale, 1987, pp 7–15).

Some selected PIMS findings are shown in Table 3.3. These findings provide some empirical guidelines that support the use of the market attractiveness-competitive position models reviewed earlier (Buzzell and Gale, 1987, Chapters 5–10). The cash flow implications of investment intensity (measured by investment as a percentage of sales) and marketing intensity (measured by marketing expenses as a percentage of sales) are given an empirical foundation. The strategic importance of market share and product quality in contributing to profitability is identified.

Limitations of PIMS

Criticisms of PIMS range from definitions of variables, data collection methods and data accuracy, to the non-causal relationships found between variables. Many of these criticisms are valid and should alert the user to treat the findings with care. The PIMS type of analysis can give the user a false sense of accuracy and predictive power. It should be viewed as another source of ideas for strategic planning to be put beside the strategist's own experience, judgement and analysis.

Practical application

The argument that the structure of an industry, the competitive position of the business, its costs/margins/investment structure and the competitive strategies it employs have a fundamental impact on profitability, has strong intuitive appeal.

Practitioners know that a dominant market leader position in a growing market with attractive margins and moderate investment requirements, will bring high profitability. Alternatively, a business ranked third or fourth in competitive position in a mature market with low margins, frequently yields low profitability or losses. PIMS demonstrates that these structural attributes have a significant effect on business profitability and that firms should seek competitive structures and positions that provide them with a profit advantage.

Table 3.3 Some PIMS findings

Attractiveness of industry – market environment

Market share is most profitable in vertically integrated industries.
R & D spending is most profitable in mature, slow growth markets.
A narrow product range in the early or middle stages of the life-cycle is less profitable than at maturity.
Capacity utilisation is important when investment intensity (investment/value added) is high.
High relative market share (>75%) improves cash flow; high growth (>7%) decreases it.

Competitive position

High relative market share (>62%) and low investment intensity (<80%) generate cash; low share (<26%) and high investment intensity (>120%) results in a net use of cash.
High R & D spending (>37% sales) depresses ROI when market share is low (<26%).
High marketing spending (>11% sales) depresses ROI when market share is low.
High R & D and marketing spending depresses ROI.
A rapid rate of new product introductions in fast growing markets depresses ROI.

Capital structure

Low or medium industry growth (<9%) coupled with low investment intensity (<80%) produces cash; high growth (>9%) and high investment intensity (>120%) is a cash drain.
A low level of new product introductions and low investment intensity (<80%) produces cash.
High investment intensity and high marketing intensity (>11% sales) drains cash.
Harvesting when investment intensity is low produces cash.
Building market share when investment intensity is high uses cash.

Source: Brownlie and Bart (1985)

The specific PIMS models and strategic relationships are useful in providing a 'reality test' for the competitive strategies under consideration. They answer questions such as:

- Does this strategy make sense in the light of the experience of others in a similar competitive structure and position?
- Are sufficient resources committed to achieve the desired competitive position and profitability?
- Are the business objectives unrealistic?
- What type of competitive pattern and future competitive structure is likely if this strategy is adopted?

These are important issues to raise, and PIMS analysis helps strategic thinking in these areas.

Industry Structure Models and Competitive Strategy

Microeconomic theory focuses on market structure and competitive position as determinants of competitive behaviour. The significance of monopolistic and oligopolistic structures in shaping competitive strategies is recognised by economists in their theories of competition.

Developments by Michael Porter (1980, pp 31–33) extend this thinking substantially and provide a practical analytical framework for developing competitive strategies involving the structural analysis of industries. He identifies the main structural forces that drive industry competitors – industry competition, supplier and customer concentration, availability of substitutes and the threat of the entry of new competitors – and suggests that industry profit is affected by these forces.

Porter indicates that the purpose of competitive strategy is to find a position where the company can best defend itself against these forces or influence them in its favour. He studies different industry structures at different stages of evolution and provides guidelines for competitive strategy. Porter goes on to identify the elements of a business that can be used to create and sustain competitive advantage. He considers defensive and offensive strategies for maintaining or improving the firm's market position. This type of analysis is useful in assessing strategic opportunities and competitive threats.

In order to influence the structure of an industry or market, it is necessary to identify the important elements of its structure and to seek to affect the competitive forces that determine profitability.

The Porter model

Porter (1985) suggests that five major forces drive industry competition. These are shown in Figure 3.23. He proposes that the structure of the industry itself, its suppliers and its buyers have a major influence on the evolution of the industry and its profit potential. The threat of substitutes and new entrants also influences the appropriate strategies to be adopted.

The implication is that the competitor should influence the balance of forces through strategic moves, thereby strengthening the firm's position. Alternatively, the strategist might reposition the firm so that its capabilities provide the best defence against the array of competitive forces. A further approach is to anticipate shifts in the factors underlying the forces and to respond to them, thus exploiting change by choosing a strategy appropriate to the new competitive balance before competitors recognise it.

A vast range of structural elements may potentially affect these competitive forces. In any particular industry, a small number of factors will be relevant. In the compressed cylinder gas market, for example, the strategic elements for management by BOC, the market leader, are the distribution system, the fragmentation of the customer base and the control of cylinder production and supply.

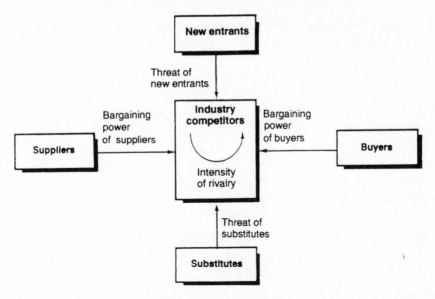

Figure 3.23 The five competitive forces and elements of industry structure
Source: Porter (1980), p4

Evolution of an industry is also affected by the life-cycle stage of its main markets. The large body of life-cycle literature provides marketing strategy guidelines for competitors at each stage. During the growth stage, it is appropriate for market leaders to adopt offensive strategies, whereas in maturity and decline, defensive strategies may be more appropriate. Effective strategies for smaller competitors, however, are different. Where the real opportunities lie for a competitor to restructure, the market will depend upon the industry value chain and the contribution of each of the companies at different levels of the supply/distribution/customer system.

Porter examined industries in different stages of evolution, from emerging product markets to declining ones. Porter considers that in the long term, the extent to which the firm is able to create a defendable position in an industry is a major determinant of the success with which it will out-perform its competitors. He proposes generic strategies by means of which a firm can develop a competitive advantage and create a defendable position:

- Overall cost leadership – aggressive pursuit of an industry-wide lowest cost position relative to competitors.
- Differentiation – development of distinctive abilities that are perceived industry-wide as unique. These may be along several dimensions such as product quality, distribution or after-sales service. In marketing terms, this is known as differentiated marketing.

- Focus – concentrated effort aimed at securing a competitive advantage in a particular market segment or niche. In marketing terms, this is referred to as concentrated marketing.

In terms of product-market evolution, a firm may change its generic strategy over time by moving from a focused strategy to an industry-wide strategy of either cost leadership or differentiation. Alternatively, a firm may adopt a cost leadership strategy, which changes over time to an emphasis on differentiation. Figure 3.24 shows the alternative strategic options and Figure 3.25 the trade-offs that occur between differentiation and productivity gains through cost leadership.

Cost leadership versus differentiation

Cost leadership
Cost leadership is one of two generic strategies in which a firm sets out to become the low-cost producer in its industry. Policy choices that tend to have the greatest impact on cost include:

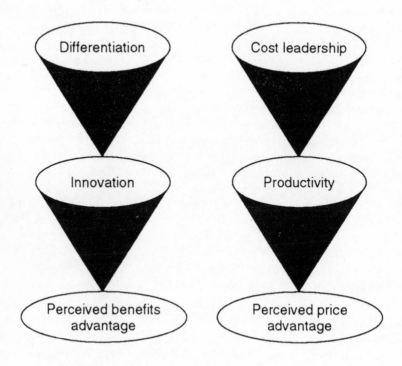

Figure 3.24 Strategic alternatives

Differentiation

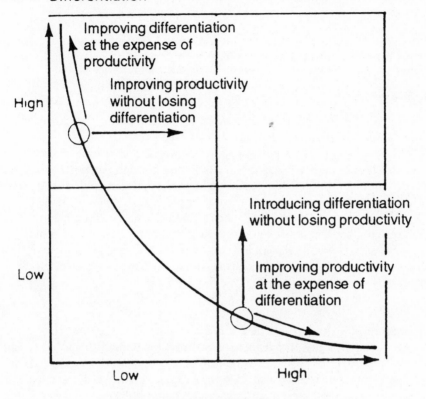

Cost leadership

Figure 3.25 Strategic directions

- product configuration, performance and features;
- mix and variety of products offered;
- level of service provided;
- channels employed (eg, few, more efficient dealers rather than many small ones).

The primary focus of the cost leadership strategy is to compete on price as the major marketing tool.

Although the advantage of a cost leadership strategy is that it provides a source of competitive advantage, particularly for market leaders who can use economies of scale, it is usually not appropriate in markets where:

- there is product parity;
- the leader is already heavily committed to an extensive product range;

- service and channel distribution are critical factors of competitive advantage.

Although cost management and reduction should be pursued where possible, it should not necessarily be the strategic focus for market leaders in declining markets.

Differentiation

In a differentiation strategy, a firm seeks to be unique in its industry along some dimensions that are widely valued by buyers.

In the gases industry, some segments of which are in decline, BOC has selected product availability as the key differentiator and has positioned itself uniquely to meet that need. In similar industries, such as auto parts and accessories, service and distribution are vital differentiators in declining markets.

Product parity usually exists between competitors, and differentiation occurs on availability, service, information provision and price. In adopting a differentiation strategy, a leader will aim for cost parity with its major competitors, but should reduce costs only in areas that do not affect favourably perceived differentiation.

Coverage versus focus

The degree of segmentation of the market and the size of the largest segments, together with the leader's competitive strengths, will determine whether a strategy of coverage or one of focus is required for leadership and dominance of the market. Usually, a leader will need coverage of the main market segments and a strategy may be adopted to attempt to combine some segments with the same product offering. This strategy of counter-segmentation may be viable in declining markets as customers decline to a hard core of users.

Sustainable competitive advantage

The task of competitive strategy is to develop, maintain or defend the firm's competitive position based on a sustainable competitive advantage. The advantage needs to be sustainable because of the considerable investment required to achieve it. Consider the following competitive advantages and their investment requirements:

- the superior product engineering and perception of product quality achieved by Mercedes Benz;
- the brand identity and preference for Coca-Cola and Foster's lager;
- the low-cost advantage achieved by Aldi Stores and British Telecom;
- the superior knowledge of the fast foods business held by McDonald's restaurants;

- the scale advantages achieved by Cadbury-Schweppes in the European market.

These represent elements of sustainable competitive advantage developed by these businesses over many years.

Market structure and competitive position

A firm's competitive position and the market structure in which it operates, acts as a pervasive influence and constraint on its competitive marketing strategies.

Market structure

Most businesses operate in oligopoly market structures defined by a situation in which supply to the market is controlled by a few large producers, the remaining supply being accounted for by small firms. There are a number of substructures of oligopoly, however, which are relevant at the product/market level of competitive strategy. These are:

- monopoly dominance;
- joint dominance (duopoly);
- oligopoly dominance;
- equal oligopoly.

Monopoly dominance refers to a market structure in which one firm has a very large share of the market (ie, share of total industry sales), while all other oligopoly firms each have a much smaller share. In this type of structure, a single firm has such clear share dominance over other firms, that it can, if it so desires, exercise monopoly-like control over both the market and its competitors' strategies. This is particularly evident on price changes. In a market structure of this type, the dominant firm will tend to lead changes in the general level of product prices, with other oligopoly firms following these changes. This is true in the European airline industry, in which the principal national airlines have held a monopoly for decades.

Joint dominance or duopoly refers to a structure in which two companies jointly dominate a market, while all other competitors, as a group, have a small market share. Two types of duopoly dominance occur in practice, one in which the two firms have approximately equal market shares, the other in which one firm has a distinct market share advantage. In both cases, the two dominant firms primarily react to each other's strategies. Either one of the two may be price leader, or it may alternate between them, with other competitors likely to follow changes. The two dominant firms jointly exercise the same types of influences on small competitors, as does the dominant firm operating in a monopoly dominance structure. This type of structure is typified in the UK telecommunications market with British Telecom and Mercury as the principal protagonists.

In oligopoly dominance, the dominant firm has a much smaller share advantage over its next competitor than is evident in a monopoly dominance structure. In such cases, the dominant firm's position is more easily challenged by other oligopolists. Nevertheless, it still remains in a position in which it can lead price changes and limit the flexibility of its competitors, particularly through the use of the price variable. The car rental market exhibits this structure, in which Budget has a clear share lead.

Equal oligopoly refers to a market structure in which no firm has clear dominance. Characteristically, two or more competitors have similar market shares, which are not sufficient to constitute duopoly or joint dominance. In such market structures, price leadership and other forms of competitive behaviour are much less predictable. It is impossible to arrive at valid generalisations on *a priori* grounds. This market structure exists in the European-oriented polypropylene market, in which ICI, Courtaulds, Mobil, Moplefan and others hold roughly equal shares. Likewise, in the European chocolate confectionery market, the leader holds only a marginal lead. The statistics given in Table 3.4 show an oligopolistic situation both in the UK and in Europe overall.

Meanwhile, the rise of European media outlets such as satellite broadcasting, will change the nature of this and many other markets, and a critical mass of product range will be needed to justify distribution costs and to fund new product launches. Also, the large-scale restructuring of the European chocolate confectionery market is expected to drive costs down and to facilitate even heavier promotional spending on brands.

In addition to these oligopoly structures, a fragmented structure, where market share is divided between many competitors, appears in some markets. In the quantity surveying market, no firm holds more than about a 5 per cent market share.

Competitive position

A firm's competitive position, usually measured by its market share, is also an important determinant of the types of strategies it adopts. The Boston

Table 3.4 European chocolate confectionery market share (% by sales volume)

Company	UK	Austria	Belgium	France	Italy	Netherlands	Switzerland	Germany	Total
Mars	24	4	6	11	1	23	9	22	17
Suchard	2	73	82	13	–	–	17	15	13
Rowntree	26	–	3	17	–	13	–	3	11
Ferrero	2	–	5	6	34	–	–	16	10
Cadbury	30	–	–	8	–	–	–	–	9
Nestlé	2	5	3	10	5	–	17	8	9

Source: Henderson Crosthwaite

Consulting Group recognises this in their product portfolio theory. The BCG growth-share model views products in terms of their market share relative to the largest shareholder in the market – ie, a measure of relative share.

The relevant measure of position is in terms of dominance. A firm may be in one of three possible positions in the market:

1. Individual dominance – in which a firm has a significantly higher market share than that of its closest competitor.
2. Joint dominance – in which a firm and one competitor have approximately equal market shares, which are significantly higher than that of their nearest competitor.
3. Non-dominance – in which the company has a significantly lower share level than one or more dominant competitors in the market.

Its position, identified in these terms, indicates its relative market power and its capability in managing the market, the competition, the direction the market takes and profitability in the market.

Limitations of industry structure analysis

The main limitation of this type of analysis, in common with other models discussed, is that it does not specifically take account of the human and behavioural dimensions of competitive strategy. It assumes that competitors will behave rationally with a profit motive and that they understand the dynamics of the market and competition, and the consequences of their own strategies. This is not so in many industries. In the building-equipment hire industry, there were many competitors operating on prices below cost at a time when capacity was falling well short of demand. Logic would suggest that prices, margins and profits could all be increased in these conditions – to everyone's benefit in the industry.

Practical significance

Industry structure and competitive position do impose constraints on the range of viable strategies available to any competitor and their results. Competitive strategies can and do change the structure and position of players in the industry, however, and the objective is to adopt strategies that provide a sustainable advantage to the business within the scope of changing structure and position.

INTEGRATION OF CONCEPTS AND MODELS

Each of the models and analytical tools reviewed in this chapter provides a contribution to strategic formulation. Indeed, there are links between them that provide a more integrated picture of strategic analysis.

Product Life-cycle and Competitive Position

Arthur D Little has linked various competitive positions ranging from dominant to weak with objectives for changing or holding those positions at different stages of the product life-cycle. Table 3.5 summarises these. Brownlie focuses on two competitive positions: market leader (with dominant market share) and market follower. Guidelines are provided for growth, maturity and decline phases, shown in Table 3.6.

Portfolio, Product Life-cycle and PIMS

Table 3.7 indicates the characteristics of strategies suggested by the portfolio approach and their relationship with the product life-cycle.

Table 3.5 Guidelines for various product life-cycle stages and competitive positions

	Embryonic	Growing	Mature	Ageing
Dominance	All-out push for share	Hold position	Hold position	
				Hold position
	Hold position	Hold share	Grow with industry	
Strong	Attempt to improve position	Attempt to improve position	Hold position	
				Hold position or harvest
	All-out push for share	Push for share	Grow with industry	
Favourable	Selective or all-out push for share	Attempt to improve position	Custodial or maintenance	Harvest
	Selectively attempt to improve position	Selective push for share	Find niche and attempt to protect	Phased withdrawal
Tenable	Selective push for position	Find niche and protect it	Find niche and hang on or phased withdrawal	Phased withdrawal or abandon
Weak	Up or out	Turnaround or abandon	Turnaround or phased withdrawal	Abandon

Source: Day (1986), p 212

Table 3.6 Competitive position and life-cycle stage

Competitive position	Growth	Product life-cycle stage maturity	Decline
Market leader (dominant market share)	Build market share; reduce prices to discourage competition; develop primary demand and channel strength	Maintain market share; advertise for brand loyalty; product differentiation; price with competitors	Harvest market share; maximise cash flow; reduce product expenditures such as advertising and selling
Market follower	Invest in research and development; advertising and distribution to increase market share; concentrate on a particular market segment; advertise for positioning	Maintain or reduce market share; price to penetrate; reduce costs below the market leaders	No product expenditure; withdraw from the market

Source: Brownlie and Bart (1985), p 24

Table 3.7 Portfolio position and life-cycle stage

Product classification	Life-cycle stage	Product stage	Strategy guideline
Question mark	Growth	Introduction	Investment
Star	Growth	Growth	Maintenance
Cash cow	Maturity	Maturity	Harvesting
Dog	Maturity	Decline	Withdrawal

It is important here not to confuse the stage of the market life-cycle with the stage of the individual product's evolution.

Question mark products may be introduced during any phase of market growth of the product category life-cycle. Cash cows may exist in markets that show significant growth, are static or even declining. Dog products may be declining when various segments of a mature market show growth prospects. The BCG model shows the evolution of a firm's own product from introduction through to maturity.

The PIMS findings tend to support the underlying concepts of growth-share, product life-cycle and the effect of learning experience on costs and profit margins. Figure 3.26 shows some of these findings.

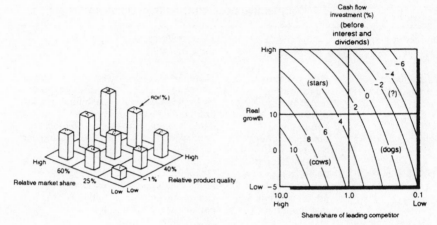

Cash flow rate contour lines for the growth-share matrix

	Market share		
		13%	27%
Early	6	20	33
Middle	11	20	29
Late	15	19	27

(Stage in life-cycle)

Figure 3.26 Portfolio life cycle and market share
Source: Day (1986) pp 162, 163 and 187

Strategic Position and Generic Strategies for Competitive Advantage

Four different strategic positions are shown in Fig. 3.27. These are based on competitive advantage in terms of differentiation or cost leadership and low or high coverage.

Low advantage in cost or differentiation and low market coverage

Here, the business is in a commodity marketing situation, where products are homogeneous, the market structure is fragmented and price competition features. Profit is usually low. It is desirable, if possible, to change this position, unless a cost leadership position can be achieved with resulting market share and profit gains.

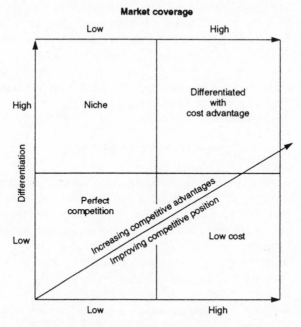

Figure 3.27 Improving competitive position

Cost advantage, low differentiation and high market coverage

This is a desirable position if the cost advantage can be protected and sustained. The volume and market share resulting from a high market coverage should yield profit.

Differentiation advantage, comparative costs and low market coverage

This is a niche position, where emphasis is necessary to protect and improve differentiation. It is viable for small competitors and for large competitors in large volume segments. Share of the overall market is relatively small.

Differentiation and cost advantages with high market coverage

This is the most profitable strategic position, because the market leader has cost, value and volume advantages over its competitors and can command a price premium, with higher margins than its competitors. This position is dominant in market share terms.

For large companies seeking dominance, competitive strategies should be directed at moving towards this strategic position, shown in Figure 3.27. There are, however, different paths from which to choose. The Japanese car manufacturers, such as Toyota, have moved from an imitation/commodity position to cost leadership, then to differentiation with cost advantages, as shown in Figure 3.28. There is evidence that smaller companies, such as Honda, have now developed niche strategies aimed at competing in specific market segments. McDonald's started as one of many in the fast foods hamburger business, moved to a niche position with product and service superiority, and then to a high volume and market share position, gaining cost advantages while maintaining differentiation (see Figure 3.29).

COMPETITIVE POSITION

A firm's competitive position is fundamental to the selection of competitive marketing strategies. In this chapter a broad view is taken of competitive position.

In essence, the factors involved in assessing competitive position are all those which have an impact on market performance, such as sales revenue, share and company/brand image, and on profit performance, such as investment levels, costs, margins, prices and productivity, and can be evaluated against major competitors.

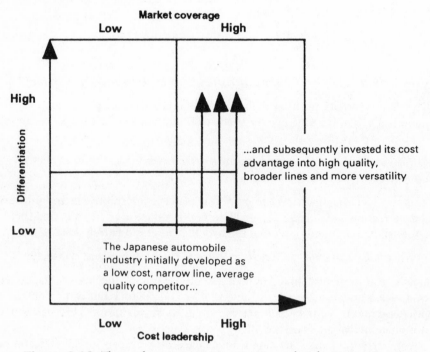

Figure 3.28 The path to competitive position taken by Japanese car manufacturers

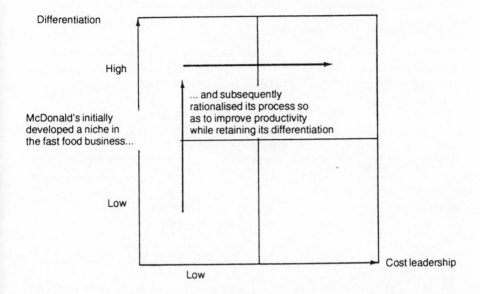

Figure 3.29 The path to competitive position for McDonald's

Assessing Competitive Position

A number of dimensions are important in practice when assessing competitive position and deciding upon strategies to maintain or change position.

Market positioning

This refers to the relevant market's recognition and perception of a firm's position in the market – what it stands for and what its offerings provide relative to its competitors' offerings. For example, in the computer market, IBM is perceived to be industry leader (the standards setter) and provider of a wide range of high quality, reliable products supported by dependable after-sales service. Companies and their products become positioned in the market's collective mind on a variety of intangible and functional dimensions, which are used by customers to distinguish them.

Market research techniques are now available to identify corporate and product positionings in a firm's target markets. Perceptions of quality, range, availability, image and other relevant dimensions are measured for competing firms. Positioning studies are used to focus a firm's attention on what target customers believe to be important, to improve areas of perceived relative weakness and to consolidate perceived advantages. This type of analysis provides direction to improve or reinforce market positioning.

Product and market coverage

An assessment of the extent of product and market coverage points to opportunities for widening or narrowing product range and segment spread. Table 3.8 shows the relative coverage of two competing firms.

Table 3.8 Product and market coverage

		Market segments				
		1	2	3	4	5
Product	1	A	A	A	A	B
variants	2	A	A	A	A	B
	3	A	A	A	A	B
	4	A	A	A	A	B
	5		A		A	B

Firm A has broad coverage of all except one market segment and has the full range of variants, except in segments one and three. Firm B specialises only in segment five with a full range.

Innovator or follower

The market stance of innovator or follower is determined by the extent and timing of the introduction of new products. Competitors frequently take a deliberate decision on whether to be innovator or follower, and structure their research and development functions and marketing departments accordingly. The advantages of being first into a market are well known, but the risks can be high and the costs of failure great. Long-term competitive position is strengthened by a record of successful innovations.

Strategic positions in the market

The market leader has the position of being first in the customer's mind. Kleenex with facial tissues, Hoover with vacuum cleaners, Heinz with baby food, IBM with computers, Budget in rental cars, Xerox with copiers. This, in the long term, is supported by the highest market share.

In some markets, there are two, or even three leaders. This characterises joint leadership. Another position in the market is the high-share flanker, which poses as a serious challenger to the market leader. The remaining positions belong to specialists who focus on market niches.

In many European markets, there is only room for two large mainstream competitors, a leader and an alternative, and the rest are niche competitors, specialising in narrow segments of the market. Viable positions in the market become strategic because they provide a basis for building, maintaining or successfully defending competitive position. These strategic positions are:

- market leader;
- market challenger;
- market follower;
- market specialist.

The general characteristics of each viable strategic position are shown in Table 3.9.

The size and structure of the market and the economics of supply will determine how many viable competitors can exist. For example, the British life insurance industry has hundreds of competitors – a market leader, a challenger, about 20 followers and the rest specialists. In the domestic airlines

Table 3.9 Strategic positions in the market

Market leader	
Largest market share	Covers mainstream market
Perceived as industry leader	Maintains share
Leads industry moves	Has the largest profit
	Protects its profit base
	Major impact on the market

Market challenger	
Number 2 or 3 in share	Covers mainstream market
Perceived as an alternative to leader	Increases share
Innovative and aggressive	Investing for future profit
Seeking leadership	Major impact on the market

Market follower	
A significant share	Covers largest segments of the market
Adequate quality lower priced alternative	Holds or increases share
Quick to follow industry moves	Cost advantages
	Limited impact on the market

Market specialist	
Largest share of a small segment	Specialises in a market niche
Small share of overall market	Holds share
Perceived as a specialist	Small, flexible and responsive
	Little impact on the overall market

industry, however, there is only a handful of competitors. The market size, structure and characteristics provide opportunities for a range of market positionings based on quality, service, price and image attributes.

The relevance of these strategic positions to competitive marketing strategy is to be able to identify what strategic position a company has, then to develop strategies to defend or reinforce that position, or to change it.

Market structure and shares

The market structure and shares of individual competitors are important dimensions of competitive position because they set the scope within which change can take place. Table 3.10 indicates a typical range of structures and share positions found in European markets.

The structure and share positions provide some guidance for formulating competitive marketing strategies. In certain conditions, such as a mature market, the dominant leader in a monopoly dominance structure may want to adopt strategies to defend its share leadership and its overall competitive position.

One of the leaders in a joint dominance structure may adopt a leadership strategy to attain clear-cut market leadership. A niche competitor may want to adopt a growth strategy to strengthen its position in one or two segments of the market or to be a leading force in the market.

Profitability and resources

This dimension of competitive position is internal to the company, but should be assessed in relation to competitors' profitability and resources. It flags the

Table 3.10 Market structure and share positions

Market structure	Monopoly dominance (1 dominates)	Joint dominance (2 dominate)	Equal oligopoly (3 or more equal share)	Fragmented structure
Market share positions	• Dominant leader (eg 50%)	• 2 leaders in share terms (eg 40%)	• 3 or more substantial shareholders (eg 5%)	• Market share spread between many competitors (eg 5%)
	• Large non-dominant (eg 25%)	• Specialist niche competitors (eg 5%)	• Specialist niche competitors (eg 5%)	
	• Small niche competitors (eg 5%)			

company's ability or otherwise to fund and continue support for its strategy in relation to competitors.

Internal sources of competitive advantage

Elements such as cost structure, specific skills, responsiveness and other internal characteristics that affect success in the industry, also form another dimension of competitive position. Frequently, as part of a competitive strategy, a business must act on costs or know-how or factors which make the company more market responsive to enable it to improve competitive position. When Lord King joined British Airways as chairman in the early 1980s, for example, he realised that his first priority was to get costs and quality into line before marketing could have any impact on the business.

These dimensions of competitive position have quantitative components (market share, profit, resources) and qualitative ones (market positioning, coverage, responsiveness, know-how). The task of competitive marketing strategy is to improve the quality of competitive position and to reduce the risk of disaster. Often, this will require action on many or all of the competitive position dimensions. Although there may be a trade-off between profit and strength of competitive position in the short term, while the firm wants to remain as a strong contender in the market, long-term profitability will be tied to a strong and defendable competitive position.

In most markets, there is room for a market leader, a differentiated number two, a substantial low-price positioned competitor, and niche specialists.

COMPETITIVE STRATEGIES

In practice, an almost infinite number of variations in competitive strategy exist, because of the multi-faceted aspects to be dealt with when changing or defending competitive position, and the vast array of different market and competitive conditions existing at any point in time.

In considering competitive position from a strategic point of view, however, there are four main directions which competitive strategy can take:

1. developing and building;
2. maintaining and holding;
3. defending;
4. withdrawing.

The fourth direction, withdrawal, involves harvesting and phased divestment strategies in which marketing's role is to maximise customer goodwill and migrate customers to other products, if that is applicable.

In reality, companies adopt a sequence of strategies that are dependent upon their objectives, competitive position, and market and industry conditions. Competitive strategies for building, maintaining and defending competitive position are addressed according to four market positions of firms:

1. dominant position – market leader;
2. position of joint dominance shared with a competitor – joint leaders;
3. a growing force and substantial share – challenger or follower;
4. a growing niche position involving dominance of a narrow segment-market specialist.

References

Aaker, DA (1984) *Strategic Market Management*, Wiley, Chichester.

Andrews, K (1984) 'Corporate strategy: the essential intangibles', *McKinsey Quarterly*, Autumn.

Ansoff, HI (1968) *Corporate Strategy*, Pelican Books, Gretna, Los Angeles.

Boston Consulting Group (1970) *Perspective on Experience*, The Boston Consulting Group Inc.

Brownlie, DT and Bart, CK (1985) *Products and Strategies*, Vol 11, No 1, MCB University Press.

Buzzell, RD and Gale, BT (1987) *The PIMS Principles: Linking Strategy to Performance*, The Free Press, New York.

Davidow, WH (1986) *Marketing High Technology: An Insider's View*, The Free Press, New York.

Day, GS (1984) *Strategic Market Planning: The Pursuit of Competitive Advantage*, West Publishing, St Paul, Minnesota.

Day, GS (1986) *Analysis for Strategic Market Decisions*, West Publishing, St Paul, Minnesota.

Kotler, P, Fakey, L and Jatusripitak, S (1986) *The New Competition: Meeting the Marketing Challenge from the Far East*, Prentice-Hall, Englewood Cliffs, New Jersey.

Lubatkin, M and Pitts, M (1985) 'The PIMS and the policy perspective: a rebuttal', *Journal of Business Strategy*, Summer.

McDonald, MHB (1989) *Marketing Plans: How to Prepare Them, How to Use Them*, Butterworth-Heinemann, Oxford.

Meenaghan, A and Turnbull, PW (1981) *Strategy and Analysis in Product Development*, Vol 15, No 5, MCB Publications.

Porter, ME (1980) *Competitive Strategy: Techniques for Analysing Industries and Competitors*, The Free Press, New York.

Porter, ME (1985) *Competitive Advantage: Creating and Sustaining Superior Performance*, The Free Press, New York.

Wasson, CR (1974) *Dynamic Competitive Strategy and Product Life-cycles*, Challenge Books.

Weitz, BA and Wensley, R (1984) *Strategic Marketing: Planning Implementation and Control*, Kent Publishing.

Windy, YJ (1982) *Product Policy: Concepts, Methods and Strategy*.

4

TECHNIQUE INTERRELATIONSHIPS AND THE PURSUIT OF RELEVANCE IN MARKETING THEORY*

Malcolm McDonald

ABSTRACT

This chapter provides evidence to show that the standard tools and techniques of marketing are hardly ever used by practising managers, which brings into question the relevance of much of what is taught in business schools.

The basic thesis is that apart from cultural and political blockages, the principal barriers to marketing theory implementation are caused firstly by methodological problems associated with the tools and techniques of marketing themselves, and secondly by the complex nature of the interrelationships between these techniques.

---

*This paper was first given at the MEG Conference held at Oxford Polytechnic, July 1990, and is reproduced with the kind permission of Norman Waite, Director of Education and Training, the Chartered Institute of Marketing.

The conclusion reached is that the human mind is largely incapable of dealing adequately with such complexity and that the only way that the academic world will be able to make a significant impact on the world of practice, particularly in more holistic domains such as strategic marketing planning, is to develop computerised support in the form of Expert Systems and the like.

DOES MARKETING THEORY HAVE ANY VALUE?

Stephen King's (1983) sensitive paper on applying research to decision-making focused attention on Britain's lack of innovation as one of the key causes of Britain's industrial demise since the war. His main argument centred around the belief that marketing research in general had failed to address the *real* marketing issues, because so much of it is *quantitative*.

He covered most forms of research in his review, including retail audits, TV ratings, multiple-choice motivational research, conjoint analysis, Fishbein, econometrics and gap analysis, concluding that they can actually be *destructive* to innovation if applied directly to decision-making.

> I believe part of our national failure to innovate has come through trying to use market research not as an *aid* to decision-making, but as a *system* that ideally reduces all personal judgement to a decision as to which of two numbers is the larger.

Many academics and practitioners have found King's paper to be an excellent and thought-provoking exposé of some of their deep-rooted concerns about the failure, not just of market research, but of marketing science in general, to storm the citadels of industry.

There can be some consolation, perhaps, in the fact that it is not only marketing people who continuously question the body of knowledge, its origins, application and usefulness to the real world of practice.

In 1981 Roger Evered (1981) wrote of the emerging realisation that the positivistic science paradigm inherited from the physical sciences has serious shortcomings for the managerial and organisational sciences, and he concluded:

> We must move beyond the objective, analytic, reductionist number-oriented, optimising and fail-safe approach to future problems, and learn to think with equal fluency in more subjective synthesising holistic, quantitative, option-increasing ways.

More recently, John Hughes (1988), in his wide-ranging review of the teaching of management education, concluded:

> The mistake we have made in teaching during the past 40 years has been to follow the logic approach to the physical sciences in teaching theory first, followed by an assumed application in practice ... The bridge from theory to practice is too hard to cross without some prior experience of the 'other side' ...

A common theme running through the substantial literature on the growing concern about the appropriateness of the positivistic science paradigm for understanding the process of management is that much of management deals with judgement, diagnosis and interpretation of events, which requires a different kind of knowing from logic and rationality.

Most people would acknowledge that in virtually any walk of life, the true expert has built up his expertise largely from experience and an intuitive grasp of problem-solving in the real world, something which is often referred to as the 'University of Life'. Indeed, many of the world's leading business people acknowledge that they owe their success not to formal business education and textbooks, but to their own experience, flair and intuitive good judgement.

Donald Schon (1984) describes scientific rigour as 'describable, testable, replicable techniques derived from scientific research, based on knowledge that is testable, consensual, cumulative and convergent', but then goes on to argue that much of what passes for scientific management is irrelevant because business problems do not come well formed. Certainly, most marketing problems are messy and indeterminate and successful practitioners make judgements using criteria which are difficult to define. Many academics would decry this as a lack of rigour, and in so doing exclude as non-rigorous much of what successful practitioners actually do.

It is this theme which is of particular relevance to marketing.

The chapter, however, will not make a plea for more attention to be paid to qualitative as opposed to quantitative research, as the author has already made the case for this (McDonald, 1985). Nor will it take up the argument against those who believe that learning by doing and feedback on performance are more valuable than knowledge in the head, and that theory is the wrong place to start when seeking to educate managers. For few would disagree with the view that theory and knowledge have a valuable part to play in helping managers to interpret, illuminate and illustrate their experience, and there *can* of course, be value in teaching marketing at school and undergraduate level and to those who lack any kind of commercial experience, provided it is done sensibly.

The last adverb brings into focus the real intention of this chapter, which is to argue that in the domain of marketing, the so-called crisis of relevancy of much of the body of knowledge has less to do with its origin in the positivistic model of science than with the failure of the academic world to understand better what needs to be done to make the bridge between theory and practice.

THE GAP BETWEEN THEORY AND PRACTICE

First, however, it is necessary to reiterate that marketing theory is not practised in industry. In no other discipline outside marketing is the gap between theory and practice so great. In March 1989, Tony McBurnie (1989), Director General of the Chartered Institute of Marketing, wrote:

> Research in the early 1980s showed that some two-thirds of British companies did not have clearly defined market strategies and did not use basic marketing disciplines.

This confirms the findings of researchers such as Greenley (1987) and McDonald (1984) about the gap between the theory of marketing planning, as written about in textbooks and as taught on management courses, and practice, with almost three-quarters of organisations relying principally on extrapolative techniques and financial husbandry. In very few cases was it possible to find any evidence of the use of some of the more substantive techniques taught on most marketing courses, such as the Ansoff Matrix, product life-cycle analysis, diffusion of innovation, the Boston Matrix, the Directional Policy Matrix, and other strategic and tactical marketing devices.

Nor is this just a European phenomenon. An interesting conclusion from the MSI Expert System Project, ADCAD (Rangaswany *et al*, 1988), was that although American companies would actually like to make use of the existing theoretical knowledge of marketing, few actually did.

The most recent study on this topic by DM Reid and LC Hinkley (1989) concluded:

> Respondents were asked which techniques they were familiar with. The results were skewed towards ignorance of all the techniques to which they were exposed. The majority were not at all familiar with any by name. The level of awareness of the techniques was not significantly different between Hong Kong and the UK.

The specific techniques which were the focus of the study included: BCG; Directional Policy Matrix; Ansoff Matrix; PIMS; Experience Curve.

Similar findings have also emerged from Australia (McColl-Kennedy *et al*, 1989): 'The awareness and usage level of planning tools is low'.

There are numerous possible explanations for this lack of usage in industry of the everyday tools of marketing teachers. For example:

- companies have never heard of them;
- companies have heard of them, but do not understand them;
- companies have heard of them, have tried them and found that they are largely irrelevant.

While all of these (and others) are distinct possibilities, it would be naïve not to recognise also that marketing is essentially a *political* process, involving organisational, interpersonal, cultural and social issues which in themselves appear to have no existence as observable entities, since they are contextual and are continuously changing and evolving.

While recent research into marketing and corporate culture (Leppard and McDonald, 1987) goes part of the way in explaining some of the blockages to the implementation of marketing theory, nonetheless there remains the question of why so many companies that genuinely strive to adopt a marketing orientated approach to doing business still repeatedly fall back on fiscal rather than marketing measures to direct and control the business (Wong *et al*, 1988). In such circumstances, one is left wondering why companies find it so difficult actually to *implement* what is taught about marketing in business schools.

MARKETING TECHNIQUES/STRUCTURES/FRAMEWORKS

Most foundation courses in marketing cover at least the following basic frameworks:

- the Ansoff Matrix;
- market segmentation;
- production life-cycle analysis;
- portfolio management (Boston Box and the Directional Policy Matrix);
- marketing research and marketing information systems.

Additionally, a host of techniques revolve around the four basic elements of the marketing mix: Product, Price, Promotion and Place. Even a cursory glance through Phillip Kotler's standard marketing management text reveals a vast and complex armoury of tools and techniques that can be used by marketing practitioners to gain a sustainable competitive advantage for their product or service.

During the past three decades, each one has been the focus of numerous academic and practitioner papers which have sought to explain their complexities and to persuade managers to adopt them as part of the process of marketing management. On the one hand, there have been several attempts to develop theories and models to explain, rationalise and justify complex phenomena in large industrial companies. On the other hand, there has been a

---

Some landmarks in this on-going debate are:

1956	W White 'The Organisation Man'	**1954**	Drucker's Management by Objectives
1957	Northcote's 'Parkinson's Law'	**1960**	General Electric introduce 'Portfolio Management
1969	Townsend's 'Up the Organisation'	**1962**	Blake & Mourton's 'The Management Grid'

1970	MBWA evolves at Hewlett Packard	1968	BCG Portfolio Management
1980	'The One Minute Manager'	1970	General Electric McKinsey's SBUs
1982	'In Search of Excellence' followed by 'Passion for Excellence'	1980	Porter's Competitive Strategies

continuous stream of iconoclasts who have sought to explain the same phenomena using a more simplistic and common-sense approach.

It is observable that, for a period, each school has its devotees, many of whom denounce or drop all the earlier received wisdom as they attempt to force their problems into the latest answer. When the latest fad fails to live up to expectations, it too begins to fade into obscurity, except at management education establishments, where it becomes part of the standard fabric of teaching.

There are, however, a number of problems with this somewhat simplistic explanation of the product life-cycle effect on each of the tools and techniques. These problems revolve firstly around methodological problems associated with the actual tools and techniques themselves, and secondly with the complexity of trying to link a number of them together.

PROBLEMS OF UNDERSTANDING

If we take a look at the more important structures and frameworks used in marketing management, we will observe a number of issues of varying degrees of difficulty in understanding, hence in application.

The product life-cycle is a case in point. There is clearly a difference between a *product* life-cycle and a *brand* life-cycle (Doyle, 1989). It is also pointless for a firm to draw a product life-cycle of one of its own products without also drawing a life cycle at least of the product class to which it belongs. But the question of how to define the product class (market) to which it belongs is fraught with difficulties. Furthermore, the linkage between the product life-cycle and the diffusion of the innovation curve needs to be properly understood. For example, high priced calculators first diffused through the scientific market, then the professional market, then the business market, then the general market, and finally the school children market. Each bell-shaped diffusion was followed by another, each time adding to the absolute sales curve depicted by the product life-cycle, with different cost and strategy implications along the way.

Failure to understand basic points such as these and others has destined plc analysis to be a topic of interest solely to interested academics. In the world of business it lies largely dormant.

Another well-known, under-utilised and misunderstood tool taught by marketing academics is the *directional policy matrix* (McDonald, 1990). For example, the criteria for the vertical axis (market attractiveness) can only be determined once the population of 'markets' has been specified. Once determined, those criteria cannot be changed during the exercise. Another common mistake is to misunderstand that unless the exercise is carried out twice – once for t.o and once for t+3, – the circles cannot move vertically. Also, the criteria have to change for *every* 'market' assessed on the horizontal axis each time a company's strength in market is assessed. Some way has also to be found of quantifying the horizontal axis to prevent every market appearing in the left-hand box of the matrix. If we add to this just *some* of the further complexities involved, such as the need to take the square root of the volume or value to determine circle diameter, the need to understand that the term 'attractiveness' has more to do with future *potential* than with any externally derived criteria, and so on, we begin to understand why practising managers rarely use the device. Indeed, one cannot help wondering whether all academics have sufficient understanding of the technique to be able to teach it competently.

Even Michael Porter's apparently more easily assimilated matrix describing the relationship between costs and degree of marketing differentiation has become the latest victim of misunderstanding and abuse through ignorance (Speed, 1989).

Reid and Hinkley (1989) drew the following conclusion from their own study:

> It reflects a failure of business schools to disseminate knowledge of strategic methodologies. Considering that tertiary per capita education provision in Hong Kong, particularly business school places, is much lower than in the UK, this indicates how they are failing in the UK to make a more significant impression.

The main problem, however, is not just that virtually every tool and technique of marketing is open to serious misunderstanding and abuse, but that no one method by itself can deliver the kinds of benefits demanded by practising managers. Most academics would readily acknowledge the singular contribution to diagnosis that can be made by each device, irrespective of whether it is from the iconoclastic school or the more rigorous academic school. For example, while it is easy (and tempting) to dismiss most of what Tom Peters says (largely because of its lack of rigour), few would deny his contribution to marketing by dint of the attention he focused on the need to service the needs of our customers effectively. Likewise, anyone who tries to run their company just on the basis of what Michael Porter says, soon discovers the inherent inadequacies of the nostra, just as those did who worshipped at the altar of Bruce Henderson and the Boston Consulting Group in the late 1960s and early 1970s. Yet few would deny the abiding relevance to business in the 1990s of what all these great writers, researchers and teachers had to offer.

To summarise, not only are most of the tools and techniques themselves inherently complex (and therefore misunderstood and misused), but no one tool on its own is adequate in dealing with the complexity of marketing.

PROBLEMS OF TECHNIQUE INTERRELATIONSHIPS

There is, then, clearly a need to be able to use a number of these tools and techniques in problem-solving, especially when a process as complex as strategic marketing planning is concerned. This raises an additional dimension of complexity for both academics and practising managers, for it then becomes necessary to understand not only the techniques themselves, but the nature of the interrelationships between them, how inputs for one model can also be used for another and how outputs from some models can also be used as inputs to others.

The problem is that the human mind just isn't capable of dealing adequately with such complexity. This view has gradually emerged as a result of working on a computer-based Expert System for Strategic Marketing Planning (McDonald, 1989a) and is confirmed by a number of researchers, including most recently Lock and Hughes (1989).

A new approach, therefore, is necessary.

A DIFFERENT APPROACH IS REQUIRED

What seems to be the common denominator of the afore-mentioned tools and techniques is that their users and those who teach them tend to concentrate on the 'medicine' itself, showing little concern for the 'patient'. This makes about as much sense as a doctor dispensing the same drug to every patient seen, irrespective of their condition. Certainly the treatment might help a proportion of the clients out for a large number of them it will be at best irrelevant, and at worst, even dangerous.

What must be recognised is that there has to be a symbiotic relationship between the doctor, the patient and the cure – it is the three working together which bring success, with the doctor taking a more holistic approach to the situation.

In the process of constructing the Expert System for Strategic Marketing Planning, it became clear that what was needed was some system to link the numerous artefacts of marketing in such a way that outputs from one technique could be used as inputs to other techniques. This was indeed the missing link, as in books and in paper-based marketing planning manuals, the process of marketing planning had of necessity to be iterative, with the onus resting on the user to understand the interrelationships between the techniques used.

The route to this discovery was the Data Model represented in Figure 4.1.

Here, the basic model consists of a Strategic Business Unit (SBU) (which can be anything from a corporate headquarters to an individual product), which is involved in a number of *markets*, and for which it produces a number of *products* (or services). The system starts with the definition of a *mission* (or pur-

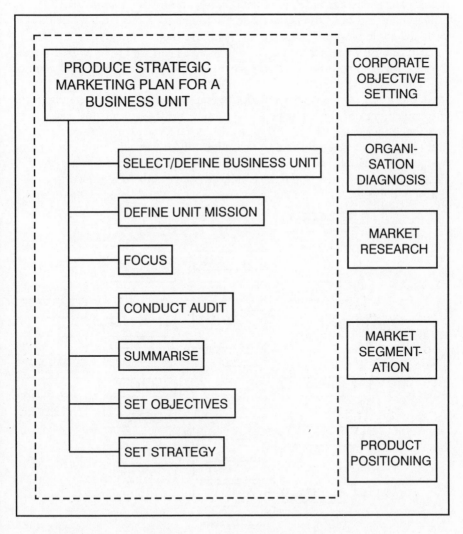

Figure 4.1 Simplified data model, in entity-relationship notation

pose) statement for the SBU and indicates very clearly the acceptable structure and content of such a document.

The next stage in the process was the definition of the contents of a strategic marketing plan and the listing of some of the principal tools and techniques which may be relevant to each of its component parts. It will be seen from Figure 4.2 that some of these techniques may be used for several parts of the plan. However, this does not delineate sufficiently clearly the nature of the technique interrelationships, so it was necessary to define in more detail the actual *process* involved in the preparation of a strategic marketing plan.

Figure 4.3 indicates the key steps in the preparation of a strategic marketing plan and some of the subsidiary tasks that have to be completed at each stage.

Each one of the boxes on the 'tree' has associated with it a number of marketing tools and techniques, so the next task was to allocate these to each of the main stages in the process.

At the *focus stage* (Figure 4.4), for example, the output is a statement of those elements of the strategic business unit (SBU) selected for analysis. In arriving at this focus, Pareto's law is clearly relevant, as are market segmentation studies (the standard industrial classification (SIC) is provided in the computer system as a possible starting point for market segmentation). Porter's cost/differentiation matrix may also be useful at this stage if there is a need to have a balance between high-volume, low-cost markets and more differentiated,

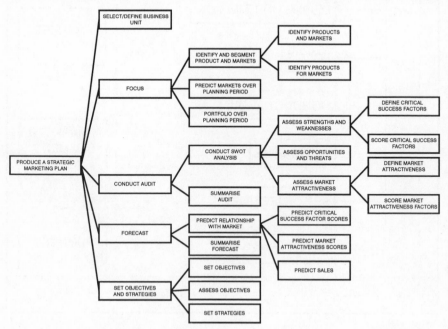

Figure 4.2 The tools and techniques of a strategic marketing plan

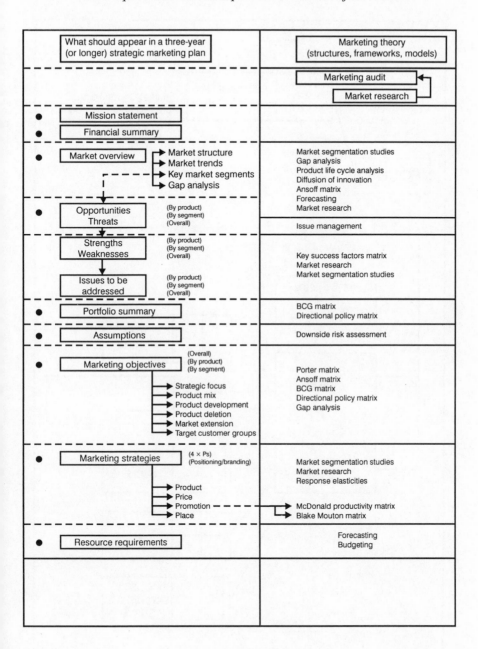

Figure 4.3 The key steps in the preparation of a strategic marketing plan

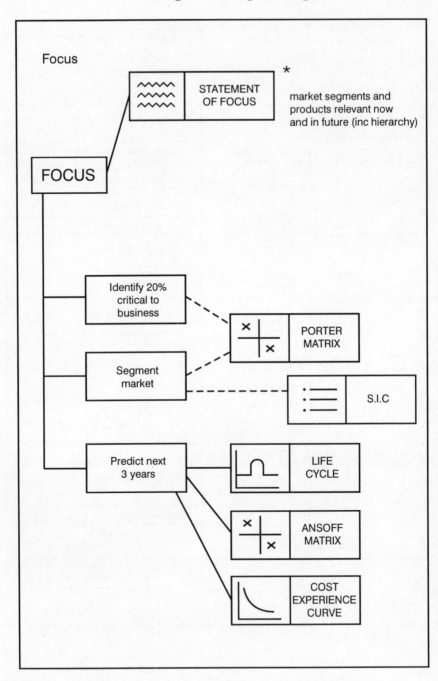

Figure 4.4 The focus stage in marketing planning

niche-type markets. The product life-cycle could clearly be useful in helping to decide which markets appear more attractive, as could a knowledge of the cost impact of experience. The Ansoff Matrix is also included here because product/market data associated with each of the four boxes could be useful in indicating the balance between existing and new activities.

The purpose of the *audit stage* (Figure 4.5) is to complete an in-depth diagnosis or analysis of the selected products and/or markets from the focus stage. Provided here are several checklists to help the program user. The Porter five force model may, for example, provide useful guidelines at this stage. Detailed instructions on how to construct tables for critical success factors and market attractiveness factors are given, as well as methodological instructions on how

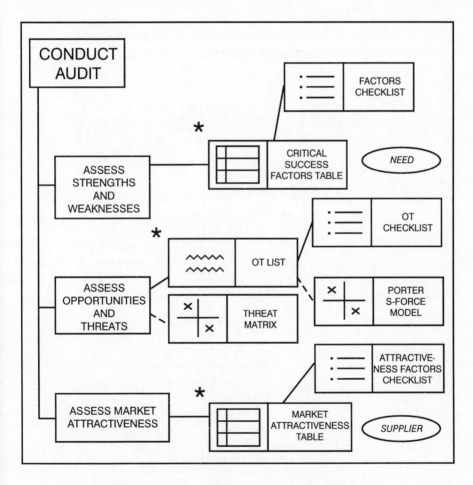

Figure 4.5 The audit stage of marketing planning

135

to deal quantitatively with external opportunities and threats. (For details of this, see McDonald, 1989b.)

The audit stage has to be summarised (Figure 4.6) and here the Boston Matrix and the Directional Policy Matrix can be useful pictorial representations of the current product/market status. Each one of these techniques emphasises different aspects of the same situation. Likewise, gap analysis provides a visualisation in summary form of the revenue and cost implications of current strategies.

It will be seen in Figure 4.7 that the same tools can also be used in the process of *setting objectives*, except that this time they are extended to indicate the desired position at some designated point of time in the future.

Figures 4.8, 4.9 and 4.10 indicate relationships between the techniques themselves.

Figure 4.8 shows the relationship between some of the principal techniques and their relevance to the basic Data Model given in Figure 4.1.

Figures 4.9 and 4.10 are attempts to indicate some of the connections between the actual techniques themselves. While it is not necessary to take the

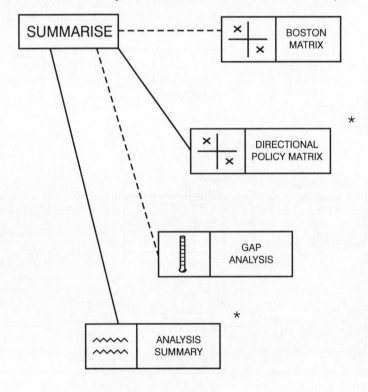

Figure 4.6 Summarising the audit stage

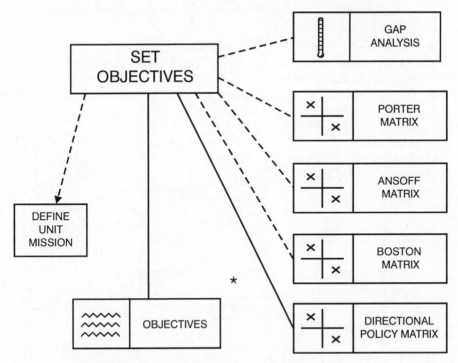

Figure 4.7 Setting objectives in marketing techniques

reader through every one of these interconnections, it would be useful to highlight at least some of the main ones.

The Directional Policy Matrix can be seen to be a central tool in strategic marketing planning (Figure 4.9). Life-cycle analysis will indicate the prospects in revenue/volume terms for the individual products/markets that are plotted on the vertical axis. The cost/experience curve of individual products/markets will provide valuable input to both the Boston Matrix and to the Porter cost/differentiation matrix, which will in turn help in determining the market attractiveness factors and critical success factors which are the basis of the Directional Policy Matrix. Gap analysis works extremely well in conjunction with the Ansoff Matrix, the output of which will be invaluable in judging the balance of the portfolio in the Directional Policy Matrix.

The reader is advised to study these figures very carefully. This advice is given because the Expert System manages these interrelationships on the computer and users (typically marketing managers) do not have to concern themselves with them.

Figures 4.9 and 4.10 show various connections identified between techniques. They assume that by using a technique, any data required by it is

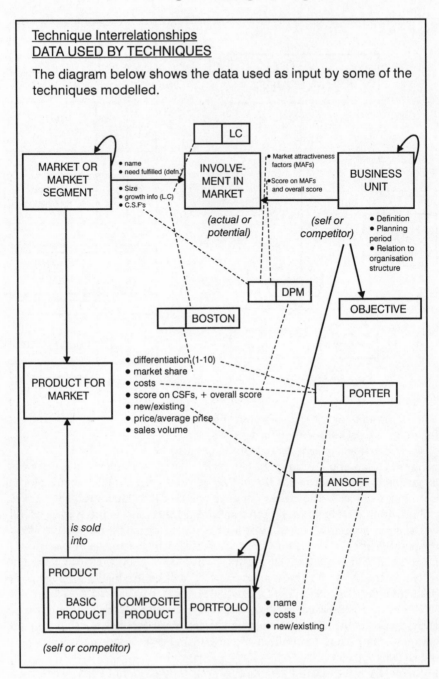

Figure 4.8 Technique interrelationships

Technique Interrelationships

The diagrams below show various connections identified between techniques. They assume that by using a technique, any data required by it is entered into the model by some means, so that data is available for another technique.

TECHNIQUE INTERRELATIONSHIPS (1)

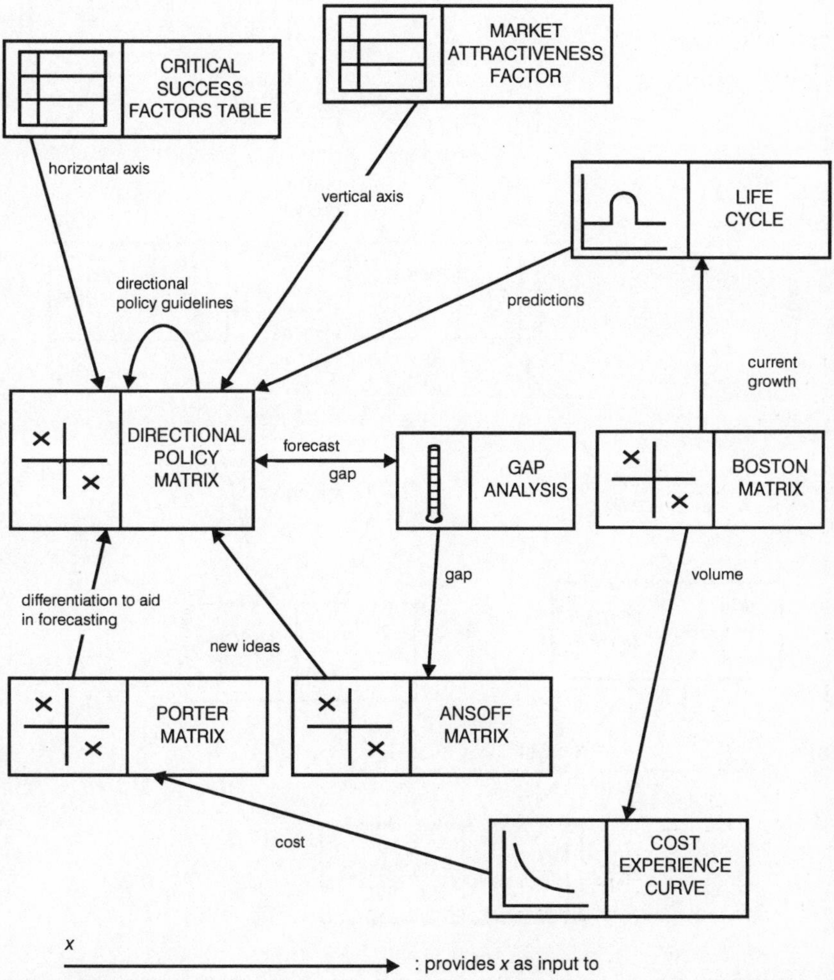

Figure 4.9 The various connections between techniques (1)

entered into the model by some means, so that data is available for another technique.

On the other hand, if you are either a practising marketing manager or a marketing lecturer, you would be advised to devote some time to thinking firstly

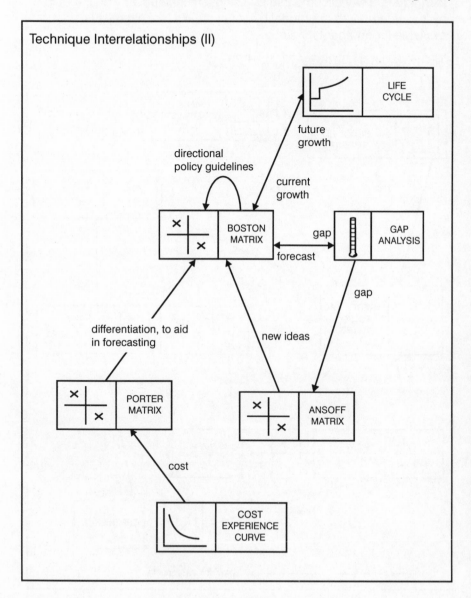

Figure 4.10 The various connections between techniques (2)

about the technical dimensions of the principal tools and techniques of marketing themselves, secondly about their specific applications, and thirdly about the interrelationships between these techniques in the process of the solving of some of the more abiding problems of strategic marketing planning.

CONCLUSIONS

The only reasonable conclusions to reach from the foregoing are:

1. Practising managers must avail themselves of better education in the understanding of the application of marketing techniques to real world problems.
2. The human mind is largely incapable of understanding and managing the complexities of the relationships between the many techniques of marketing.
3. In view of 2 above, expert systems will need to be developed so that these complexities are managed by the computer in a way which is helpful to practising managers in solving their complex problems.

References

Doyle, P (1989) 'Building Successful Brands: The Strategic Options', *Journal of Marketing Management*, Vol 5, No 1.

Evered, R (1981) 'Management Education for the Year 2000' in Cooper, CL (ed) 'Developing Managers for the 1980s', Macmillan, London.

Greenley, G (1987) 'An Exposition into Empirical Research into Marketing Planning', *Journal of Marketing Management*, Vol 3, No 1, July.

Hughes, JM (1988) 'The Body of Knowledge in Management Education', *Management Education and Development*, Vol 19, Part 4, pp 301–310.

King, S (1983) 'Applying Research to Decision-Making', MRS Conference, Spring.

Leppard, J and McDonald, MHB (1987) 'A Re-appraisal of the Role of Marketing Planning', *Journal of Marketing Management*, Vol 3, No 2.

Lock, AR and Hughes, DR (1989) '"Soft" Information Systems for Marketing Decision Support', *Marketing Intelligence and Planning*, Vol 7, Nos 11–12.

McBurnie, A (1989) 'The Need for a New Marketing Perspective', *MBA Review*, Vol 1, No 1, March.

McColl-Kennedy, IR, Uau, OHM and Kiel, GC (1989) 'Marketing Planning Practices in Australia: A companion across company types', Graduate School of Management, The University of Queensland Research Paper.

McDonald, MHB (1984) 'The Theory and Practice of Marketing Planning for Industrial Goods in International Marketing', Cranfield Institute of Technology, PhD thesis.

McDonald, MHB (1985) 'Methodological Problems Associated with Qualitative Research: Some Observations and a Case Analysis of International Marketing Planning', *International Studies in Management Organisation*, Vol XV, No 2.

McDonald, MHB (1985) 'Marketing Planning and Expert Systems: An Epistemology of Practice', *Marketing Intelligence and Planning*, Vol 7, Nos 7–8.

McDonald, MHB (1989a) 'Marketing Plans: how to prepare them; how to use them', Heinemann, London.

McDonald, MHB (1990) 'Some Methodological Problems Associated with the Directional Policy Matrix', *MBA Review*, Spring.

Rangaswany, A, Burke, R, Wind, J and Eliashberg, J (1988) 'Expert Systems for Marketing', Marketing Science Institute Working Paper Report, Nos 87–107.

Reid, DM and Hinkley, LC (1989) 'Strategic Planning: The Cultural Impact', *Marketing Intelligence and Planning*, Vol 7, Nos 11–12.

Schon, D (1984) 'The Crisis of Professional Knowledge and the Pursuit of an Epistemology of Practice', research paper for the Harvard Business School 75th Anniversary Colloquium on teaching by the case method, April.

Speed, RJ (1989) 'Oh Mr Porter! A Re-Appraisal of Competitive Strategy', *Marketing Intelligence and Planning*, Vol 6, No 5.

Wong, V, Saunders, J and Doyle, P (1988) 'The Quality of British Marketing: a comparative investigation of international competition in the UK market', proceedings of the 21st Annual Conference of the Marketing Education Group, Huddersfield Polytechnic, July.

5

STRATEGIC MARKETING PLANNING: WHAT IT IS AND HOW TO DO IT

Malcolm McDonald

The purpose of this chapter is to remind readers about the key elements of marketing planning and to explain how it can be done. It is in three sections: the first examines marketing planning myths; the second outlines the main steps involved in marketing planning; and the third looks briefly at the implementation and design of marketing planning systems.

MARKETING PLANNING MYTHS

Whatever the precise balance between the many underlying causes for the relative economic decline of nations such as the UK, part of it can be explained by an almost total lack of understanding of marketing on the part of senior managers. This was explained in some considerable detail in Chapters 1 and 2. However, when it comes to *marketing planning*, the widespread ignorance is devastating. This conclusion is based on a four-year study carried out at Cranfield into how industrial goods companies selling internationally carry out their marketing planning (McDonald, 1982). This survey showed that while all managers agree that it is logical to find some rational way of identifying objectives, to choose one or more of them based on the firm's distinctive competence, and then to schedule and cost out what has to be done to achieve the chosen objectives, 90 per cent of UK companies don't do this. Instead, they complete budgets and forecasts.

What most companies think of as planning systems are little more than forecasting and budgeting systems. These give impetus and direction to tackling the current operational problems of the business, but tend merely to project the current business unchanged into the future – something often referred to in management literature as 'tunnel vision'.

The successes enjoyed in the past were often the result of the easy marketability of products, and during periods of high economic prosperity there was little pressure on companies to do anything other than solve operational problems as they arose. Careful planning for the future seemed unnecessary. However, most companies today are experiencing difficulties precisely because of this lack of planning and there is a growing realisation that survival and success in the future will come only from patient and meticulous planning and market preparation. This entails making a commitment to the future.

Today, there is widespread awareness of lost market opportunities through unpreparedness and real confusion over what to do about it. It is hard not to conclude, therefore, that there is a strong relationship between these two problems and the systems most widely in use at present – ie, sales forecasting and budgeting systems.

Marketing's contribution to business success in manufacturing, distribution or merchanting activities lies in its commitment to detailed analysis of future opportunities to meet customer needs and a wholly professional approach to selling to well-defined market segments those products or services that deliver the sought-after benefits. While prices and discounts are important, as are advertising and promotion, the link with engineering through the product is paramount. But such a commitment and activities must not be mistaken for budgets and forecasts. Those, of course, we need and we have already got (our accounting colleagues have long since seen to that). Put quite bluntly, the process of marketing planning is concerned with identifying what and to whom sales are going to be made in the longer term to give revenue budgets and sales forecasts any chance of achievement. Furthermore, chances of achievement are a function of how good our intelligence services are; how well suited are our strategies; and how well we are led.

Let us begin with a reminder of some of the basics. Marketing planning is a logical sequence and a series of activities leading to the setting of marketing objectives and the formulation of plans for achieving them. It is a management process. Conceptually, the process is very simple. Marketing planning by means of a planning system is, *per se*, little more than a structured way of identifying a range of options, for the company, of making them explicit in writing, of formulating marketing objectives which are consistent with the company's overall objectives and of scheduling and costing out the specific activities most likely to bring about the achievement of the objectives. It is systemisation of this process which is distinctive and which lies at the heart of the theory of marketing planning.

Naïvety about Marketing Planning

It has long been a source of bemusement that many meticulous marketing planning companies fare badly, while the sloppy or inarticulate in marketing terms do well. Is there any real relationship between marketing planning and commercial success and, if so, how does that relationship work its way through?

There are, of course, many studies which identify a number of benefits to be obtained from marketing planning, but there is little explanation for the commercial success of those companies that do not engage in formalised planning. Nor is there much exploration of the circumstances of those commercially unsuccessful companies that also have formalised marketing planning systems.

It is very clear that the simplistic theories do not adequately address the many contextual issues in relation to marketing planning, which may well account for the fact that so few companies actually do it. In fact, 90 per cent of companies in the Cranfield study, by their own admission, did not produce anything approximating to an integrated, co-ordinated and internally consistent plan for their marketing activities. This included a substantial number of companies that had highly formalised procedures for marketing planning. Certainly, few of these companies enjoyed the claimed benefits of formalised marketing planning, which in summary are as follows:

- co-ordination of the activities of many individuals whose actions are interrelated over time;
- identification of expected developments;
- preparedness to meet changes when they occur;
- minimisation of non-rational responses to the unexpected;
- better communication among executives;
- minimisation of conflicts among individuals which would result in a subordination of the goals of the company to those of the individual.

Indeed, many companies have a lot of the trappings of sophisticated marketing planning systems but suffer as many dysfunctional consequences as those companies that have only forecasting and budgeting systems.

Operational Problems Resulting from the Forecasting and Budgeting Approach

The following are the most frequently mentioned operating problems resulting from a reliance on traditional sales forecasting and budgeting procedures in the absence of a marketing planning system:

- lost opportunities for profit;
- meaningless numbers in long-range plans;
- unrealistic objectives;
- lack of actionable market information;
- interfunctional strife;
- management frustration;
- proliferation of products and markets;
- wasted promotional expenditure;
- pricing confusion;
- growing vulnerability to environmental change;
- loss of control over the business.

It is not difficult to see the connection between all of these problems. However, what is perhaps not apparent from the list is that each of these operational problems is in fact a symptom of a much larger problem which emanates from the way in which the objectives of a firm are set.

The meaningfulness, and hence the eventual effectiveness, of any objective, is heavily dependent on the quality of the information inputs about the business environment. However, objectives also need to be closely related to the firm's particular capabilities in the form of its assets, expertise and reputation that have evolved over a number of years. The objective-setting process of a business, then, is central to its effectiveness. What the Cranfield research demonstrated conclusively is that it is inadequacies in the objective-setting process which lie at the heart of many of the problems of UK companies.

Some kind of appropriate system has to be used to enable meaningful and realistic marketing objectives to be set. A frequent complaint is the preoccupation with short-term thinking and an almost total lack of what has been referred to as 'strategic thinking'. Also, that plans consist largely of numbers, which are difficult to evaluate in any meaningful way because they do not highlight and quantify opportunities, emphasise key issues, show the company's position clearly in its markets, nor delineate the means of achieving the sales forecasts. Sales targets for the sales-force are often inflated in order to motivate them to higher achievement, while the actual budgets themselves are deflated in order to provide a safety-net against shortfall. Both act as demotivators and both lead to the frequent use of expressions such as 'ritual', 'the numbers game', 'meaningless horsetrading', and so on. It is easy to see how the problems listed at the start of this section begin to manifest themselves in this sort of environment.

Closely allied to this is the frequent reference to profit as being the only objective necessary to successful business performance. There is in the minds of many business people the assumption that in order to be commercially successful, all that is necessary is for the 'boss' to set profit targets, to decentralise the firm into groups of similar activities and then to make managers accountable for achieving those profits. However, even though most companies in the UK made the making of 'profit' almost their sole objective, many of their industries have gone into decline, and ironically, there has also been a decline in real profitability. There are countless examples of companies pursuing decentralised profit goals that have failed miserably.

Here, it is necessary to focus attention on what so many companies appear to be bad at – ie, determining strategies for matching what the firm is good at with properly researched market-centred opportunities, and then scheduling and costing out what has to be done to achieve these objectives. There is little evidence of a deep understanding of what it is that companies can do better than their competitors or of how their distinctive competence can be matched with the needs of certain customer groups. Instead, overall volume increases and minimum rates of return on investment are frequently applied to all products and markets, irrespective of market share, market growth rate, or the longevity of the product life-cycle. Indeed, there is a lot of evidence to show that many companies are in trouble today precisely because their decentralised units manage their business only for the current profit and loss account, often at the expense of giving up valuable and hard-earned market share, failing to invest in research and development and running down the current business.

Thus, financial objectives, while being essential measures of the desired performance of a company, are of little practical help, since they say nothing about *how* the results are to be achieved. The same applies to sales forecasts and budgets, which are *not* marketing objectives and strategies. Understanding the real meaning and significance of marketing objectives helps managers to know what information they need to enable them to think through the implications of choosing one or more positions in the market. Finding the right words to describe the logic of marketing objectives and strategies is infinitely more difficult than writing down numbers on a piece of paper and leaving the strategies implicit. This lies at the heart of the problem. For, clearly, a number-oriented system will not encourage managers to think in a structured way about strategically relevant market segments, nor will it encourage the collection, analysis and synthesis of actionable market data. And in the absence of such activities within operating units, it is unlikely that headquarters will have much other than intuition and 'feel' to use as a basis for decisions about the management of scarce resources.

How Can These Problems be Overcome?

One of the main difficulties is how to get managers throughout an organisation to think beyond the horizon of the current year's operations. This applies universally to all types and sizes of company. Even chief executives of small companies find difficulty in breaking out of the fetters of the current profit and loss account. The problem, particularly in large companies, is that managers who are evaluated and rewarded on the basis of current operations find difficulty in concerning themselves about the corporate future. This is exacerbated by behavioural issues in the sense that it is safer, and more rewarding personally, for a manager to do what he knows best, which in most cases is to manage his *current* range of products and customers in order to make the *current* year's budget.

Unfortunately, long-range sales forecasting systems do not provide the answer. This kind of extrapolative approach fails to solve the problem of identifying precisely what has to be done today to ensure success in the future. Exactly the same problem exists in both large diversified companies and in small undiversified companies, except that in the former the problem is magnified and multiplied by the complexities of distance, hierarchical levels of management, and diversity of operations. Nevertheless, the problem is fundamentally the same.

Events that affect economic performance in a business come from so many directions, and in so many forms, that it is impossible for any manager to be precise about how they interact in the form of problems to be overcome and opportunities to be exploited. The best a manager can do is to form a reasoned view about how they have affected the past and how they will develop in the future, and what action needs to be taken over a period of time to enable the company to prepare itself for the expected changes. The problem is *how* to get managers to formulate their thoughts about these things, for until they have, it is unlikely that any objectives that are set will have much relevance or meaning.

Accordingly, they need some system which will help them to think in a structured way about problem formulation. It is the provision of such a rational framework to help them to make explicit their intuitive economic models of the business that is almost totally lacking from the forecasting and budgeting systems of most companies. It is apparent that in the absence of any such synthesised and simplified views of the business, setting meaningful objectives for the future seems like an insurmountable problem, and this in turn encourages the perpetuation of systems involving merely the extrapolation of numbers. There is also substantial evidence that those companies that provide procedures for this process, however informal, have gone some considerable way to overcome the problem. Although the possible number of analyses of business situations is infinite, procedural approaches help managers throughout an organisation at least to consider the essential elements of problem definition in a structured way. This applies even to difficult foreign markets, where data and information are hard to come by, and even to markets which are being managed by agents, who find that these structured approaches, properly managed, help *their* businesses as well as those of their principals.

Each of the stages illustrated in Figure 5.1 will be discussed in more detail later in this chapter. The dotted lines joining up steps 5, 6 and 7 are meant to indicate the reality of the planning process, in that it is likely that each of these steps will have to be gone through more than once before final programmes can be written.

Although research has shown these marketing planning steps to be universally applicable, the degree to which each of the separate steps in the diagram needs to be formalised depends to a large extent on the size and nature of the company. For example, an undiversified company generally uses less formalised procedures because top management tends to have greater functional knowledge and expertise than subordinates and because the lack of diversity of operations enables direct control to be exercised over most of the key determinants of success. Thus, situation reviews, the setting of marketing objectives, and so on, are not always made explicit in writing, although these steps have to be gone through.

In contrast, in a diversified company, it is usually not possible for top management to have greater functional knowledge and expertise than subordinate management, hence the whole planning process tends to be more formalised in order to provide a consistent discipline for those who have to make the decisions throughout the organisation.

Either way, however, there is now a substantial body of evidence to show that formalised marketing planning procedures generally result in greater profitability and stability in the long term and also help to reduce friction and operational difficulties within organisations.

Where marketing planning has failed, it has generally been because companies have placed too much emphasis on the procedures themselves and the resulting paperwork, rather than on generating information useful to and consumable by management. Also, where companies relegate marketing planning to someone called a 'planner' it invariably fails, for the single reason that planning for line management cannot be delegated to a third party. The real role of the 'planner' should be to help those responsible for implementation to plan. Failure to recognise this simple fact can be disastrous. Finally, planning failures often result from companies trying too much, too quickly, and without training staff in the use of procedures. *) the reason for ineffective plan*

We can now look at the marketing planning process in more detail, starting with a look at the marketing audit. So far we have looked at the need for marketing planning and outlined a series of steps that have to be gone through in order to arrive at a marketing plan. However, any plan will only be as good as the information on which it is based, and the marketing audit is the means by which information for planning is organised.

What is a marketing audit?

Auditing as a process is usually associated with the financial side of a business and is conducted according to a defined set of accounting standards, which are well documented, easily understood, and which therefore lend themselves readily to the auditing process. The total business process, although more complicated, innovative and relying more on judgement than on a set of rules, is still nevertheless capable of being audited.

An audit is a systematic, critical and unbiased review and appraisal of the environment and of the company's operations. A marketing audit is part of the larger management audit and is concerned with the marketing environment and marketing operations.

Why is there a need for an audit?

Often the need for an audit does not manifest itself until things start to go wrong for a company, such as falling sales and margins, lost market share and so on. At times like these, management often attempts to treat the wrong symptoms, the most frequent result of which is to reorganise the company! But such measures are unlikely to be effective if there are more fundamental problems which have not been identified. Of course, if the company could survive long enough, it might eventually solve its problems through a process of elimination! Essentially, the argument is that problems have to be properly defined, and the audit is a means of helping to define them.

To summarise, the audit is a structured approach to the collection and analysis of information and data in the complex business environment and an essential prerequisite to problem solving.

The form of the audit

Any company carrying out an audit will be faced with two kinds of variables. First, there are variables over which the company has no direct control: these usually take the form of what can be described as environmental and market variables. Second, there are variables over which the company has complete control: these we can call operational variables. This provides a clue as to how we can structure an audit – that is to say, in two parts: external audit and internal audit. The external audit is concerned with the uncontrollable variables such as the economy and the markets served by the company, while the internal audit is concerned with the controllable variables, which are usually the firm's internal resources. Table 5.1 contains a checklist of areas that should be investigated as part of the marketing audit. Each one of these headings will need to be examined with a view to building up an information base relevant to the company's performance.

Table 5.1 The marketing audit checklist

External audit *Business and economic environment*	**Internal audit** *Marketing operational variables (own company)*

External audit
*Business and economic
environment*

- Economic
- Political/fiscal/legal
- Social/cultural
- Technological
- Intra-company

The Market

- Total market, size, growth and trends (value/volume)
- Market characteristics, developments and trends
  - Products
  - Prices
  - Physical distribution
  - Channels
  - Customers/consumers
  - Communication
  - Industry practices

Competition

- Major competitors
- Size
- Market shares/coverage
- Market standing/reputation
- Production capabilities
- Distribution policies
- Marketing methods
- Extent of diversification
- Personnel issues
- International links
- Profitability
- Key strengths and weaknesses

Internal audit
*Marketing operational variables
(own company)*

- Sales (total, by geographical location, by industrial type, by customer, by product)
- Market shares
- Profit margins/costs
- Marketing information/ research
- Marketing mix variables as follows:
  - Product management
  - Price
  - Distribution
  - Promotion
  - Operations and resources

When should the audit be carried out?

A mistaken belief held by many people is that the marketing audit should be some kind of final attempt to define a company's marketing problem, or at best something done by an independent body from time to time to ensure that a company is on the right lines. However, since marketing is such a complex function, it seems illogical not to carry out a pretty thorough situation analysis at least once a year at the beginning of the planning cycle.

There is much evidence to show that many highly successful companies, as well as using normal information and control procedures and marketing research throughout the year, also start their planning cycle each year with a formal review (through an audit-type process) of everything that has had an important influence on marketing activities. Certainly, in many leading consumer goods companies, the annual self-audit approach is a tried and tested discipline integrated into the management process.

Who should carry out the audit?

Occasionally it may be justified to hire outside consultants to carry out a marketing audit to check that a company is getting the most out of its resources. However, it seems an unnecessary expense to have this done every year. The answer, therefore, is to have an audit carried out annually by the company's own line managers on their own areas of responsibility.

Objections to this usually revolve around the problems of time and objectivity. In practice, these problems are overcome by institutionalising procedures in as much detail as possible so that all managers have to conform to a disciplined approach, and secondly by thorough training in the use of the procedures themselves. However, even this will not result in achieving the purpose of an audit unless a rigorous discipline is applied from the highest down to the lowest levels of management involved in the audit. Such a discipline is usually successful in helping managers to avoid the sort of tunnel vision that often results from a lack of critical appraisal.

What happens to the results of the audit?

The only remaining question is what happens to the results of the audit? Some companies consume valuable resources carrying out audits that bring very little by way of actionable results. There is a mistaken belief that a marketing audit is a marketing plan. But it isn't. It is just a database that has been translated into relevant information. The task remains of turning the marketing audit into intelligence, which is information that is essential for making decisions.

Since the objective of the audit is to indicate what a company's marketing objectives and strategies should be, it follows that it would be helpful if some format could be found for organising the major findings. One useful way of doing this is in the form of a SWOT analysis. This is a summary of the audit under the headings of internal strengths and weaknesses as they relate to external opportunities and threats. This SWOT analysis should contain, if possible, not more than four or five pages of commentary focusing on key factors only. It should highlight internal differential strengths and weaknesses *vis-à-vis* competitors and key external opportunities and threats. A summary of reasons for good or bad performance should be included. It should be interesting to read, contain concise statements, include only relevant and important data, and give emphasis to creative analysis.

Where relevant, the SWOT should contain life cycles for major product/market segments for which the future share will be predicted using the audit information. Also, major products/markets should be plotted on some kind of portfolio notice to show their desired position over the full planning method. Guidelines on completing the SWOT include:

1. Start with a market overview:

   — has the market declined or grown?
   — how does it break down into segments?
   — what is your share of each?
   Keep it simple; if you do not have the facts, make estimates. Use life-cycles, portfolios, bar charts, pie charts, and so on to make it all crystal clear.

2. Now identify the key segments for you, and do a SWOT for each one:

   — list the key factors for success;
   — outline the major outside influences and their impact on each segment;
   — give an assessment of your company's strength and weaknesses *vis-à-vis* competitors. Highlight differential strengths and weaknesses;
   — give an explanation for good or bad performance.

Assumptions

Having completed the marketing audit and SWOT analysis, assumptions now have to be written.

There are certain key determinants of success in all companies about which assumptions have to be made before the planning process can proceed. It is really a question of standardising the planning environment. For example, it would be no good receiving plans from two product managers, one of whom believed that the market was going to increase by 10 per cent, while the other believed that the market was going to decline by 10 per cent.

Examples of assumptions might be, 'with respect to the company's industrial climate, it is assumed that:

1. Industrial overcapacity will increase from 105 per cent to 115 per cent as new industrial plants come into operation.

2. Price competition will force price levels down by 10 per cent across the board.
3. A new product in the field of *x* will be introduced by our major competitor before the end of the second quarter.'

Assumptions should be few in number, and if a plan is possible irrespective of the assumptions made, then the assumptions are unnecessary.

Marketing objectives and strategies

The next step in marketing planning is the writing of marketing objectives and strategies, the key stage in the whole process – if this is not done properly, everything that follows is of little value.

This is an obvious activity to follow on with, since a thorough situation review, particularly in the area of marketing, should enable the company to determine whether it will be able to meet the long-range financial targets with its current range of products in its current markets. Any projected gap can be filled by the various methods of product development or market extension.

We discuss below marketing objectives and strategies in more detail. For now, the important point to make is that this is the time in the planning cycle when a compromise has to be reached between what is wanted by the several functional departments and what is practicable, given all the constraints that any company has. For example, it is no good setting a marketing objective of penetrating a new market if the company does not have the production capacity to cope with the new business and if capital is not available for whatever investment is necessary in additional capacity. At this stage, objectives and strategies will be set for five years, or for whatever the planning horizon is.

An *objective* is what you want to achieve. A *strategy* is how you plan to achieve your objectives. Thus, there can be objectives and strategies at all levels in marketing: for example, advertising objectives and strategies and pricing objectives and strategies. However, the important point to remember about marketing objectives is that they are about products and markets only. Common sense will confirm that it is only by selling something to someone that the company's financial goals can be achieved, and that advertising, pricing, service levels, and so on are the means (or strategies) by which we might succeed in doing this. Thus, pricing objectives, sales promotion objectives, advertising objectives and the like should not be confused with marketing objectives.

Marketing objectives are simply about one or more of the following:

- existing products in existing markets;
- new products for existing markets;

156

- existing products for new markets;
- new products for new markets.

They should be capable of measurement, otherwise they are not objectives. Directional terms such as 'maximise', 'minimise', 'penetrate', 'increase', etc are only acceptable if quantitative measurement can be attached to them. Measurement should be in terms of sales volume, sterling, market share, percentage penetration of outlets, and so on.

Marketing strategies are the means by which marketing objectives will be achieved and generally are concerned with 'the four Ps', as follows:

- Product: the general policies for product deletions, modifications, additions, design, packaging, etc.
- Price: the general pricing policies to be followed for product groups in market segments.
- Place: the general policies for channels and customer service levels.
- Promotion: the general policies for communicating with customers under the relevant headings, such as advertising, sales-force, sales promotion, public relations, exhibitions, direct mail, etc.

Having completed this major planning task, it is normal at this stage to employ judgement, analogous experience, field tests, and so on, to test out the feasibility of the objectives and strategies in terms of market share, sales, costs, profits, and so on. It is also normally at this stage that alternative plans and mixes are delineated, if necessary.

Programmes

The general marketing strategies are now developed into specific subobjectives, each supported by more detailed strategy and action statements.

A company organised according to functions might have an advertising plan, a sales promotion plan, a pricing plan, and so on. A product-based company might have a product plan, with objectives, strategies and tactics for price, place and promotion as necessary.

A market or geographically based company might have a market plan, with objectives, strategies and tactics for the four Ps as necessary. Likewise, a company with a few major customers might have a customer plan. Any combination of the above might be suitable, depending on circumstances.

Marketing Plans and Budgets

A written marketing plan is the backcloth against which operational decisions are taken on an on-going basis. Consequently, too much detail should not be attempted. Its major function is to determine where the company is now, where it wants to go to, and how to get there. It lies at the heart of a company's revenue-generating activities and from it flow all other corporate activities, such as the timing of cash flow, the size and character of the labour force, and so on.

The marketing plan should be distributed on a 'need-to-know' basis only and used as an aid to effective management. It cannot be a substitute for it.

It will be obvious from all of this that the setting of budgets becomes not only much easier, but the resulting budgets are more likely to be realistic and related to what the *whole* company wants to achieve rather than just one functional department.

The problem of designing a dynamic system for budget setting rather than the 'tablets of stone' approach, which is more common, is a major challenge to the marketing and financial directors of all companies. The most satisfactory approach would be for a marketing director to justify all his marketing expenditure from a zero base each year against the tasks he wishes to accomplish. A little thought will confirm that this is exactly the approach recommended in this chapter. If these procedures are followed, a hierarchy of objectives is built up in such a way that every item of budgeted expenditure can be related directly back to the initial corporate financial objectives. For example, if sales promotion is a major means of achieving an objective in a particular market, when sales promotional items appear in the programme, each one has a specific purpose which can be related back to a major objective.

Doing it this way not only ensures that every item of expenditure is fully accounted for as part of a rational, objective and task approach, but also that when changes have to be made during the period to which the plan relates, such changes can be made in such a way that the least damage is caused to the company's long-term objectives.

The incremental marketing expense can be considered to be all costs that are incurred after the product leaves the factory, *other than* costs involved in physical distribution, the costs of which usually represent a discrete subset. There is, of course, no textbook answer to problems relating to questions such as whether packaging should be a marketing or a production expense, and whether some distribution costs could be considered to be marketing costs. For example, insistence on high service levels results in high inventory carrying costs. Only common sense will reveal workable solutions to issues such as these.

Under price, however, any form of discounting that reduces the expected gross income, such as promotional discounts, quantity discounts, overriders and so on, as well as sales commission and unpaid invoices, should be given the most careful attention as incremental marketing expenses. Most obvious incremental marketing expenses will occur, however, under the heading 'promotion' in the form of advertising, sales salaries and expenses, sales promotional expenditure, direct mail costs, and so on.

The important point about the measurable effects of marketing activity is that anticipated levels should be the result of the most careful analysis of what is required to take the company towards its goals, while the most careful attention should be paid to gathering all items of expenditure under appropriate headings. The healthiest way of treating these issues is a zero-based budgeting approach.

MARKETING PLANNING SYSTEMS, DESIGN AND IMPLEMENTATION

In the first section of this chapter we described the widespread confusion between marketing planning and forecasting and budgeting, and the consequences of this, while in the second section the main steps in the marketing planning process were outlined. In this final section, some of the *contextual* issues of marketing planning are examined.

The truth is, of course, that the actual process of marketing planning has been described only in outline. Any book will tell us that it consists of: a situation review; assumptions; objectives; strategies; programmes; and measurement and review. What the books do not tell us is that there are a number of contextual issues that have to be considered that make marketing planning one of the most baffling of all management problems. Here are some of those issues:

- When should it be done, how often, by whom, and how?
- Is it different in a large and a small company?
- Is it different in a diversified and an undiversified company?
- Is it different in an international and a domestic company?
- What is the role of the chief executive?
- What is the role of the planning department?
- Should marketing planning be top-down or bottom-up?
- What is the relationship between operational (one year) and strategic (longer term) planning?

A Battle Against Complexity

Many companies currently under siege have recognised the need for a more structured approach to plan their marketing and have opted for the kind of standardised, formalised procedures written about so much in textbooks. These rarely bring any benefits and often bring marketing planning itself into disrepute.

It is quite clear that any attempt at the introduction of formalised marketing planning systems has serious organisational and behavioural implications for any company, as it requires a change in its approach to managing its business.

It is also clear that unless a company recognises these implications, and plans to seek ways of coping with them, formalised marketing planning will be ineffective. The Cranfield research showed that the implications are principally as follows:

- Any closed loop marketing planning system (but especially one that is essentially a forecasting and budgeting system) will lead to dull and ineffective marketing. Therefore, there has to be some mechanism for preventing inertia from setting in as a result of introducing too much bureaucracy into the system.

- Marketing planning undertaken at the functional level of marketing, in the absence of a means of integration with other functional areas of the business at general management level, will be largely ineffective.

- The separation of responsibility for operational and strategic marketing planning will lead to a divergence of the short-term thrust of a business at the operational level from the long-term objectives of the enterprise as a whole. This will encourage a preoccupation with short-term results at the operational level, which normally makes the firm less effective in the long term.

- Unless the chief executive understands and takes an active role in marketing planning, it will never be an effective system.

- A period of up to three years is necessary (especially in large firms) for the successful introduction of an effective marketing planning system.

Some indication of the potential complexity of marketing planning can be seen in Figure 5.2. Even in a generalised model such as this, it can be seen that in a large diversified group operating in many foreign markets, a complex combination of product, market and functional plans is possible. For example, what is required at regional level will be different from what is required at headquarters level, while it is clear that the total corporate plan has to be built from the individual building-blocks. Furthermore, the function of marketing itself may be further functionalised for the purpose of planning, such as marketing research, advertising, selling, distribution, promotion, and so forth, while different customer groups may merit having separate plans drawn up.

A number of points concerning requisite planning levels seem clear. First, in a large diversified group, irrespective of such organisational issues, anything other than a systematic approach approximating to a formalised marketing planning system is unlikely to enable the necessary control to be exercised over the corporate identity. Secondly, unnecessary planning, or over-planning, could easily result from an inadequate or indiscriminate consideration of the real planning needs at the different levels in the hierarchical chain. Thirdly, as size and diversity increase, so the degree of formalisation of the marketing

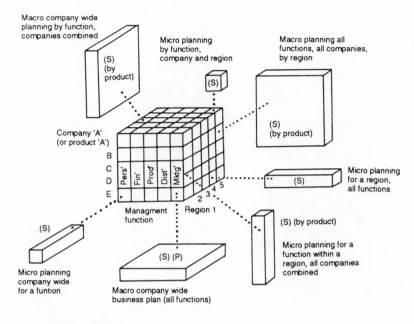

Macro company wide
planning by function,
companies combined

(S)
(by
product)

Micro planning
by function,
company and region

(S)

Macro planning all
functions, all companies,
by region

(S)
(by product)

Company 'A'
(or product 'A')

B
C
D
E

Pers' Fin' Prod' Dist' Mktg'

Managment
function

Region 1

2 3 4 5

(S)

Micro planning
company wide
for a funtion

Micro planning
for a region,
all functions

(S)

(S) (by product)

Micro planning for a
function within a
region, all companies
combined

(S) (P)

Macro company wide
business plan (all functions)

Key P = parent company
     S = subsidary company

Figure 5.2 Macro business plan: all functions, all companies, all regions,
together with constituent building-blocks

planning process must also increase. This can be simplified in the form of a
matrix (Figure 5.3).

The degree of formalisation must increase with the evolving size and diversity of operations. However, while the degree of formalisation will change, the
need for an effective marketing planning system does not. The problems that
companies suffer, then, are a function of either the degree to which they have
a requisite marketing planning system or the degree to which the formalisation
of their system grows with the situational complexities attendant upon the size
and diversity of operations.

The Results of Planning

Figure 5.4 explores four key outcomes that marketing planning can evoke. It
can be seen that systems I, III and IV – ie, where the individual is totally subordinate to a formalised system, or where individuals are allowed to do what
they want without any system, or where there is neither system nor creativity –
are less successful than system II, in which the individual is allowed to be
entrepreneurial within a total system. System II, then, will be an effective

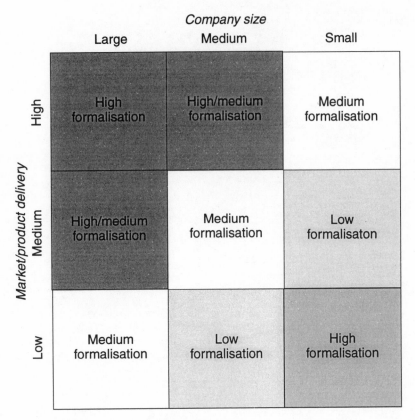

Figure 5.3 Market/product diversity by company size

marketing planning system, but one in which the degree of formalisation will be a function of company size and diversity.

Creativity cannot flourish in a closed loop formalised system. There would be little disagreement that in today's abrasive, turbulent and highly competitive environment, it is those firms that succeed in extracting entrepreneurial ideas and creative marketing programmes from systems that are necessarily yet acceptably formalised, that will succeed in the long run. Much innovative flair can so easily be stifled by systems. Certainly there is ample evidence of international companies with highly formalised systems that produce stale and repetitive plans, with little changed from year to year, that fail to point up the really key strategic issues as a result. The scandalous waste this implies is largely due to a lack of personal intervention by key managers during the early stages of the planning cycle.

There is clearly a need, therefore, to find a way of perpetually renewing the planning life-cycle each time around. Inertia must never set in. Without some

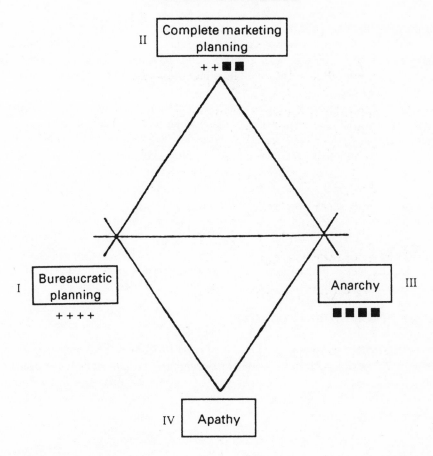

+ Degree of formalisation
■ Degree of openness

Figure 5.4 Four outcomes of marketing planning

such valve or means of opening up the loop, inertia quickly produces decay. Such a valve has to be inserted early in the planning cycle during the audit, or situation review stage. In companies with effective marketing planning systems, whether such systems are formalised or informal, the critical intervention of senior managers – from the chief executive down through the hierarchical chain – comes at the audit stage. Essentially what takes place is a personalised presentation of audit findings, together with proposed marketing objectives, strategies and outline budgets for the strategic planning period. These are discussed, amended where necessary, and agreed in various synthesised formats at the hierarchical levels in the organisation *before* any detailed operational planning takes place. It is at such meetings that managers are called upon to justify their views, which tends to force them to be more bold and creative than they would have been had they been allowed merely to send in their proposals.

Obviously, however, even here much depends on the degree to which managers take a critical stance, which is likely to be much greater when the chief executive takes an active part in the process. Every hour of time devoted at this stage by the chief executive has a multiplier effect throughout the remainder of the process. And it should be remembered that we are not talking about budgets at this juncture, in anything other than outline form.

One of the most encouraging findings to emerge from the Cranfield research is that the theory of marketing planning is universally applicable. While the planning task is less complicated in small, undiversified companies, and there is less need for formalised procedures than in large, diversified companies, the fact is that exactly the same framework should be used in all circumstances and that this approach brings similar benefits to all.

Role of the Chief Executive

The Cranfield research showed that few chief executives have a clear perception of the purposes and methods of planning, the proper assignment of planning responsibilities throughout the organisation, the proper structures and staffing of the planning department, and the talent and skills required in an effective planning department.

The role of the chief executive is generally agreed as being to:

- define the organisational framework;
- ensure that the strategic analysis covers critical factors;
- maintain the balance between short- and long-term results;
- display his or her commitment to planning;
- provide the entrepreneurial dynamic to overcome bureaucracy;
- build this dynamic into the planning operation (motivation).

In respect of planning, the principal role is to open up the planning loop by means of the chief executive's personal intervention. The main purpose of this is to act as a catalyst for the entrepreneurial dynamic within the organisation, which can so easily decay through too much bureaucracy. This is not sufficiently recognised in the literature.

When considering the point in the context of the reasons for failures of marketing planning systems it is clear that, for any system to be effective, the chief executive requires to be conversant with planning techniques and approaches, and to be committed to and to take part in the marketing planning process.

Role of the Planning Department

This role is to:

- provide the planning structure and systems;
- secure rapid data transmission in the form of intelligence;
- act as a catalyst in obtaining inputs from operating divisions;
- forge planning links across organisational divisions – eg, R&D and marketing;
- evaluate plans against the chief executive's formulated strategy; and
- monitor the agreed plans.

The planner is a co-ordinator who sees that the planning is done – not a formulator of goals and strategies.

Marketing Planning Cycle and Horizons

The schedule should call for work on the plan for the next year to begin early enough in the current year to permit adequate time for market research and analysis of key data and market trends. In addition, the plan should provide for the early development of a strategic plan that can be approved or altered in principle.

An important factor in determining the planning cycle is bound to be the degree to which it is practicable to extrapolate from sales and market data, but, generally speaking, successful planning companies start the planning cycle formally somewhere between nine and six months from the beginning of the next fiscal year. It is not necessary to be constrained to work within the company's fiscal year: it is quite possible to have a separate marketing planning schedule if that is appropriate, and simply organise the aggregation of results at the time required by the corporate financial controller.

One- and five-year planning periods are by far the most common. Lead time for the initiation of major new product innovations, the length of time necessary to recover capital investment costs, the continuing availability of customers and raw materials, and the size and usefulness of existing plant and buildings are the most frequently mentioned reasons for having a five-year planning horizon. Many companies, however, do not give sufficient thought to what represents a sensible planning horizon for their particular circumstances. A five-year time-span is clearly too long for some companies, particularly those with highly versatile machinery operating in volatile fashion-conscious markets. The effect of this is to rob strategic plans of reality. A five-year horizon is often chosen largely because of its universality. Secondly, some small subsidiaries in large conglomerates are often asked to produce strategic plans for seven, ten and sometimes fifteen years ahead, with the result that they tend to become meaningless exercises.

The conclusion to be reached is that there is a natural point of focus into the future beyond which it is pointless to look. This point of focus is a function of the relative size of a company. Small companies, because of their size and the way they are managed, tend to be comparatively flexible in the way in which they can react to environmental turbulence in the short term. Large companies, on the other hand, need a much longer lead time in which to make changes in direction. Consequently, they tend to need to look further into the future and to use formalised systems for this purpose, so that managers throughout the organisation have a common means of communication.

Positioning of Marketing Planning

There is one other major aspect to be considered. It concerns the requisite location of the marketing planning activity in a company. The answer is simple to give: in the first instance, marketing planning should take place as near to the market-place as possible, but such plans should then be reviewed at high levels within an organisation to see what issues, if any, have been overlooked.

It has been suggested that each manager in the organisation should complete an audit and SWOT analysis on his own area of responsibility. The only way that this can work in practice is by means of a hierarchy of audits. The principle is simply demonstrated in Figure 5.5. This illustrates the principle of auditing at different levels within an organisation. The marketing audit format will be universally applicable: it is only the detail that varies from level to level and from company to company within the same group.

Because, in anything but the smallest of undiversified companies, it is not possible for top management to set detailed objectives for operating units, it is suggested that at this stage in the planning process, strategic guidelines should be issued. One way of doing this is in the form of a 'strategic planning letter'. Another is by means of a personal briefing by the chief executive at 'kick-off' meetings. As in the case of the audit, these guidelines would proceed from the broad to the specific, and would become more detailed as they progressed through the company towards operating units. These guidelines would be under the headings of 'financial', 'manpower and organisation', 'operations', and of course 'marketing'.

Under marketing, for example, at the highest level in a large group top management may ask for particular attention to be paid to issues such as the technical impact of microprocessors on electro-mechanical component equipment, leadership and innovation strategies, vulnerability to attack from the flood of Japanese and European products, and so on. At operating company level, it is

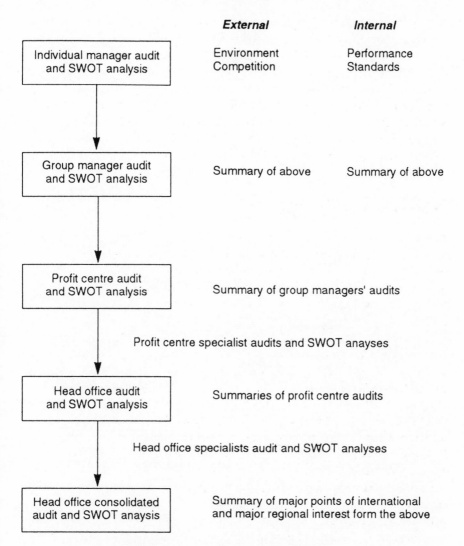

Figure 5.5 A marketing audit hierarchy

possible to be more explicit about target markets, product development, and the like.

Having carefully explained the point about *requisite* marketing planning, Figure 5.6 illustrates the principles by which the process should be implemented in any company. It shows a hierarchy of audits, SWOT analyses, objectives, strategies and programmes.

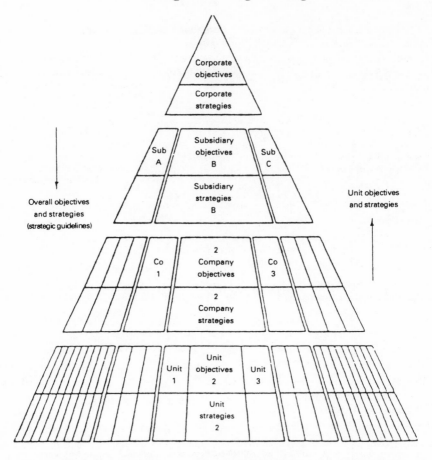

Figure 5.6 Strategic and operational planning – the hierarchy

Figure 5.7 is another way of illustrating the total corporate strategic and planning process. This time, however, a time element is added, and the relationship between strategic planning letters, long-term corporate plans and short-term operational plans is clarified. It is important to note that there are two 'open loop' points on this last diagram. These are the key times in the planning process when a subordinate's views and findings should be subjected to the closest examination by his superior. It is by taking these opportunities that marketing planning can be transformed into the critical and creative process it is supposed to be, rather than the dull, repetitive ritual it so often turns out to be. These figures should be seen as one group of illustrations showing how the marketing planning process fits into the wider context of corporate planning.

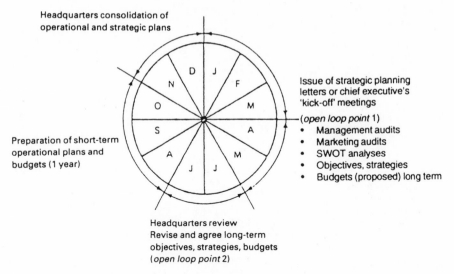

Headquarters consolidation of
operational and strategic plans

Issue of strategic planning
letters or chief executive's
'kick-off' meetings

(*open loop point* 1)
• Management audits
• Marketing audits
• SWOT analyses
• Objectives, strategies
• Budgets (proposed) long term

Preparation of short-term
operational plans and
budgets (1 year)

Headquarters review
Revise and agree long-term
objectives, strategies, budgets
(*open loop point* 2)

Figure 5.7 Strategic and operational planning – timing

A *Final Thought*

In conclusion, it should be stressed that there can be no such thing as an off-the-peg marketing planning system, and anyone who offers one must be viewed with great suspicion.

In the end, marketing planning success comes from an endless willingness to learn and to adapt the system to people and circumstances. It also comes from a deep understanding about the *nature* of marketing planning, which is something that in the final analysis cannot be taught.

The next chapter takes the discussion a stage further. Based on the 1980s Cranfield research, it provides a state-of-the-art review of the latest developments in strategic marketing planning.

Reference

McDonald M (1982) 'The Theory and Practice of Marketing Planning for Industrial Products in International Markets', PhD thesis, Cranfield University.

6

THE ROLE OF EXPERT COMPUTER SYSTEMS*

Malcolm McDonald and Hugh Wilson

OVERVIEW

During the 1980s, Japanese activity in the field of expert systems and related technologies prompted the EC to give birth to the ESPRIT programme in an attempt to integrate European efforts. This in turn led to the DTI-sponsored ALVEY and IED programmes, and other initiatives. An outcrop of these is a DTI-sponsored club called EXMAR – comprising ten major British companies. Formed in 1987, its objectives are to investigate the possibility of computerised assistance for strategic marketing planning by the development of a prototype, and to spread awareness of expert systems in club member organisations. It is funded by contributions from the member companies, and by the Department of Trade and Industry.

The purpose of this chapter is to examine the potential of expert systems, to outline the progress of the EXMAR project and to draw conclusions about appropriate computer support for marketing planning.

*Reproduced by permission of John Wiley & Sons Ltd. This paper first appeared in the *British Journal of Management,* Vol 1, No 3, as 'State of the Art Developments in Expert Systems and Strategic Marketing Planning', copyright Professor David Otley.

It is in two parts. This chapter catalogues the early efforts in the late 1980s to develop an expert system. Chapter 7 continues the story by cataloguing the progress of EXMAR into the mid-1990s.

INTRODUCTION

A surprising fact about expert systems is that although they have inspired a number of new programming languages and powerful new computer architectures, they have made virtually no progress in the domain of marketing, and while most interested parties view them as a potentially powerful way of beating the competition, there are few products and no on-line systems available (Foster, 1985; Moutinho and Paton, 1988). Because artificial intelligence has become the latest buzzword, many software houses are hyping up their old software in advertisements, but most of these can be discounted as irrelevant in the real world of expert systems.

The principal reasons for this lack of progress revolve around the technical problems associated with getting computers to mimic experts and the costs involved. There are no shortcuts to building good expert systems. It takes a considerable amount of skill, patience and several years of effort to develop an expert system in a new area and get it into the field (Rangaswamy *et al*, 1988).

WHAT ARE EXPERT SYSTEMS?

Expert systems are a branch of what is known as artificial intelligence, which is a loosely grouped activity in which a number of researchers of varying backgrounds have done some research since the mid-1950s. But artificial intelligence is still not tightly defined.

Conventional computing deals with simple and unambiguous facts with existing packages being little more than moronic number crunchers. Most software is written in the form of an algorithm, which is a list of commands for the computer to carry out in the order prescribed. It uses data held in a separate file, which is stored in a particular way. Thus, software is data plus algorithm and is useful for boring, repetitive, numerical tasks. The largest selling software has been spreadsheets and word processing packages. Database management was developed from this.

However, managers handle more than words and numbers. They are concerned about knowledge, which is information interpreted for a particular application. The British Computer Society definition of an expert system is:

> The embodiment within a computer of a knowledge-based component, from an expert skill, in such a form that the system can offer intelligent advice or take an intelligent decision about a processing function. A desirable additional characteristic, which many would consider fundamental, is the capability of the system, on

demand, to justify its own line of reasoning in a manner directly attributable to the enquirer. The style adopted to attain these characteristics is rule-based programming.

Put more simply, expert systems, capture not only the knowledge of a human expert, but also the rules that he or she uses to reach conclusions. This knowledge is then made available to others by means of a computer program.

The two main components of an expert system are the knowledge base and the inference engine. The rules used by an expert and his knowledge and experience about a certain domain are interrogated and the captured knowledge becomes the knowledge base, which is the heart of the system.

The inference engine accesses the knowledge base, makes the necessary connections, draws conclusions, and generates the answers. The general reasoning strategies are separated from the knowledge base so as to allow the system to use knowledge in a variety of ways, requesting additional information, if required, to solve a particular problem and explaining the reasoning behind its questions and recommendations by reporting the rule and facts used. Since the knowledge base and inference engine are separate, an inference engine can be bought to be used in association with other databases. This is called a shell.

An expert system will usually have the following characteristics. It will:

- relate to one area of expertise or knowledge rather than to a set of data;
- be restricted to a particular topic;
- have collected the rules (heuristics) and knowledge of an expert;
- have an inference engine;
- be capable of extension;
- be able to cope with uncertainty;
- give advice;
- explain its reasoning.

WHY HAS PROGRESS BEEN SO SLOW IN MARKETING?

During the 1960s, attention was focused on specific problem-solving applications in scientific fields. Many successful expert systems have been built, including MYCIN for diagnosing infectious diseases (Buchan and Shortcliffe, 1984), and PROSPECTOR, a system for evaluating geographical locations for possible mineral deposits (Duda *et al*, 1979).

Management problems, however, do not lend themselves to quite the same precise logic as scientific problems. People do not solve most of life's problems by mathematical means, but rather by experience, knowledge and intuition. Marketing problems are dealt with in the same way, as most of them are logical rather than mathematical, and problem-solving knowledge, while available, is incomplete.

Decision-support systems and the like use hard facts and static formulae which, given the correct data, provide correct answers. They belong more naturally to the logical, black-or-white, right-or-wrong world of computers. But managers in the world of marketing deal with uncertainties and often with vague concepts. Decisions invariably are built on a set of 'rules', or heuristics, that reflect the expert's own knowledge and experience about the problem in question. These rules are hard to specify and quantify, because the expert's experience enables him or her to think in terms of shades of grey, 'more or less', and 'approximately'. Such fuzzy reasoning is commonly used by human beings to find a path through situations that are too complex and amorphous for the human mind to handle in a totally conscious, rational, scientific way.

Most people would acknowledge that in virtually any walk of life, true experts have built their expertise largely from experience and an intuitive grasp of problem-solving in the real world, something which is often referred to as the 'University of Life'. Indeed, many of the world's leading business people acknowledge that they owe their success not to formal business education and textbooks, but to their own experience, flair and intuitive good judgment.

Schon (1984) describes this phenomenon as follows: 'Competent practitioners usually know more than they can say. They exhibit a kind of knowing-in-practice, most of which is tacit'. He cites an investment banker, who makes his decisions based on 70–80 per cent instinct, and only 20–30 per cent calculable rules. This 'gut feel' was a major asset to the bank in question. His point is that artistry is not reducible to discernible routines.

He describes scientific rigour as 'describable, testable, replicable techniques derived from scientific research, based on knowledge that is testable, consensual, cumulative and convergent', but then goes on to argue that much of what passes for scientific management is irrelevant because business problems do not come well formed. Certainly, most marketing problems are messy and indeterminate and successful practitioners make judgements using criteria and rules which are difficult to define. Many academics would decry this as a lack of rigour, and in so doing exclude as non-rigorous much of what successful practitioners actually do.

Accounting for Artistry

The problem to be addressed by expert systems in the marketing domain, then, revolves around how to take account of the intuitive artistry displayed by experts in situations of complexity and uncertainty in a way that is describable and susceptible to a kind of rigour that falls outside the boundaries of technical rationality. The question is, how an epistemology of practice can be captured and represented in an expert system.

For an expert system to mimic an expert, it needs to be able to deal with the uncertainties, complexities and vague concepts that human beings deal with routinely, even though such 'rules' are neither simple nor straightforward. For example, a simple rule for a marketing manager might be: 'If the market is growing, increase promotional expenditure'. This would appear to be easy for a human being to understand, but in reality words like 'market', 'growing', 'increase' and 'promotional expenditure' are open to many different interpretations, as indeed is the whole lexicon of marketing.

One way of dealing with this problem is the development of 'fuzzy sets'. A 'growing market', for example, is a fuzzy set in the sense that its meaning can vary from situation to situation. Fuzzy numbers approximate the response figures from marketing experts and these numbers are then loaded into, for example, sales projections and promotion analyses.

The foundation of any expert system is the knowledge base, which can be extracted from one or more experts in a particular field. The expertise is usually stored in the form of rules-of-thumb (heuristics), which are, typically 'if then' statements. For example, if A is true, then B is true; or if X is true, do Y. Given an initial set of circumstances, the system can map out a set of contingencies and further contingencies.

A heuristic differs from an algorithm in that it does not give a correct answer, nor does it guarantee results. It merely suggests a general direction that is more or less likely to prove more useful than another direction. An example of a heuristic in chess might be: 'If a player stays in control of the centre of the board, he or she is more likely to win'. In marketing, a heuristic might be: 'If the market is growing and if you have appropriate business strengths, then an appropriate marketing objective would be to grow market share'.

A system of interlinking heuristics in the form of a decision tree is one way of representing knowledge. This is sometimes 'backwards inferencing' and sometimes 'forward inferencing'. Backwards inferencing starts with an objective and tries different combinations of rules and/or actions until it is reached. Forward inferencing reasons from initial information until it reaches useful conclusions. This can give rise to what is termed 'combinatorial explosion', which can be avoided by pruning and the use of heuristics that are correct most of the time. This gives probable solutions to less rigorously defined problems that are too complex to be dealt with algorithmically.

To date, however, no one has seriously tackled the world of marketing with expert systems other than the MSI ADCAD (Rangaswamy *et al*, 1988) system developed to advise on advertising design. After considering a variety of consumer and environmental factors, advertisers use a combination of empirical research, communication theory and rules-of-thumb to select communication objectives and to select appropriate creative approaches.

The authors themselves list a number of weaknesses in ADCAD, but conclude: 'As one advertising executive put it: "it helps us to think a little deeper about the issues we have to consider in developing ads that are both strategically and executionally sound"'. Another interesting and relevant conclusion was that most managers, when asked, said they would like to make use of existing theoretical and empirical knowledge of marketing when making decisions. However, few actually did use such knowledge. Expert systems can bridge this gap by structuring, validating and disseminating marketing knowledge while, at a theoretical level, they challenge their creators to understand and critically evaluate the elements of marketing knowledge and their interrelationships.

In the next section, the approach taken to the analysis phase at the start of the EXMAR project is outlined, and the system objectives that were derived are described. The nature of the logical model that emerged is discussed, and the demonstrator system based on it is described, emphasising the nature and style of the support to the user provided by the system, how this reflects the logical model, and how this meets the system objectives.

EXMAR – PREVIOUS WORK AND EARLY OBSERVATIONS

The initial requirements analysis produced a number of interesting problems for the project, which were to sow the seeds of expensive and time-consuming delay. These problems can be summarised as follows:

- It became clear that not many of the member companies were particularly *au fait* with the methodology of marketing planning. This led to the problem of setting clear objectives for the project.
- The diversity of company industry types, ranging from capital goods to service industries, meant that no subsequent system could possibly be suitable for all circumstances.
- Problems and subsequent proposed objectives ranged from 'To support a formal planning framework to improve discipline during the planning process' and 'To support further understanding of the effects of currency fluctuations' to 'To promote discipline in pricing control'.

For these reasons, it was decided to focus on the process of marketing planning itself rather than on any situation-specific system. A firm of software consultants was appointed project manager and a knowledge-based systems house was appointed principal contractor.

The systems house began a series of 12 half-day interviews with the author in order to develop a formal paper model as a basis for computerisation. Unfortunately, although taped and transcribed, they were largely unfocused due to the inexperience of the interviewers and little progress was made towards formal modelling of the marketing planning process. The problem centred around lack of proper project control by the project managers, confused expectations by members of the club based on marketing planning naïvety, the inexperience of the knowledge engineers, and the passive role of the domain expert, which was necessary in view of the nature of the project.

The result was that the paper outlining the tasks to be performed by the computer system targeted the whole marketing planning process rather than any subset, and because of this breadth, the process to be computerised was not documented in any detail, nor backed up by any substantive models and interrelationships. Other specifications required by the development methodology in use, such as financial requirements, system structure, and so on, were never produced.

New Management

At this point, the project manager appointed new software consultants to take over the feasibility study and the delivery system. The new contractor set about finding some common requirements among end-users in order to outline the domain model, with a boundary definition showing which parts of the model would be tackled by the computer system. They set about establishing the following areas:

- scope;
- constraints;
- organisational impact;
- maintainability;
- extensibility;
- technology;
- time-scales;
- risk and cost versus quantifiable benefits.

Artificial Intelligence Ltd, the new software consultants, drew various conclusions about the appropriate technical approach.

The need for focus

The previous work had been on a broad front, involving analysis into all aspects of strategic marketing planning. This is a vast topic, tackling many of the most fundamental problems inherent in business activity, and progress was therefore slow. There was a need to focus on a subset of the overall problem.

Feasibility and utility to be established

The very title of the club, 'Expert Systems in Marketing', suggested that the use of expert systems techniques in this area was possible and appropriate. This assumption of feasibility was based on the observation that there existed demonstrable expertise, but why this might imply a classic rule-based expert system had not been addressed. This was a doubly large assumption as no previous systems (or work towards systems) were known in this application area.

There was a need to address this early, as well as the related issue of how any system would be of use to the marketing planner.

Modelling and representation

It was decided that the appropriate first step was to carry out analysis in a closely scoped subset of the problem, with the emphasis on modelling the area using whatever formal techniques were appropriate. An example of the choice deliberately not made at the start was whether any modelling of expertise adopted the 'low road' of embedding the expertise in data structures and code, the 'high road' of an explicit 'deep' representation, or the 'middle road' of an explicit but heuristic representation (Brown, 1984). In this modelling work, the emphasis would be on representation rather on computation, as the essential first step towards any computer system.

The marketing swamp

Marketing will be referred to later in this chapter as a swamp of intuitive, experience-based practice with the occasional rocky peak of formal techniques. In the experience of Artificial Intelligence Ltd the best place to start when modelling such 'soft' domains was often on the boundary between the soft area and neighbouring more readily formalisable areas. In this case, that meant starting with the established formal techniques and working out from there.

RESULTS OF ANALYSIS WORK – AND THE DEMONSTRATOR

Several analysis sessions were held with the author and with marketing practitioners in club member organisations. This resulted in an overall EXMAR system objective, an outline model that was used as the basis for a demonstrator system, and a list of areas where further work was required.

The overall EXMAR system objective was defined to be:

> To provide assistance for the marketing planning process in such a way as to spread knowledge and further understanding of how and why the various factors of the market interact and serve to define the parameters of the business activity.

The remainder of this section describes features of the model and how these were exploited in the demonstrator. The structure is an interleaved description of the two. Each subsection describes a model feature and the relevant aspects of the demonstrator.

Assistance in Interpretation and Understanding

The model covers the data manipulated by a marketing planner when developing a strategic marketing plan, and structures the marketing planner's task. Many of the individual subtasks or processes of this task involve modelling by the user of the business context, or interpretation by the user of the information entered. There is much that a computer system based on the model cannot do for the user, and it became increasingly clear that its most appropriate aim is to assist.

The objective of the demonstrator was therefore to provide an interactive system that supports a marketing planner by providing tools that help the user to represent the state of the markets and products under consideration; to interpret this information so as to gain an understanding of the markets and one's place within them; and to determine a course of action based on this understanding.

Model of the Process of Generating a Marketing Plan

A hierarchical breakdown of the process the marketing planner should adopt to generate a marketing plan was defined. Encouraging the user to adopt this process is of value in itself, as the process incorporates much experience that helps to avoid common pitfalls – for example, the need to arrive at an appropriate understanding of the current situation before setting objectives for the future.

The demonstrator uses this hierarchy as a basis for the user's navigation around the system. The initial screen display is shown to illustrate this (Figure 6.1). Also shown is a window for more detailed navigation around a particular stage.

Each box in the graphical browser represents a stage of the process. The user carries out a stage by selecting a box with the mouse: the system then takes the appropriate action, which may, for example, be to present the user with a form to fill in, or to open a more detailed browser of the process for that stage.

To give an overview of the process, *Select/Define Business Unit* identifies which area of the business the marketing plan is for and records the purpose of the business area. *Focus* identifies which of the unit's markets and products are of interest. *Conduct Audit* assesses the current position of the products and markets. *Forecast* predicts the future position of the products and markets, assuming that we do not intervene, as a base-line for objective setting. Finally, *Set Objectives and Strategies* sets objectives for the business unit based on the information collected, analysed and summarised, and defines strategies by which the objectives are to be met.

Detailed browsers contain icons showing the nature of the support offered for a particular stage: for example, there are icons for graphical displays of information, for tables of numbers, and for free text. The *Predict Relationship with Markets* browser is illustrated as an example, also in Figure 6.1.

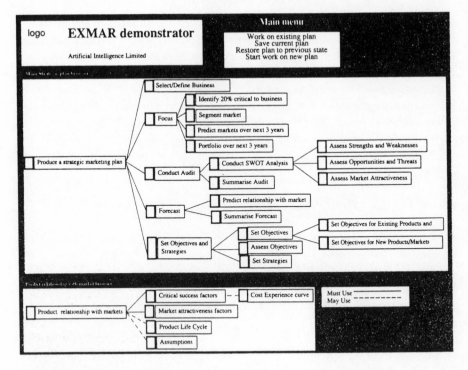

Figure 6.1 Initial screen display, with an example of a detailed browser

Users will largely go through the process depth first and top-to-bottom; but they are free to do otherwise, as there are many cases where they may legitimately wish to do so.

A Generally Applicable, Sound Data Model

A data model was developed that captured and related the information considered during production of a strategic marketing plan. It has proved essentially sound and of general applicability to the wide range of marketing situations represented by the diverse club member companies.

The model has three cornerstone entities: *business unit*, the part of the organisation for which the plan is being developed; *product*, the products of services offered by the unit; *market*, the markets in which it operates.

Critical success factors model the workings of a market by documenting the factors critical to the success of any product in the market, from the consumers' viewpoint. They are an objective assessment of how the market works, independently of the business unit's presence in it. The matching of products to markets is represented by the important 'product for market' entity: a product's score on the critical success factors relates to this entity.

Market attractiveness factors model the priorities of the business unit by documenting the factors determining how attractive a market is to the unit. Being a subjective assessment of the business unit's priorities, the criteria for their correctness must be the result of agreement between key executives. The matching of markets to business units is represented by the important 'involvement in market' entity: a market's score on the market attractiveness factors relates to this entity.

Time-dependent information is held in 'snapshot entities', which are 'forms' which must be completed by the user, whose role is to supply the relevant information such as product costs, prices, unit definitions, and so on. For each plan, the demonstrator system holds data structures closely based on the data model. The user's primary means of manipulating the data is by using these forms, one of which is illustrated in Figure 6.2.

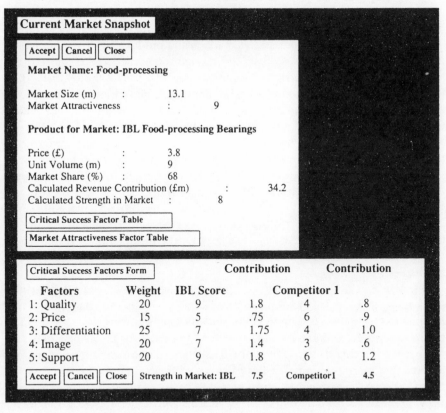

Figure 6.2 Typical forms for data notation

The top form shows current information about the food-processing market for the fictional International Bearings Limited (IBL) company, which sells bearings into a variety of markets. The bottom form shows the critical success factors defined for this market, with weights to illustrate their relative importance. For example, while price is important in this market, it is less so than several other factors, such as product differentiation and quality, the product's image, and the engineering support provided. It also shows a score for IBL and its main competitor against these factors, and a weighted average computed by the system, to represent IBL's overall strength in the market. This is copied to the top form by the system. The market attractiveness score on the top form results from a similar weighted average form for the attractiveness of the market against such criteria as the market's size, growth and profitability.

The Use of Techniques in the Data Model

The 'rocky peaks' with which the analysis work started are 'textbook' techniques for analysing an organisation's markets and products, such as the directional policy matrix, which is illustrated in Figure 6.3, the Boston and Porter matrices, and so on. These view different aspects of the data model using differing graphical representations, to aid in interpretation of the data. To extend our analogy, the data model thus forms the bridges between the rocky peaks to enable us to navigate the intervening swamp.

The screen snapshot in Figure 6.3 gives an example of how the demonstrator exploits these features by showing the underlying data presented in the standard formats. The directional policy matrix plots, for each of IBL's markets, the market attractiveness against IBL's strength in the market. The size of the circles is proportional to the market's contribution to IBL's revenue (although it could have been set to any useful metric). Different circle shadings illustrate the current, forecast and objective situations for the product/market. (In terms of the data model discussed earlier, each circle strictly represents a 'product-for-market'.)

The matrix aids in understanding both the situation of an individual product/market, and the balance of the portfolio of products. An example of the matrix's interpretation is that, in all its markets, IBL is moving downwards and rightwards from the current to the forecast situation. This indicates a general weakening of IBL's position: the matrix illustrates what IBL intends to do about this for the automotive market by maintaining its competitive position while cutting costs where possible.

On request, the demonstrator also provides standard, 'textbook' advice for a product-for-market in a given position on the matrix, as a guide to the planner in setting objectives. For example, for the automotive market, the system

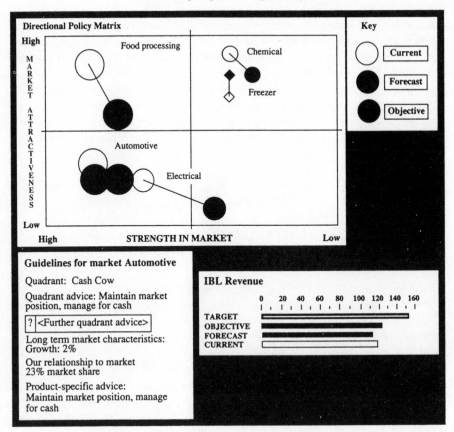

Figure 6.3 Data presentation to aid understanding

advises that the market position (strength in market and market share) be maintained, but that subject to this the market be managed for cash to fund development of more attractive markets. This is the only case in the demonstrator where it was felt appropriate that the system should take an active role of giving advice, rather than the passive role of presenting information in differing forms to aid the user in interpretation.

The diagram also shows a 'gap gauge' – a bar chart showing the financial gap between the business unit's target revenue and the sum of the individual objectives so far set for the various markets.

Less Structured Information: Checklists and Free Text

Some parts of the marketing plan were best expressed in text – for example, the business unit's mission statement, and lists of opportunities and threats.

Also, in several areas, marketing expertise was identified that was not formalised beyond free text in the model. Examples are checklists of common critical success factors; assistance with definition of a business unit's mission statement; and checklists of possible opportunities and threats to consider. This unstructured information was related, however, to specific points in the planning process, or to specific items in the data model. The demonstrator exploited this by making available text windows at appropriate points with icons on the browsers and elsewhere. This was implemented using the *NoteCards* hypertext system.

DEMONSTRATOR FEEDBACK AND THE DEVELOPMENT OF A PROTOTYPE

The demonstrator model was first seen by club members in December 1988 and was given unanimous acclaim by all. The following were the features which they especially recommended:

- The initiative is with the user – the demonstrator leaves the user to decide what to do next. This was liked by the club members, who felt it to be appropriate for this application.
- Evidence of utility – club members felt an operational system based on the demonstrator's ideas could be of significant use in the vital process of strategic marketing planning. This is an example of utility being addressed by the client rather than by the developers.
- Communication of the nature of the proposed prototype – the demonstrator served to communicate the nature of the support that would be offered to a marketing planner by a fuller computer system, to club members and to the author. With this innovative system, this was difficult to achieve on paper.
- Use in specification of prototype – the demonstrator was extremely effective in discussions with club members to aid with the specification of the prototype which was subsequently developed.

THE ROLE OF THE COMPUTER

The potential benefits shown by the EXMAR demonstrator are due mainly to its assistance with the understanding and interpretation of the information entered. The end results may include a marketing plan, but it also includes an enhanced and readily communicable understanding of the business gained by the marketing planner. These benefits are largely due to appropriate and varied display of the information.

Apart from data presentation, a computer system in this domain can perform the tasks for which computers have traditionally been used: managing data, maintaining constraints between data items like a spreadsheet, and performing routine calculations. These free up the user's thoughts for higher-level problems.

Finally, in some cases the computer can be more proactive, offering advice, pointing out decisions that go against conventional wisdom, and so on.

The most appropriate technology for this mix of roles will itself be a mix. In the case of EXMAR, the software techniques included object-oriented programming, hypertext and use of windows-based programming environments, to enable swift development and a carefully tailored user interface. We have not found rule-based representations so far to be relevant, although they may be in future developments.

To some expert systems workers this emphasis on data presentation and low-level data management, as opposed to sophisticated calculation or reasoning, would constitute some sort of failure. We consider, however, that the objective of computer systems is to make the combination of user and system more effective than the user alone, not to build 'clever' computer systems. Even in the classic scientific expert systems such as those quoted earlier, the user interface frequently constituted more of the work, and more importantly delivered more of the benefits, than emphasis in the literature would suggest. This may apply even more in such 'soft' and ill-understood areas as marketing planning. The rapid recent progress in the power, and price, of the underlying software tools that enable graphical user interfaces to be provided will ensure that more such areas will be tackled effectively in the future.

Analysis Approach

The analysis approach used for EXMAR was undogmatic and modest: to model the available expertise with whatever modelling techniques proved most appropriate, starting with the most well-established, documented and verified expertise. 'Don't run before you can walk' should not need emphasising, but the early experience of the club shows that perhaps it still does. The very term 'expert systems' has led some to unjustified assumptions not just about the feasibility of building computer systems based on expertise, but also of their utility and of the most appropriate modelling and system-building tools (Bobrow et al, 1986). The alternative is classic software engineering, with an expanded tool-kit of analysis and implementation techniques to draw upon as appropriate.

This may lead to the question about how and to what extent the model and demonstrator may be said to incorporate expertise. All aspects of the model and demonstrator can reasonably be said to be based on expertise: the process; the data model; the means of presentation of information; the checklists provided; and the one case where data-dependent advice is given. The system thus takes the 'low road' according to Brown's categorisation discussed earlier. There is certainly much available (but not necessarily formalisable) expertise that has not been captured. The critical design task has been the effective definition of the boundary between the system and the user such that the user is encouraged to think about the issues that the system cannot of itself address. This conforms to the stated EXMAR system objective quoted earlier, of providing assistance for the marketing planning process in such a way as to spread knowledge and further understanding of the business and its markets.

CONCLUSIONS

A number of conclusions can be drawn from the EXMAR experience:

1. The development of EXMAR shows that it is possible to use expert system methodologies to built support systems in complex areas of marketing management, especially if the domain is well defined, has a large number of factors to be considered and relevant expert knowledge is available.
2. The more complex and amorphous the expertise to be captured, the longer it takes both the expert and the knowledge engineer to reach an acceptable approximation. It is clear that to develop an expert system that is of some practical use requires both time and resources of massive proportions. This is supported by the MSI research paper (Rangaswamy *et al*, 1980) which concludes: 'There are no shortcuts to building a good expert system. It takes a considerable amount of skill, patience, and years of effort to develop an expert system in a new area and get it into the field'.
3. Expert systems provide a consistency to human decision-making which is valuable, since people tend to forget or ignore knowledge.
4. EXMAR has generated considerable interest and support among the major multinational companies that form the club, because it forces them to think deeply and in a structured way about the issues that need to be considered in developing a strategic marketing plan.
5. Expert systems are useful in helping both academics and practitioners to structure, validate and use marketing knowledge and to better understand the interrelationships between the elements of marketing.
6. Tight project control is vital. This view is supported by Mumford (1988). Many issues need to be considered, such as clear definition of subject matter, availability of inputs, and clear agreement with users on objectives, timescales and resourcing. The close involvement of the EXMAR club members has been essential in this respect. It has been achieved through an active working party, through agreed quality assurance criteria for each stage of the work, and through the use of a demonstrator.

7. The potential advantages of expert systems in marketing are consistent advice, secure knowledge bases, making better use of experts, enhanced decision-making and improved analysis.

8. Since we live in an imperfect world, with imperfect problems and imperfect tools, it is unreasonable to expect a perfect expert system until there are perfect experts and perfect technology. On the other hand, if an expert system gives better advice than you would have had without it, it is probably worthwhile.

In conclusion, it is unlikely that expert systems will ever be able to give the same value as real human experts, although clearly they can offer reasonable advice. Nor will they guarantee that you make the right decisions. But they can help you to gain a proper perspective of the alternatives.

In a sense, expert systems will always be a bit like distance-learning programmes, which can replace a bad teacher, but never a good one.

References

Bobrow, DG, Mittall, S and Stefik, M (1986) *Expert Systems: Perils and Promise*, Commun ACM, September, pp 880–894.

Brown, JS (1984) 'The low road, the middle road and the high road', in Winston, PH and Prendergast, K (eds) *The AI Business*, MIT Press, Cambridge, Massachusetts.

Buchan, B and Shortcliffe, E (1984) *Rule-based Expert Programs: The MICIN Experiments of the Stanford Heuristic Programming Project*, Addison-Wesley, Reading, Massachusetts.

Duda, R, Gaschning, J and Hart, P (1979) 'Model design in the PROSPECTOR consultant system for mineral exploration', in Michie, D (ed) *Expert Systems in the Microelectronic Age*, Edinburgh University Press, Edinburgh.

Foster, E (1985) 'Artificial intelligence', *Personal Computing*, April.

Moutinho, L and Paton, R (1988) 'Expert systems: a new tool in marketing', *Quarterly Review of Marketing*, Summer.

Mumford, E (1988) 'Designing computer-based systems', *University of Wales Business and Economics Review*, 3.

Rangaswamy, A, Burke, RA, Wind, J and Eliashberg J (1988) *Expert Systems for Marketing*, Marketing Science Institution Working Paper Report, Nos 87–107.

Schon, D (1984) *The Crisis of Professional Knowledge and the Pursuit of an Epistemology of Practice*, paper for the Harvard Business School Colloquium on Teaching by the Case Method, April.

7

CRITICAL PROBLEMS IN MARKETING PLANNING: THE POTENTIAL OF DECISION SUPPORT SYSTEMS*

Hugh Wilson and Malcolm McDonald

OVERVIEW

Chapter 6 catalogued the early stages of the development of EXMAR. This chapter continues the story up to the 1990s.

Few companies use a comprehensive marketing planning process, despite wide agreement on the benefits to be gained. This results from cognitive, procedural, resource, organisational, cultural, informational and environmental problems. While computers in marketing are mainly used for operational tasks, research in other domains suggests that decision support systems could assist in reducing some of these problems. A research project is, therefore, under way to examine whether and how software can be used to improve strategic marketing planning practice. An initial report on findings to date is

*This paper first appeared in the *Journal of Strategic Marketing*, 2, 1994, pp 249–269 and is reproduced with the kind permission of Chapman & Hall.

given, based on a qualitative evaluation with six organisations using a proto-type system. There is some evidence that appropriate software support can increase marketing skills, encourage wider evaluation of alternatives, support wider managerial involvement in strategy formation, improve internal data flows and enhance plan quality. Provisional guidelines on the nature of such systems are presented. Future research stages are outlined.

INTRODUCTION

Marketing planning provides a process and techniques which can deliver well-documented benefits, but these benefits are not widely obtained. To explain this, a number of barriers to effective marketing planning have been identified. Some are organisational and cultural, such as the isolation of the marketing function from the company's operations. Others are cognitive and procedural – for example, the need for marketing knowledge and skills, and for a flexible approach to planning.

Research in decision support systems applied to other areas of management provides some indication that their application to marketing planning might reduce some of these barriers. There is a need to test this notion, both in terms of the feasibility of building such systems and in terms of their utility in reducing the barriers to effective marketing planning. Testing feasibility involves work both on how to apply emerging software technologies and on formalising and simplifying the marketing planning process as a basis for com-puterisation. This work can only be validated by the design of working soft-ware. Testing utility involves the evaluation of software by practising managers.

In this chapter, we explore in depth the rationale for applying decision sup-port technology to the definition of marketing strategy, through a review of relevant research in marketing planning and in decision support systems (the following two sections). We then give a report on findings to date from Cranfield School of Management's research in this area, which has involved the design of a working prototype and its evaluation in six organisations (the fourth and fifth sections). Finally, we outline the research currently in progress with 35 organisations using the prototype for live planning.

MARKETING PLANNING IN THEORY AND PRACTICE

There is a wide body of broadly consistent prescriptive literature on how and why marketing plans should be developed (for example, Abell and Hammond, 1979; McDonald, 1989b; Kotler, 1991) covering the information to be collected and the process to be followed, as well as appropriate analytical techniques (Meldrum *et al*, 1987; Kotler and Armstrong, 1989; Brooksbank, 1990; McDonald, 1991).

DECISION SUPPORT SYSTEMS IN MARKETING PLANNING

We have identified a number of problems with marketing planning in practice. Are there grounds for hoping that decision support systems (DSS) can reduce some of these? To answer this question, we will first consider the research into decision support systems applied to other domains of managerial decision-making, to look for promising analogies. We will then look at how managers currently use software in this domain. Finally, we will examine the previous research that focuses specifically on decision support for marketing planning.

Why Apply Decision Support Systems to Marketing Planning?

We will look at each group of marketing planning barriers in Table 7.1 to explore whether similar problems have been reduced by DSS use in other areas of managerial activity.

Roles people play

Intuitively, this is not the most promising area for computers to offer assistance. It seems unlikely, for example, that the use of a DSS would of itself increase senior management's support for marketing planning. Relationships such as this have been more frequently hypothesised the other way round – for example, in a number of studies that have found top management's support for a DSS project to be a factor contributing to project success (Sanders and Courtney, 1985; Guimaraes et al, 1992). It is plausible, nevertheless, that a system could indirectly increase top management support for marketing planning due to the learning effect of system use, discussed later.

Greater involvement in marketing planning from top management or from staff outside marketing could also result from a group decision support system's facilitation for group working. Experiments on groups (Nunamaker et al, 1988; Pinsonneault and Kraemer, 1989) show that support for group decision-making can result in greater participation among members. In the laboratory, though, members have to be present to participate: if within the organisation they are not consulted at all or do not make themselves available, the computer system cannot reduce this barrier to effective planning.

Any impact of decision support on these barriers, then, is likely to be limited.

Cognitive

An early objective of decision support systems was to make management science models, little understood and little used by practising managers, more available and usable (Little, 1970). Decision support systems have been found to result in a greater depth of analysis (Pinsonneault and Kraemer, 1989), suggesting perhaps a measure of success with this objective in cases where decision support systems have been applied.

A number of marketing tools and techniques involve the graphical display of information as well as analysis, such as portfolio matrices and product life-style curves. Appropriate graphical display has been shown to impact decision-making positively (Benbasat and Dexter, 1986; Jarvenpaa, 1989), suggesting that if a decision support system reduces the effort involved in generating the display, it will render the marketing tools more usable. But it is not just the effort involved that holds practitioners back from using graphical tools: some of the cognitive difficulties found by practitioners relate to technical aspects of the graphics, such as logarithmic scales on a portfolio matrix (McDonald, 1990b). It is plausible that computer support could overcome these difficulties. As many decision support systems have a substantial graphical component, this is a factor, unexplored in many studies, that may contribute widely to the impact of the technology.

A related goal of decision support systems has been to encourage the consideration of more alternative solutions to a problem (Lodish, 1981). Some studies have found that system users consider more alternatives (Sainfort *et al*, 1990), in some cases through explicit support for brainstorming (Nunamaker *et al*, 1988). The role of the system in challenging previous perceptions is evidenced by Dickmeyer (1983), who found DSS users more likely to change their minds due to a planning exercise. Other studies, though, have not found a significant difference in the alternatives considered (Sharda *et al*, 1988).

As well as compensating for a lack of knowledge and skills, using a decision support system may actually teach the user some of the skills he or she lacks. If a DSS helps a user to perform a task, the user may learn by example how to perform similar tasks (Little, 1970). Van Horn (1990), for instance, found this effect with a telecommunications planning DSS.

Systems and procedures

The extensive work on group decision support for planning at the University of Arizona (Nunamaker *et al*, 1988) concentrates on support for a planning process. The researchers report that this works well whether the process is prescribed by the system designers or is defined by the participants. As we discuss in the next section, this contrasts with most software that is currently available for marketing strategy, which concentrates on assisting with specific tools and techniques, resulting in some calls for more support for a planning process that combines the techniques together (Waalewijn and Boulan, 1990; editorial in *International Journal of Research in Marketing*, Vol 8, 1991).

The Arizona researchers recognise the importance of text to complement numerical data in planning and claim to have achieved good results with the incorporation of suitable facilities in their DSS. This might be expected to assist with the common problem of planning forecasts being made without documentation of how they are to be achieved.

A formalised marketing planning process has for some companies proved a mixed blessing. There is perhaps, a trade-off between formalisation and flexibility. The Arizona research found that the larger the group, the more the participants appreciated the structure provided by the system. Little (1970), in this seminal paper that coined the term 'decision calculus' as a philosophy for building decision support systems, recognised the importance of leaving the user in control of the decision-making process, a point emphasised by Lodish (1981). Describing experience with CALLPLAN, which helped salespeople to allocate their time among accounts and prospects, Lodish (1981) wrote:

> Before the salesmen got their first results at the computer terminal, their initial reaction was one of caution and skepticism. However, experience with the interactive program transformed this attitude into varying levels of enthusiasm as the salesman realised that he was controlling the program, rather than it controlling him.

This contrasts with the language used by authors from the decision analysis school of decision support (Wind and Saaty, 1980) who discuss how the arguably complex and opaque analytic hierarchy process:

> forces them [managers] to explicate the environmental scenarios most likely to affect their business decisions ... the discipline forced by the need to structure the problem hierarchically may help achieve consensus over the dimensions of the problem.

We speculate that this more controlling philosophy may contribute to the difficulties described by the authors in persuading managers to participate in the process they advocate. This would be consistent with recent research into sales force automation, which found that systems which were seen as 'empowering' were used much more extensively than those seen as 'controlling' (Hewson and Hewson, 1994).

Expert systems have a similar flavour in that the system often (but not always) has control of the decision-making process. There is no agreement on whether expert systems are a subset of decision support systems or a separate technology (Alter, 1977; Stabell, 1986). Luconi *et al* (1986) distinguish expert systems, decision support systems and 'expert support systems', the distinguishing characteristic being where the control lies for 'flexible strategies' – procedures to explore and analyse the problem and possible solutions. According to their definitions, in expert systems, the control lies with the computer, while in decision support systems the user is in charge. With expert support systems, however, responsibility is shared between computer and user.

In marketing planning, many authors have called for some formalisation of the planning process, but as we have seen, over-rigid processes can cause difficulty. The lesson from other research would appear to be that there needs to be some flexibility in the process supported by a computer system, with a shared responsibility for the planning process between the system and the user.

Resources

Although many case studies claim that the systems they describe save time (Alpar, 1991; Bayer and Harter, 1991), experimental results are inconsistent on this point (Pinsonneault and Kraemer, 1989). There are a number of possible explanations:

1. Most studies have been carried out with novice users, who are likely to be slower than experienced users at performing any given task on the computer. This explanation is cited by Sharda *et al* (1988), who found in their experiments that DSS users took longer to begin with than those using pen and paper, but caught up after three weeks or so.
2. If systems encourage more analyses to be made, this may compensate for any time savings on each individual analysis.
3. The computer system may encourage users to apply techniques unthinkingly that are not appropriate, resulting in excessively detailed analysis (Rangaswamy *et al*, 1991).

Whether decision support would save time in marketing planning, then, is an open question.

Organisational environment/culture

Analogous research is only known for one barrier in this group: that of a corporate culture which stifles idea generation and open expression of views. Nunamaker *et al* (1988) found that system use made participants in planning sessions less likely to be unduly influenced by organisational roles and responsibilities and less likely to be intimidated by their colleagues' status. This resulted in a greater openness.

Data

Lack of information was mentioned by five of the six marketing planning studies examined in Table 7.1. A computer system that is internal to the company cannot generate, of course, external information that has not been collected, but it may provide a convenient central point for the data and provide more efficient dissemination within the organisation. This is rarely the focus for decision support research, as these benefits are shared with management information systems, which have been well researched (Jarvenpaa *et al*, 1985).

Environmental

There are no known studies relating the use of a decision support system to particular environmental problems such as turbulence.

Summary

With some of the barriers to successful marketing planning, there is little reason to believe that computer systems could help and it is likely that these barriers must be reduced by other means. With many of the barriers, though, there are parallels from other domains where decision support systems have been of assistance. This suggests that it is worth investigating whether the same holds true in marketing planning.

We will now look at what software is available to support marketing planning and to what extent it is currently being used.

Use of Decision Support Systems in Marketing Planning

To what extent are computers currently used to support marketing planning? Surveys indicate (Higgins and Opdebeek, 1984; Morris *et al*, 1989; Andersen Consulting, 1989; Hirst 1991a,b; Shaw, 1994) that computerisation of the marketing function has to date concentrated on the following:

1. The 'big four' personal productivity tools for microcomputers: spreadsheets, graphics packages, word processing and databases. These are now being supplemented by group working tools such as electronic mail.
2. Marketing and sales productivity systems, often based on a general-purpose database management system (DBMS), which provide specific facilities such as lead tracking, order taking and mailshots (Moriarty and Swartz, 1989). These have as yet a relatively small, but increasing, penetration.
3. Statistics packages for analysis of market research data, and so on.

The facilities provided are biased towards either purely numerical or purely textual work. Most applications are routine and operational rather than strategic; forecasting is a relatively common exception. The 'semi-structured' tasks that are the preserve of decision support systems (Gorry and Scott Morton, 1971; Keen and Scott Morton, 1978) have been little addressed as yet.

It seems likely, then, that support for marketing planning is in the main restricted to the provision of some relevant information from operational systems, supplemented by the use of personal productivity tools for document creation, presentation authoring, and so on.

This is confirmed by the small number of commercial products targeted at marketing planning and marketing strategy. An informal search for relevant commercial products has been carried out. Information has been obtained from advertisements in the marketing and strategic planning press, reports from management consultancies, trade body publications and discs listing marketing software published by the American marketing press. Relevant software can be categorised as follows:

1. Product marketing planning software: packages aimed at product managers and looking at one product/market. PPAM from a small UK company, Lysia, is an example which was formerly marketed in the UK. Business Insight from Simcon can be regarded as in this category, as the analysis focuses on one product/market. Both have an expert systems approach, asking questions and offering advice.

2. Marketing planning software for multiple products and markets: targeted at marketing managers. Other than the EXMAR software arising from this research, three examples have been found. SMPS from Partners in Marketing includes SWOP analysis and portfolio analysis; there is one UK user currently. Lysia's Smartplan (not thought to be marketed currently) includes competitive analysis, strategy setting and the generation of parts of a three-year marketing plan. It is purely quantitative. Stratex from Nokia Data is a strategic marketing planning tool for small businesses; it appears to provide a tailorable framework for the construction of systems, rather than an end-user system in itself.

3. Corporate planning systems with a marketing dimension: targeted at corporate planners. Examples are Ansoff's ANSPLAN and Alacrity Strategy from Alacritour Inc in Toronto. Where these incorporate a definition of multiple products/markets, the analysis typically stops at the level of market share and growth, and product differentiation as a single dimension.

4. Marketing technique packages: these support individual marketing tools and techniques, with little or no attempt to integrate the tools or to provide a planning framework. The key benefit offered is the graphical presentation of the data to aid understanding, in some cases supplemented by advice based on the underlying theory for the technique. An example is Portfolio Planner, developed by the authors after the early work on this research project. Other commercial products of this type believed to have been influenced by the current research are named StratMar and MatMar.

There are, then, few relevant off-the-shelf products. A small proportion of companies, however, have developed bespoke systems for internal use. Some examples are listed below:

1. ICL developed a system (Aitken and Bintley, 1989) for use with the aid of a facilitator to enhance marketing skills as well as to develop marketing plans. The system supports tools such as perceptual maps and efficiency frontiers for pricing, providing some links between the tools by shared data, but it is not a fully integrated system. Interestingly, the paper by its developers used the term 'expert system', which was not used at any point by its users or sponsors. The system certainly did not fit the technology-based definitions of expert systems, displaying information graphically and doing arithmetic rather than generating advice. It was felt to have the drawback of having

been built piecemeal and not supporting a planning process. As the principal sponsor said, by contrast with EXMAR, there was no 'washing line to hang the pegs [of marketing techniques] on'.

2. A large chemicals multinational demonstrated to the authors a system with more of an expert system flavour, which asked the user a series of questions about a product market and then generated advice, drawing on specific knowledge of the chemical industry coded into the program. Its take-up was significant, though it tended to be used once only to generate ideas in a single session.

3. A pharmaceuticals multinational demonstrated a marketing planning system with a lesser advice component. Guiding the user through a form-filling process, financial information and more qualitative information was collected. While some advice was given based on portfolio theory, this was not the primary thrust of the system. For ease of analysis across business units, the system included definitions of markets and product groups specific to the company. The system was used to standardise planning across the world and to ease aggregation of country plans into a corporate plan.

In general, then, decision support systems are as yet little used to support marketing planning, although some companies are doing pioneering work with bespoke systems and commercial products are beginning to appear. The hypothesis that decision support systems could enhance marketing planning effectiveness is thus largely untested in the market-place. To what extent has it been tested by research? We will now review previous research into decision support systems for marketing planning specifically.

Previous Research in DSS for Marketing Planning

Only one major study has been identified on decision support systems involving marketing planning: Bovich's (1987) PhD thesis, on 'Marketing management decision-making and the role of decision support systems'. This described an experiment typical of those described by Pinsonneault and Kraemer (1989) in their review of group DSS studies, although the DSS is not termed a group decision support system by Bovich. Students in two groups performed a task defined by a scenario from MARKSTRAT, one group being offered use of a decision support system called FCS:EPS, a system which 'allowed its users to perform a wide range of spreadsheet, graphic, and statistical analyses'. The task included presentation of results in the form of a paper report as if to senior management, broadly covering the contents of a product marketing plan. Bovich examined the efficiency and effectiveness of the decision-making process, the decision quality and the users' confidence in the decisions they reached.

The DSS group were told to use the DSS, but only to the extent that they thought it would be useful. Both groups were trained in the relevant techniques. The DSS group had an extra hands-on training session in how to use the software. The quality of the solutions was measured by three means: by MARKSTRAT, by how close the predictions were to the MARKSTRAT model's predictions and by experts.

Bovich concluded that the users of the system had greater confidence in the solutions they proposed, but did not have greater process efficiency, as measured by solution time or greater breadth in alternative design and evaluation. Critically, DSS use had no significant effect on solution quality. There was some support for the notion that training with the DSS led to a more synthetic and forward looking perspective.

Methodological weaknesses reported by Bovich included the use of individuals rather than groups, the individuals' inexperience in system use and the study's short time-scale. The study had several other limitations: students were used rather than practising managers, the presence of a facilitator for DSS users in the form of 'an experienced DSS consultant' did not seem to be controlled for, and no evidence was presented on how close the MARKSTRAT scenario was to the problems encountered by managers in the field.

This study, then, gave useful evidence of the training benefits of DSS use, which alone could justify the further investigation of DSS in the area of marketing planning. It left many questions unanswered, however. First, the software used and the task set were not specifically aimed at the generation of a marketing plan, so they were not tackling issues such as support for a marketing planning process. Secondly, the laboratory experiment method only shed limited light on many factors of interest to marketing planners, such as the ability of systems to overcome communications barriers and hostile corporate cultures. Thirdly, the study only set out to address *whether* a specific system helped with marketing planning, providing little indication of *how* the system helped and how this assistance might be improved.

We speculate that the importance of evaluating systems more broadly than on whether their costs exceed their benefits might also apply in decision support system domains other than marketing planning. The paucity of empirical research allowing for these subtleties would seem inappropriate at such an early stage in the development of computer systems, a point made by Mumford (1988) and a number of other applied IT researchers: 'we should currently be generating ideas, theories and hypotheses, rather than simply testing them, and ... anything which restricts or constrains this process is inappropriate'.

No further literature has been identified specifically concerning decision support systems for marketing planning, although other decision support systems may in practice contribute information or analyses of relevance to a marketing plan (Curry and Moutinho, 1991; Rita, 1991).

In summary, the research into the application of DSS to marketing planning shows some limited benefits but without shedding much light on what caused the benefits or how they should be extended. We will now describe the objectives of the authors' current research, which are rich enough to address these issues.

OBJECTIVES

The aim of the research is to explore the efficacy of the application of decision support systems to marketing planning. As we have seen, it is clear that, at best, a system will reduce only some of the problems preventing more effective marketing planning. It is also clear that the design of a system must be appropriate to the domain. A system must also be appropriately implemented or applied to the organisation: implementation issues such as user training and support, facilitation in using the system, the phasing of system introduction and top management support for the system, have been widely found to impact upon the success of the introduction of the system (Ginzberg, 1981; Montazemi, 1988). Therefore, our research proposition is that an appropriately designed and implemented decision support system can improve strategic marketing planning practice.

We investigate this proposition by the development and formative evaluation of one specific system, named EXMAR. This is for several reasons. EXMAR has the largest known user base for a DSS in this domain, the users are accessible for research purposes, the marketing theory and design decisions underlying the system are known and changes requested by users can be built into future versions to provide an improved test-bed for research.

The research proposition leads to two objectives, the first relating to the nature of the improvement to marketing planning practice and the second exploring what constitutes an appropriately designed and implemented system.

1. The primary research objective is to explore what benefits, if any, are gained by users of the EXMAR prototype.

This includes exploring which barriers to marketing planning are reduced by the system, if any, whether system use results in any other benefits or dysfunctional effects and whether the benefits vary across organisations. The research is exploratory in that the system, its use by organisations and the research instruments used are all at an early stage of development.

2. The secondary research objective is to explore what aspects of the design and implementation of the system have led to these benefits and how they might be improved, in the following areas:
   - Marketing planning model: how the marketing planning process and relevant marketing techniques are formalised to provide a basis for computerisation.

- Nature of the system: how the system's scope is defined, what nature of support is provided by the system and how software technologies are applied to enable this support.
- System implementation: who uses the system and in what context, how the system is introduced into the organisation and how the system is applied.
- Development method: how the system is developed, including how requirements are defined, what development process is followed, how user interface design is approached and within what organisational and business context the development occurs.

To place this paper in context, the stages of this long-term research project are as follows:

1. Initial modelling: conceptual research to develop a marketing planning model as a basis for computerisation.
2. Demonstrator development: development of an initial demonstrator system to explore ideas on the nature of support offered by the system.
3. Prototype development: development of a sufficiently robust prototype system to allow evaluation in the field.
4. First qualitative evaluation: a qualitative evaluation with six companies from different market sectors, using semi-structured interviews and user-completed reports.
5. Questionnaire: a survey of users exploring factors contributing to DSS success.
6. Second qualitative evaluation: a set of user case studies, to complement the questionnaire.
7. Full system specification: a third development iteration involving further modelling and system design to incorporate feedback from the evaluation exercises.

The initial modelling, demonstrator and prototype development have been documented previously (McDonald, 1990a,b; McDonald and Wilson, 1990, 1993). We will now turn to the method and results from the first qualitative evaluation. The work in progress on subsequent stages is described in the final section.

First Qualitative Evaluation

Marketing managers from six companies were trained in how to use the software. They then developed a marketing plan using the system within their organisations and wrote a report on their conclusions. The companies were chosen to cover a variety of market sectors and to incorporate capital, other industrial, consumer and service products. The vertical markets covered were aerospace, engineering, consumer goods, computing, banking and insurance.

The results of feedback on the prototype from users during the development process were used to define the categories under which information was to be collected. These were incorporated in a report structure that the companies were asked to follow in their reports. The report template included open-ended questions under each heading: the wording of these followed questionnaire design guidelines in avoiding bias and so on. In addition, 13 semi-structured group interviews, typically lasting 3 hours, were carried out to gather background information on the companies and their planning, and to explore selected areas in more depth.

The reports received were rich and extensive. They did not all follow the report template closely, however, covering in general subsets of the report's questions. In analysing the responses, it therefore proved useful to combine as well as contrast the information gained from interviews and from the written reports, resulting in at least four full responses to most categories. The data was summarised in an evaluation summary which followed the report template's headings.

Interviewing is subject to well-known dangers, particularly when the researchers have another role for the interviewees, in this case as systems designers (MacIntyre, 1978, provides a persuasive parallel in health care). The use of user-completed reports as well as interviews was intended to counteract this weakness to some extent through methodological pluralism (Gill and Johnson, 1991).

FINDINGS TO DATE

The findings are considered under the headings defined in the previous section.

Can Decision Support Systems be Used to Improve Strategic Marketing Planning Practice?

The views of the six participating companies constitute a qualitative assessment of user satisfaction (O'Keefe, 1989). Five of the six companies were very positive on this point, reporting benefits as follows:

1. The systematic guidance through a logical process was thought to be very valuable. This ensured that key aspects of planning were covered.
2. The system also prompted for key data. This provided a useful central store for this data and also highlighted areas where information was required, influencing activities including market research and management information systems development.

3. The system provided a 'powerful visual display of key information', aiding understanding and communication.
4. The system 'does not necessarily pinpoint the correct action, but highlights where attention must be placed'. 'EXMAR provides the "fresh pair of eyes" that are essential if planning is to be able to break the accepted truths that have been built up by the organisation'.
5. The system 'takes the "mystique" out of using marketing tools'.

The marketers also found the evaluation exercise useful, leading to 'improved marketing strategy through involvement in process', due to new insights into the company's position and changed paper procedures.

The sixth company was more sceptical, although still sufficiently interested to wish to stay involved. They warned that as the (prototype) system stood, 'anyone able to work through the steps ... with the limited help given ... would have sufficient information and expertise to write a marketing plan anyway'. This company seemed substantially influenced by the 'expert systems' label that had been attached to the system, leading to expectations of a 'cleverer' system that were fed by advertising of other software. Their expectations were nevertheless useful in generating ideas for ways in which the system could add more value, most of which have been included in the full system specification.

Several other companies thought that the 'expert systems' term raised the wrong expectations and should be dropped. One company described how their model of the system's objective had evolved from a highly proactive expert system to an electronic assistant helping the human expert to add his/her judgement. The term 'tool-kit' was used by another, while a third described its role as providing a focal point for discussions on all topics of marketing planning.

In conclusion: there is some evidence, in terms of user satisfaction, that decision support systems can be used to improve strategic marketing practice.

If Decision Support Systems Can Assist, How?

We consider briefly the support for the notion that system use reduces barriers to marketing planning effectiveness.

1. There is some support for the cognitive hypothesis that the system increases knowledge and skills in marketing planning. Several companies reported having understood the tools and techniques of marketing better and having improved paper-based procedures as a result of using the system. These included the company that was sceptical about use of the system itself. It is difficult, however, to isolate the effect of the use of the system in itself from the effects of the users' training and their involvement in the evaluation exercise.

2. The procedural impact of the system, in the encouragement of a plan features such as better documentation of intervention, is also supported – again, indicated by user comments as well as by changed procedures.
3. Lack of innovation/non-recognition of alternatives: this was impacted by the system during evaluation of the prototype software, users having reported that new insights have been gained into their companies' positions as a result. Users believed that this would also occur in normal use.
4. Roles people play: there is some evidence for the system impacting this, with several companies becoming more 'marketing planning friendly' with system use. If attitudes are too frozen, however, the system will not thaw them. An example is a company that was involved in the earlier EXMAR developments, which lost interest when the marketing department was taken over by an accountant who did not consider marketing planning worth a single internal meeting to discuss the club's work. Recent changes in senior management have led to a reawakening of interest in EXMAR.
5. Hypotheses relating to organisational barriers are as yet open. There is some indication from one company, involved in system development from an early stage, that the system's role as a catalyst for change in attitudes may have impacted positively on organisational structure.

We will now consider the lessons on the nature of the support offered by the software, using as headings the subsidiary research questions.

Scope

Focus on strategy not tactics

Marketers can and do produce budgets and monitor their performance against budgets adequately already.

Focus on the product/market dimension

The very act of defining market segments and product groups and defining critical success factors for each market caused debate and fresh insights in many companies. The focus of the analysis on product markets, how customers buy in the markets, the company's performance in the markets and the competition from others, acted as a catalyst to focus minds on customers and 'break the accepted truths that have been built up by the organisation'.

Keep financial information high-level but complete

Collaborating companies were very aware of the dangers of bogging down the analysis by excessive detail. There was, nevertheless, a desire in many companies to go beyond revenue to some representation of cost and 'profit', at least in the sense of marketing contribution.

Marketing Model

Use a model integrating techniques around their common data and organised around the marketing planning process

A model was developed that integrated a number of key marketing techniques by defining a common data model on which they drew for information. The benefit of this is that information entered once by the user can be used to multiply in different analyses. This reduces the effort involved, increasing the depth of analysis. Organising around a logical data model also helps the user to understand the tools and techniques by making transparent the interrelationships between techniques. Tying the tools and techniques to stages in a logical process means that the user is encouraged to use appropriate tools at appropriate times, which reduces learning barriers and enables the user to concentrate on interpretation.

Represent the model on paper to enable communication and validation of the marketing theory

Diagrams were developed (McDonald, 1990a) to define a common representation around which marketers and IT specialists could communicate. It was found necessary to adapt standard systems analysis diagrams for this domain to make them more intuitive to marketers. This use of standard systems analysis techniques is not universally advocated for decision support systems, as some of the extensive 'knowledge engineering' literature for the development of expert systems shows (Hickman *et al*, 1989). We believe, however, that the communication barriers between the 'expert' and the systems developers in the EXMAR work before the author's involvement started was at least partly due to the lack of a common language. As DeMarco (1978) writes in a classic systems analysis paper:

> Since user and analysis have a long-standing history of failure to communicate, it is essential that their discussions be conducted over some workable negotiating instrument, something to point to as they labor to reach a common understanding. Their discussion concerns systems, both past and present, so a useful system model is the most important aid to communication.

The model itself is a research output from this study and will described fully elsewhere. Specific contributions to marketing theory from this study are as follows:

1. Techniques interrelate in a surprisingly elegant and rich way. The complexity involved provides an additional hypothesis as to why the techniques are not used more in practice and, incidentally, provides an argument for the use of software technology as an aid.

2. The directional policy matrix has been developed to make it more usable and to avoid common pitfalls in its use (McDonald, 1990b). For example, a clustering of circles on top of each other, typically in the top left quadrant, was found to be frequent in practice. This has been addressed by making the strength in the market axis relative to the best of the competition (borrowing an idea from the Boston matrix), encouraging the user to spread out market attractive scores by gentle advice where necessary and automatically scaling the axes. Users do not have to concern themselves with these subtleties or with their implications such as the use of a logarithmic horizontal axis.

3. Provisional conclusions have been reached on the relationship between Porter's definition of 'differentiation' and the use of critical success factors to model 'strength in market' extending recent research into applying Porter's (1980) work more precisely (Speed, 1989; Sharp, 1991).

The Nature of Systems

Leave the user in control

This research supports the decision calculus school in the belief that the user should be left in control of decisions (Little, 1970). This implies no hidden logic and little jargon. Users should also be able to control the process they adopt in planning. The system can encourage but it should not dictate. In sessions at which the authors have been present (normally as facilitators), users have switched from one task to another, left the system to gain information, made changes to illustrate a point to a colleague, and so on. This implies a free interface, almost certainly based on windowing technology, following the edict of the developers of the seminal Xerox Star interface: 'Never pre-empt the user' (Bewley *et al*, 1983).

Guide the user through a logical planning process

Users nevertheless appreciate being guided through a logical process. This guidance is different in nature from the support for rigorous clerical processes traditionally addressed by transaction processing systems and from the totally free interface of a word processing package or a spreadsheet. The approach to this has accordingly taken some time to evolve: the demonstrator was too close to the former, the prototype to the latter and the full system specification we hope about right. We speculate that this conclusion is generalisable to a number of decision support domains.

Display information graphically to help understanding

Graphical display using marketing matrices and business graphics can in itself add value. Differing views on the same information can help the user to gain perspective and come to balanced conclusions.

Semi-structured tasks imply a need to integrate text and data

Several companies emphasised the benefits of being able to relate data to text – for example, the source of market size information, assumptions made in market size prediction, documentation of how specific increases in revenue will be achieved, and so on.

'Hypertext' is a computer science research area concentrating on ideas for displaying and manipulating these mixed representations (Ritchie, 1993). This work has been drawn on for this project by use of the NoteCards hypertext system in the demonstrator (Halasz *et al*, 1987) and the Analyst system in the prototype. This reflects our belief that tasks such as marketing planning are as much concerned with idea processing as they are with decision-making, the representation of ideas being naturally made in words and pictures as well as numbers.

Explicit predictive models are not necessary in order to add value

The software has so far not attempted to incorporate predictive models where volume, market share or unit costs are dependent variables. This goes against the assumption in much DSS literature, starting with Little (1970) and continuing with much of the expert systems school, that predictive models are where computers can add value. This reflects, however, the advances in user interfaces in the last ten years and the consequent ability of systems to add value by other means, such as the effective display of information. This does not imply, of course, that good predictive models could not be usefully incorporated where they can be defined.

Ensure the learning curve is low

The software will not get used otherwise. Making the software easier to learn must be traded off, if necessary, against ease of use for experienced users.

Organisational Fit

Use at any level of aggregation

Most user group members thought the system could contribute at different levels of detail within their companies; from a corporate overview of key business sectors to in-depth studies of individual market segments. One company thought that this would enable them to decentralise their planning internationally, spreading the expertise and 'best practice' of the central groups and the more sophisticated business units to weaker parts of the business.

Don't restrict use to the marketing department

EXMAR has been used by chief executives, strategic planners and line managers, as well as by marketing directors and managers. Two of the collaborating managers had strategic planning titles; interestingly, this did not cause them to suggest a wider scope for the system, as the tight focus on the product/market dimension was thought to be important. The software was regarded by one company as valuable for getting line managers more involved in planning and at an earlier stage in the planning process.

Don't restrict the mode of use more than necessary

Software should allow for a variety of contexts: performing specific analyses rather than developing a complete plan, developing a plan over a number of sessions, leaving the system to collect further information or perform other tasks, data entry by clerical staff, and so on. All of these have been requested by managers. Software making more idealistic assumptions about planning (such as the chemical company's in-house software reviewed earlier) will not be used as an integral part of the planning process.

The software built during this study has run on a single personal computer (PC), although in practice it is often used with a cluster of users around a screen or displaying the screen on to the wall with an overhead projector. The PC revolution has in part been caused by the added sense of control that users have over their own computer (Morris *et al*, 1989). Enabling users to exchange plans readily on a floppy disk has so far proved adequate and there has been little pressure to extend the system to a multi-user client-server architeture, although no firm conclusions can be drawn on this point.

Development Method

Use prototyping

Our experience supports the argument (Keen, 1980; Iivari and Karjalainen, 1989) that new areas of application in decision support systems should be proto-typed.

Development should be 'expert driven' as well as 'user driven'

While the intial model was developed in close co-operation with a domain expert (one of the authors), in much of the prototype software development the expert was less involved, the software engineer (the other author) relying on feedback from potential users, in line with conventional systems analysis theory. The problem with this approach is that in a domain where management practice does not reflect the best of prescriptive theory, users don't know what they want – or, in some cases, they know what they want but don't know the marketing formalisms to get it. The result is that the prototype is less easy to use than it could have been. To this extent, we dispute the implementation process writers' assumption (Keen, 1980) that the objective of development is purely to produce a system that the users will use. Users may need to be gently steered in a specific direction, as advocated by the 'decision research' school (Stabell, 1986).

Ensure the software is tailorable and adaptable

Management theory changes with time, as do companies' procedures, information flows and people. Software must therefore be capable of being adapted with time or being tailored to a specific company – by programmers or preferably by users. A number of users confirmed that the introduction of marketing planning may involve compromises. Even if the will is there, it may simply be impossible to set up the necessary information flows quickly. One company expected to wait for years for some of the information requested by EXMAR. There may also be cases where the general textbook theory does not apply to a specific company. A case in point is modelling in the financial services sector of the variables leading to revenue in a product/market, traditionally 'price' and 'volume'. Object-oriented programming is claimed to aid considerably in ensuring that software is flexible and adaptable, largely through the ease of software reuse due to the inheritance concept (Deutsch, 1989; Lazarev, 1991). Our experience supports this.

CONCLUSIONS AND FURTHER RESEARCH

The evaluation reported here has provided valuable guidance on what the features of a marketing planning system should be in terms of scope, the underlying model of marketing planning, user interface style, and so on, in order to best assist with marketing planning. This is guiding the further software development that is in progress.

The evaluation has produced evidence that software can lower some of the barriers to marketing planning, particularly inadequate marketing knowledge and skills, poor documentation of the interventions that will be made, lack of innovation and non-recognition of alternatives, inadequate senior management involvement in the process of strategy formation and poor cross-functional communication. Software can also clarify information requirements, leading to better-targeted market research and clear requirements for internal information systems.

This evidence is, however, tentative. The participants were using the system for evaluation purposes and over a relatively short period of three months. This suggests further evaluation work with 'live' users as a matter of priority.

Further research stages are under way that explore the experience of organisations who have been using the prototype system for up to three years.

1. A questionnaire is being circulated to the 35 companies using the prototype system, who are mostly by chance in South Africa. The questionnaire is based on a theoretical framework for research in decision support systems

for marketing planning, which has been derived by integrating previous IT/DSS research (eg, Ives *et al*, 1980; Sanders and Courtney, 1985; Snitkin and King, 1986; Money *et al*, 1988) with the barriers to marketing planning described earlier. The objectives are to validate and refine instruments for the measurement of system success and benefits, as a contribution to future research and as a first step in questionnaire analysis; to examine implementation factors affecting system success, such as user training and support and top management support for the system; and to provide some indications of system success.

2. Case studies are being conducted on ten companies, primarily by semi-structured interviews, using Glaser and Strauss' (1967) grounded theory approach to theory generation and representation. Whereas the questionnaire is testing hypotheses that can be defined at this stage, these case studies are extending the theory itself through a goal-free evaluation approach (Scriven, 1972).

We are still some distance, then, from conclusive evidence on the impact of software in marketing planning. But although it is clear that software systems could never be a panacea, there is much to encourage us that IT can contribute strongly to this vital field of managerial practice.

References

Abell, D and Hammond, J (1979) *Strategic Market Planning*, Prentice-Hall, Englewood Cliffs, New Jersey.

Aitken, S and Bintley, H (1989) 'Building a marketeer's workbench: an expert system applied to the marketing planning process', *ICL Technical Journal* November, pp 721–736.

Alpar, P (1991) 'Knowledge-based modeling of marketing managers' problem solving behaviour', *International Journal of Research in Marketing*, 8, pp 5–16.

Alter, SL (1977) 'A taxonomy of decision support systems', *Sloan Management Review*, Vol 19, No 1, pp 39–56.

Ames, BC (1968) 'Marketing planning for industrial products', *Harvard Business Review*, Vol 46, No 5, pp 100–111.

Andersen Consulting (1989) *IT in Marketing and Sales '89*, Andersen Consulting, London.

Bayer, J and Harter, R (1991) 'Miner', 'manager', and 'researcher': three modes of analysis of scanner data', *International Journal of Research in Marketing*, 8, pp 17–27.

Benbasat, I and Dexter, AS (1986) 'An investigation of the effectiveness of color and graphical information presentation under varying time constraints' MIS Quarterly, March, pp 59–83.

Bewley, WL, Roberts, TL, Schoit, D and Verplank, WL (1983) 'Human factors testing in the design of Xerox's 8010 "Star" Office Workstation', in *CHI '83 Human Factors in Computing Systems, ACM*.

Bovich, EP (1987) 'Marketing management decision making and the role of decision support systems', unpublished PhD thesis, University of Michigan.

Brooksbank, RW (1990) 'Marketing planning: a seven-stage process', *Marketing Intelligence and Planning*, Vol 8, No 7, pp 21–28.

Cosse, TJ and Swan, JE (1983) 'Strategic marketing planning by product managers', *Journal of Marketing*, 47, pp 92–102.

Curry, B and Moutinho, L (1991) *Environmental Issues in Tourism Management: Computer Modelling for Judgemental Decisions*, Working Paper, Cardiff Business School.

DeMarco, T (1978) 'Structured analysis and system specification', in *GUIDE 47 Proceedings*, GUIDE International Corporation, reprinted in EN Yourdon (ed) *Classics in Software Engineering*, Yourdon Press, Englewood Cliffs, New Jersey.

Deutsch, LR (1989) 'The past, present and future of Smalltalk', in *Proceedings of the 1989 European Conference on Object-oriented Programming*, S Cook (ed), Cambridge University Press, Cambridge, pp 73–87.

Dickmeyer, N (1983) 'Measuring the effects of a university planning decision aid', *Management Science*, 29, 673–685.

Gill, J and Johnson, P (1991) *Research Methods for Managers*, Chapman, London.

Ginzberg, MJ (1981) 'Key recurrent issues in the MIS implementation process', *MIS Quarterly*, June, pp 47–59.

Glaser, BG and Strauss, AL (1967) *The Discovery of Grounded Theory: Strategies for Qualitative Research*, Aldine, New York.

Gorry, GA and Scott Morton, MS (1971) 'A framework for management information systems, *Sloan Management Review*, Vol 13, No 1, pp 55–70.

Greenley, GE (1982) 'An overview of marketing planning in UK manufacturing companies', *European Journal of Marketing*, Vol 16, No 7, pp 3–15.

Greenley, GE (1983) 'An overview of marketing planning in UK service companies', *Marketing Intelligence and Planning*, Vol 1, No 3, pp 55–68.

Greenley, GE (1987) 'An exposition of empirical research into marketing planning', *Journal of Marketing Management*, Vol 3, No 1, pp 83–102.

Guimaraes, T, Igbaria, M and Lu, M (1992) 'The determinants of DSS success: an integrated model', *Decision Sciences*, 23, pp 409–30.

Halasz, FG, Moran, TP and Trigg, RH (1987) 'Notecards in a nutshell', in *Proceedings of the ACM CHI + GI Conference*, Toronto, 5–9 April.

Hewson, N and Hewson, W (1994) *The Impact of Computerised Sales and Marketing Systems in the UK* (4th edn), HCG Publications, Milton Keynes.

Hickman, FR, Killin, Land, Mulhall, Porter and Taylor (1989) *Analysis For Knowledge-based Systems: A Practical Guide to the KADS Methodology*, Ellis Horwood, Chichester, UK.

Higgins, JC and Opdebeek, EJ (1984) 'The microcomputer as a tool in marketing decision aids: some survey results', *Journal of the Market Research Society*, Vol 26, No 3, pp 243–254.

Hirst, M (1991a) 'Personal computer software for use in marketing education, part 1,' *Journal of Marketing Management*, 7, pp 77–192.

Hirst, M (1991b) 'Personal computer software for use in marketing education, part 2,' *Journal of Marketing Management*, 7, pp 167–188.

Hooley, GJ, West, CJ and Lynch, JE (1984) *Marketing in the UK: A Survey of Current Practice and Performance*, Institute of Marketing, Maidenhead.

Hopkins, DS (1981) *The Marketing Plan*, Research Report No 801, The Conference Board, New York.

Iivari, J and Karjalainen, M (1989) 'Impact of prototyping on user information satisfaction during the IS specification phase', *Information and Management*, 17, pp 31–45.

Ives, B, Hamilton, S and Davis, GB (1980) 'A framework for research in computer-based management information systems', *Management Science*, Vol 26, No 9, pp 910–934.

Jarvenpaa, SL (1989) 'The effect of task demands and graphical format on information processing strategies', *Management Science*, Vol 35, No 3, pp 285–303.

Jarvenpaa, SL, Dickson, KW and DeSanctis, K (1985) 'Methodological issues in experimental IS research: experiences and recommendations', *MIS Quarterly*, 59, June, pp 141–56.

Keen, PGW (1980) Adaptive design for decision support systems, *Data Base*, 12, pp 15–25.

Keen, PGW and Scott Morton, MS (1978) *Decision Support Systems: All Organizational Perspective*, Addison-Wesley, Reading, Massachusetts.

Kotier, P and Armstrong, G (1989) *Principles of Marketing* (4th edn), Prentice-Hall, Englewood Cliffs, New Jersey.

Kotler, P (1991) *Marketing Management: Analysis, Planning, Implementation and Control* (7th edn), Prentice-Hall, Englewood Cliffs, New Jersey.

Lazarev, GL (1991) 'Reusability in Smalltalk: a case study', *Journal of Object-oriented Programming*, Vol 4, No 2, pp 11–20.

Leppard, JW. (1987) 'Marketing planning and corporate culture: a conceptual framework which examines management attitudes in the context of marketing planning', MPhil thesis, Cranfield Institute of Technology.

Little, JDC (1970) 'Models and managers: the concept of a decision calculus, *Management Science*, Vol 16, No 8, B466–B485.

Lodish, LM (1981) 'Experience with decision-calculus models and decision support systems', in RL Shultz and AA Zoltners (eds), *Marketing Decision Models*, North Holland.

Luconi, FL, Malone, TW. and Scott Morton, MS (1986) 'Expert systems: the next challenge for managers', *Sloan Management Review*, Vol 27, No 4, pp 7–14.

Macintyre, S (1978) 'Some notes on record-taking and making in an antenatal clinic', *Sociological Review*, Vol 26, No 3, pp 595–611.

McDonald, MHB (1984) 'The theory and practice of marketing planning for industrial goods in international markets, PhD thesis, Cranfield Institute of Technology.

McDonald, MHB (1989) *Marketing Plans* (2nd edn), Heinemann, Oxford.

McDonald, MHB (1990a) 'Technique interrelationships and the pursuit of relevance in marketing theory', *Quarterly Review of Marketing*, Summer, pp 1–11.

McDonald, MHB (1990b) 'Some methodological comments on the directional policy matrix', *Journal of Marketing Management*, 6.

McDonald, MHB (1991) *The Marketing Audit: Translating Marketing Theory into Practice*, Butterworth-Heinemann, Oxford.

McDonald, MHB and Wilson, HN (1990) 'State-of-the-art developments in expert systems and strategic marketing planning', *British Journal of Management*, 1, pp 159–170.

McDonald, MHB and Wilson, HN (1993) 'Why apply software to marketing strategy? Mapping the sources of competitive advantage', in MHB McDonald, W Hewson and HN Wilson (eds), *Emerging Information Technologies – A Marketing Opportunity*, HCG Publications, Milton Keynes, pp 92–97.

Meldrum, MJ Ward, K and Srikanthan, S (1987) 'Needs, issues and directions in the marketing accountancy divide', *Quarterly Review of Marketing*, Spring/Summer, pp 5–12.

Money, A, Tromp, D and Wegner, T (1988) 'The quantification of decision support benefits within the context of value analysis', *MIS Quarterly*, June, pp 223–236.

Montazemi, AR (1988) 'Factors affecting information satisfaction in the context of the small business environment', *MIS Quarterly*, June, pp 239–256.

Moriarty, RT and Swartz, GS (1989) 'Automation to boost sales and marketing', *Harvard Business Review*, Vol 67, No 1, pp 100–108.

Morris, MH, Burns, AC and Avila, RA (1989) 'Computer awareness and usage by industrial marketers', *Industrial Marketing Management*, Vol 18, No 3, pp 223–232.

Mumford, E (1988) 'Designing computer based systems', *University of Wales Review Business and Economics*, 3.

Nunamaker, JF, Applegate, LM and Konsynski, BR (1988) 'Computer-aided deliberation: model management and group decision support', *Operations Research*, Vol 36, No 6, pp 826–848.

O'Keefe, RM (1989) 'The evaluation of decision-aiding systems: guidelines and methods', *Information and Management*, 17, pp 217–226.

Pinsonneault, A and Kraemer, KL (1989) 'The impact of technological support on groups: an assessment of the empirical research', *Decision Support Systems*, 5, pp 197–216.

Porter, ME (1980) 'Competitive Strategy: Techniques for Analysing Industries and Competitors', Free Press, New York.

Rangaswamy, A, Harlam, BA and Lodish, LM (1991) 'INFER: an expert system for automatic analysis of scanner data', *International Journal of Research in Marketing*, 8, pp 29–40.

Ritchie, I (1993) 'Hypertext: navigating the information explosion', in MHB McDonald, W Hewson and HN Wilson (eds), *Emerging Information Technologies – A Marketing Opportunity*, HCG Publications, Milton Keynes, pp 217–221.

Rita, P (1991) 'Expert systems and marketing strategy: an application to portfolio management decisions in tourism', in *Preparing Marketing for the New Millenium, 24th Annual Conference of the Marketing Education Group*, Cardiff.

Sainfort, FC, Gustafson, DH, Bosworth, K and Hawkins, RP (1990) 'Decision support systems effectiveness: conceptual framework and empirical evaluation', *Organisational Behavior and Human Decision Processes*, 45, pp 232–252.

Sanders, GL (1984) 'MIS/DSS success measure', *Systems, Objectives, Solutions*, 4, pp 29–34.

Sanders, GL and Courtney, JF (1985) 'A field study of organizational factors influencing DSS success', *MIS Quarterly*, March, pp 77–92.

Scriven, M (1972) 'Pros and cons about goal-free evaluation', *Evaluation Comment 3*, pp 1–7.

Seddon, RR (1991) 'Front-ending intelligent computer systems: designing a windows-based graphical user-interface for ExMar', MSc thesis, School of Industrial and Manufacturing Science, Cranfield Institute of Technology.

Sharda, R, Barr, SH and McDonnell, JC (1988) 'Decision support system effectiveness: a review and an empirical test', *Management Science,* Vol 34, No 2, pp 139–159.

Sharp, B (1991) 'Competitive marketing strategy: Porter revisited', *Marketing Intelligence and Planning,* Vol 9, No 1, pp 4–10.

Shaw, R (1994) *How to Transform Marketing Through IT*, Business Intelligence, London.

Snitkin, SR and King, WR (1986) 'Determinants of the effectiveness of personal decision support systems, *Information and Management,* 10, pp 83–89.

Speed, RJ (1989) 'Oh Mr Porter! A re-appraisal of Competitive Strategy', *Marketing Intelligence and Planning,* Vol 6, No 5, pp 8–11.

Stabell, CB (1986) *Decision Support Systems: Alternative Perspectives and Schools*, Working Paper No 1986/6, Norwegian School of Management, Oslo.

Stasch, SF and Lanktree, P (1980) 'Can your marketing planning procedures be improved?' *Journal of Marketing,* Vol 44, No 3, pp 79–90.

Van Horn, HH (1990) 'The telecom planner – a training tool for a collaborative approach to integrating telecommunications into the business plan', unpublished PhD thesis. The Union Institute, Cincinnati.

Waalewijn, P and Boulan, R (1990) 'Strategic planning on a personal computer', *Long Range Planning,* Vol 23, No 4, pp 97–103.

Wind, Y and Saaty, TL (1980) 'Marketing applications of the analytic hierarchy process, *Management Science*, Vol 26, No 7, pp 641–658.

8

THE CHANGING FACE OF MARKETING IN THE 1990s

Malcolm McDonald

We have seen from earlier chapters that marketing planning is not fairyland textbook stuff, but a flesh-and-blood, real-life struggle. Ego, greed, stupidity and other forms of human folly conspire to defeat the planner.

It is surprising, to say the least, when it is considered that research has shown a direct link between long-run profitability and an effective approach to marketing planning, that eight out of ten companies hardly bother with it at all, preferring to stick with forecasting, budgeting and financial husbandry (Greenley, 1989). Yet the sheer speed of change, growing economic turbulence and intense global competition, make the task of forcing an organised approach to the identification of competitive advantage more pressing than it has ever been before. For, without competitive advantage, there will be no guaranteed growth in the 1990s and many more well-known names will disappear by the turn of the century.

This chapter suggests some scenarios for the next few years on the way that marketing is thought about and practised in companies.

MARKETING AND PROFIT

Although it has taken a very long time to begin to realise it, it is finally dawning on organisations that a tactical, short-term, purely financial approach, which seemed to work well in the past, no longer works. Of Tom Peters' 43 'excellent' companies, only 6 remain excellent at the time of writing (Pascale, 1990). Of *Management Today*'s top British companies over the past 11 years, only 5 are still profitable (Doyle, 1992). Doyle's research in 1988 showed that almost 9 out of 10 British companies regarded short-term profits to be their main aim (compared with 80 per cent of US companies and only 27 per cent of Japanese companies, Wong *et al*, 1988).

It will not have escaped the notice of the discerning observer of British industry, that exceptionally high profits today seem to be correlated with low or no profits tomorrow. Nor that the financial community has long recognised that short-run profits are a poor guide to shareholder value. Accounting practices are, of course, somewhat arbitrary, and short-run profits can be boosted, depending on how depreciation and stock valuation, acquisitions, foreign currency and research and development are handled. Financing growth through debt rather than through equity and boosting profits by trading off the future for the present (R&D, headcount, service, and so on) always lead to growth in earnings per share, but to a drop in the capital value of the shares due to the financial risks involved. The only conclusion that can be reached is that, contrary to popular belief, it is *managers*, not the financial institutions, that are short-term in their outlook.

All of this will have to change, however, otherwise the organisations that continue to espouse such outdated business management methods will disappear in ever-increasing numbers. Companies will begin to measure *customer* profitability, as well as product profitability, as it is becoming increasingly obvious that it is the way we deal with customers that makes or loses us profit.

While this is not the place to raise the complex issue of how to treat intangible assets in the balance sheet, suffice it to say that with the compliance of the Accounting Standards Authority, more companies are beginning to place a value on their brand names. Some companies actually put this value in their balance sheets – a practice which the author believes is dangerous. A better practice by far, in the author's opinion, is to value intangible assets such as brands for the sole purpose of building them up and managing them appropriately. Marketing managers should be measured in terms of the return they get on these assets rather than on tangible assets.

Additionally, the overriding emphasis on return on sales as a measure of performance will be seen in a more well-balanced perspective. We all remember the basic accounting ratios set out in Figure 8.1.

Quite simply, RONA measures how well an organisation is making use of the money invested in the business. It measures the annual trading profit (return), as a percentage of the investment in assets. Net assets are fixed assets (such as land, buildings, plant, machinery, furniture, cars, office equipment, etc) at their net book value, plus working capital employed (such as stocks, raw materials

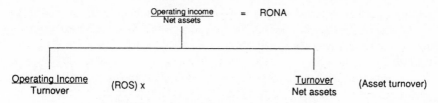

Figure 8.1 RONA, ROS and asset turnover

and work-in-progress, plus debtors minus creditors). Understanding how working capital is used in the cash-to-cash cycle is key to improving RONA (see Figure 8.2).

The distance around the circle, and the spaces between the steps, is the time it takes to achieve a return on the money invested in the business. So, the larger the circle, the longer it takes to complete the loop and the lower the RONA. By working to make the cash-to-cash cycle smaller, it is possible to move faster around the loop, making the money in the business work harder and harder and more efficiently to generate a better RONA.

While all of this may seem obvious, it is none the less surprising that so many organisations still place too much emphasis on the first part of the equa-

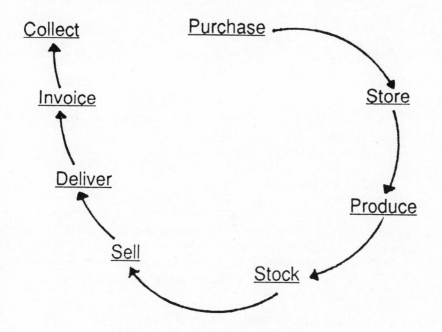

Figure 8.2 The cash-to-cash cycle

tion – ie, return on sales (margin) – and not enough on asset turnover, for, clearly, a better result may be obtained by accepting a lower ROS and gaining a higher asset turnover. The truth, of course, is that organisations need to concentrate on both sides of the equation. For example, working capital can be tightened by reducing surplus raw material stocks, manufacturing on a just-in-time basis, and only stocking what is essential to deliver on time and in full. Margin can be improved by cutting out waste, by reducing non-essential costs and by selling higher value goods and services to meet customer needs.

The main point is that looking at the absolute profitability of individual products and services, and making management decisions about important issues such as product launches, product deletions, promotional effort, and so on, is unlikely to be as acceptable in the future as it has been in the past. This raises the important issue of portfolio approaches.

PORTFOLIO APPROACHES

More than any other management tool, portfolio management will emerge as being key to an organisation's success. It is clear, for instance, that while few would disagree with the fundamental common sense of the need to balance margin and asset turnover, the difficulty arises in working out exactly when and how to do this.

For a full and detailed methodological approach to the subject of portfolio management, readers should refer to a paper by the author (McDonald, 1990). In this chapter, all that is necessary is to review briefly why portfolio management is so important in relation to what has been said thus far and in relation to what follows.

Most readers will recognise the box in Figure 8.3, developed by General Electric some years ago. It can be seen that they used *industry attractiveness* and *business strengths* as the main axes.

It is not necessary, however, to use a nine-box matrix, and many managers prefer to use a four-box matrix similar to the Boston box. Indeed, this is the author's preferred methodology as it seems to be more easily understood by, and useful to, practising managers. The four-box directional policy matrix is shown in Figure 8.4. Here, the circles represent sales into an industry, market or segment and, in the same way as in the Boston matrix, each is proportional to that segment's contribution to turnover.

The difference in this case is that rather than using only two variables, the criteria which are used for each axis are totally relevant and specific to each company using the matrix. It shows:

- markets categorised on a scale of attractiveness to the firm;
- the firm's relative strengths in each of these markets; and
- the relative importance of each market.

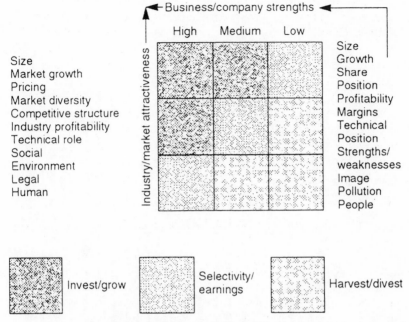

Figure 8.3 General Electric's matrix

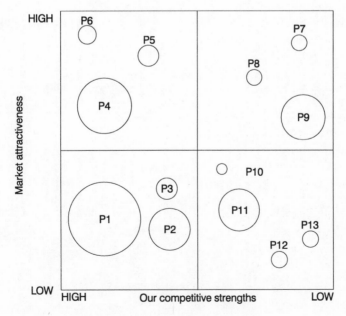

Figure 8.4 A four-box matrix

Figure 8.5 Programme guidelines suggested for different positioning on the directional policy matrix

Main Thrust	Invest for growth	Maintain market position, manage for earnings	Selective	Manage for cash	Opportunistic development
Market Share	Maintain or increase dominance	Maintain or slightly milk for earnings	Maintain selectively; Segment	Forego share for profit	Invest selectively in share
Products	Differentiation – line expansion	Prune less successful, differentiate for key segments	Emphasise product quality. Differentiate	Aggressively prune	Differentiation – line expansion
Price	Lead – aggressive pricing for share	Stabilise prices/raise	Maintain or raise	Raise	Aggressive – price for share
Promotion	Aggressive marketing	Limit	Maintain selectively	Minimise	Aggressive marketing
Distribution	Broaden distribution	Hold wide distribution pattern	Segment	Gradually withdraw distribution	Limited coverage
Cost Control	Tight control – go for scale economies	Emphasise cost reduction viz. variable costs	Tight control	Aggressively reduce both fixed & variable	Tight – but not at expense of entrepreneurship
Production	Expand, invest (organic acquisition, joint venture)	Maximise capacity utilisation	Increase productivity, eg specialisation/automation	Free up capacity	Invest
R & D	Expand – invest	Focus on specific projects	Invest selectively	None	Invest
Personnel	Upgrade management in key functional areas	Maintain, reward efficiency, tighten organisation	Allocate key managers	Cut back organisation	Invest
Investment	Fund growth	Limit fixed investment	Invest selectively	Minimise & divest opportunistically	Fund growth
Working Capital	Reduce in process – extend credit	Tighten credit – reduce accounts receivable, increase inventory return	Reduce	Aggressively reduce	Invest

222

When executives begin to think clearly about the criteria for judging the relative potential of each of their markets, products, regions, countries, distributors (or whatever) in achieving their growth and profit objectives, it becomes clear that there is a logical pecking order. It also becomes clear that the ones with less potential for growth are often the ones that provide much of the profit today, while the ones with more potential for the future still require some considerable effort and investment to build up or to keep good positions in these attractive, growing 'markets.' Equally, it becomes clear that in some of these 'markets', organisations have greater strengths than in others.

This categorisation into four boxes has wide-ranging implications for any organisation, in terms of its personnel, production, R&D, distribution, finance and, most of all, marketing. The 'guidelines' in Figure 8.5 indicate some of the more obvious considerations that should be taken account of in setting objectives and strategies for each of the organisation's 'markets', depending on where they are positioned in their four-box directional policy matrix.

When categorised thus, there is no problem in deciding, for example, when the focus should be on ROS as opposed to asset turnover, where problems should be treated as marketing problems, what kind of people to put into different roles, when to be tough or flexible on credit control, where to direct the advertising and selling effort, and so on.

Alas, too many organisations preface their actions with the phrase 'Our policy is ...' which really means that they treat all 'markets' in more or less the same way and use the same financial measures of efficacy for all, 'shooting themselves in the foot' in the process.

The author's prediction, then, is that of necessity, there will be a much greater sense of portfolio and that appropriate policies will be developed that reflect the market position and the organisation's strengths. Only in this way will the crude, short-term financial husbandry that has decimated British industry be replaced.

MARKETING AND INFORMATION TECHNOLOGY

Billions of pounds have been spent on information technology (IT) during the past two decades, most of it with little effect. Departmental, or functional, problems have attracted swarms of IT providers, all keen to solve the problem with yet more 'tin'. Each project has been justified in ROI terms, usually in the form of number of bodies saved, with little or no post-investment check on the actual ROI. Another feature of this contagious IT disease has been the fragmentation of information systems (IS), with little interconnection between one departmental IT solution and another.

All this has succeeded in doing is to focus the hearts and minds of managers more on their narrow departmental interests and away from the correct organisational focus – customers. The author predicts that customer market focus will surface in a way never experienced before, with real bonding between supplier and customer. For this to happen, companies are already beginning to realise that they need a complete overhaul of their IS and IT strategies, which will have to be based on the key issues that emerge from a genuine desire to be customer responsive.

This will inevitably mean breaking down the functional barriers and building IS and IT systems that are much more future orientated than financially driven.

MARKETING QUALITY

Marketing will no longer be only a function within the organisation. There will be an attitude of mind which uses all the appropriate marketing artefacts to build relationships, not only with customers, but with suppliers, shareholders, financial institutions, employees and, above all, internal customers.

Already, leading companies like Rank Xerox, Procter and Gamble, 3-M and General Electric are using competitive benchmarking to monitor the best operators in any function, in any industry, anywhere in the world, in order to transfer best practice into their own internal operations. They are doing this as part of a relentless drive to give customers a better deal.

It is unfortunate that much of what passes for total quality is internally orientated, with little reference to the customer. Up to now, quality in the main has referred to operations, and in particular to manufacturing. Such laudable initiatives, driven by BS 5750, ISO 9000 and ES 29000 have had a beneficial effect on product quality, but have achieved little for the customer. Customers demand and should receive, by rights, flawless products. All of this is to little avail, however, if such quality initiatives are internally driven. Product quality in its broader sense involves much more than the tangible product, as can be seen from Figure 8.6.

Unfortunately, real customer need has been excluded from much of the extant legislation. As can be seen from Figure 8.7, none of the existing standards tackle the real issues surrounding customer need. It is only the shaded area that is covered by existing legislation.

The author predicts that the tentative start made by Marketing Quality Assurance (MQA) in defining international standards for marketing quality will drive a whole new code of behaviour in relation to the way that companies treat customers. This organisation, with an independent governing board, has defined 35 standards for marketing quality, under the three key headings shown in Table 8.1.

It is clear to the author that, before long, companies that cannot demonstrate that they have achieved an independent international standard in relation to marketing, will not be able to deal with the world's leading companies.

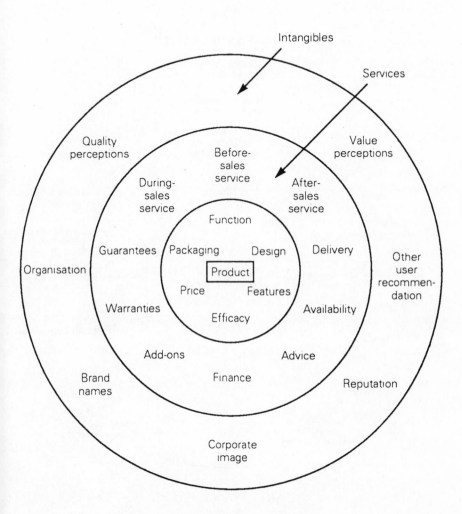

Figure 8.6 Product quality

THE PURSUIT OF QUALITY

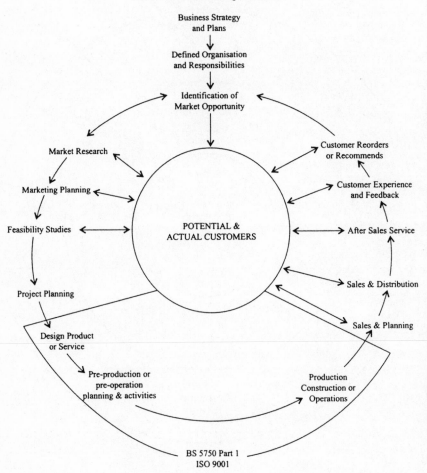

Figure 8.7 The pursuit of quality

Table 8.1 MQA specification – the three key areas

Customer focus	Business, marketing and sales plans	Management responsibility
• Continually identifying and reassessing customer needs, preferences and competition • New products, meeting customer requirements, market readiness • Customer communications, care information, monitoring and feedback • Customer support programmes – after-sales service • Code of conduct	• Business plans – strategy – customer input • Marketing and sales plans – marketing audits – objectives/strategies – role of contributing departments • Marketing and sales operations • Performance measurement • Purchasing • Administration • Contributing depts.	• Quality policy • Organisation • Management review • Quality systems • Resources, personnel, training • Controls and procedures

PROFESSIONAL MARKETING

Throughout this book, frequent reference has been made to the fact that few organisations use any of the well-known tools and techniques of marketing. This is largely because so few marketing managers actually understand how to use them in a technical sense.

It is a pity that few practising marketing managers are professionally qualified, a situation which, until it is rectified, will lead to the supremacy of finance and accounting and the subservience of marketing as a discipline. The Diploma of the Chartered Institute of Marketing will become an essential starting point in a marketing career, with BA, BSc and MBA degrees with a marketing specialisation becoming the norm. Only when most people holding a marketing job hold a professional qualification will marketing as a function be truly elevated to its rightful position alongside finance, personnel and production. Such people will need to be excellent communicators, politicians and general managers, as well as excellent marketing practitioners, as marketing will occupy a much more central role than hitherto, with marketing as a concept and a code of behaviour driving the organisation.

As already stated in Chapter 5, computers will become a more accepted part of marketing. In particular, expert systems and knowledge-based systems will bring marketing techniques within the marketing office, so that they become a part of everyday life rather than being confined to textbooks and courses.

ORGANISATION

The author was recently asked to run a series of in-house marketing pro-grammes for a major global company that had narrowly avoided a hostile takeover. Its shares had consistently underperformed the FTSE average. The chairman decided that his company should be more market-orientated, and marketing programmes were to be a significant part of the change process.

One such event revolved around the important subject of marketing creativi-ty. Yet the expressions of fathomless vacuity on the faces of participants revealed a massive disjuncture between the aims and content of the course and the deeply hierarchical structure within the organisation that penalised ini-tiative, rewarded compliance and subservience, and discouraged anyone but the most senior managers from using their initiative.

Facing this situation, managers on such a course would clearly be stupid to change their behaviour, as to do so would lead to punishment. The result, of course, was that they paid lip-service to the course, and no tutor, no matter how skilled, could possibly succeed.

Likewise, as organisations are essentially political structures, in which groups of people acquire, wield and defend power aggressively in highly specialised groups, or departments, it is unlikely that another, probably newer, marketing department would have much influence or sway over the company's strategy. Accountants are unlikely to publicise the irrelevancy of much of the informa-tion produced by their systems. IT departments are unlikely to admit that they have contributed absolutely nothing to the customer's or to the company's prosperity. Personnel are hardly likely to admit to failing to respond effectively to the company's changed environment. Nor are production people likely to admit that their preoccupation with MRP 2, Right-first-Time, Just-in-Time pro-grammes, and the like, often have little to do with anything that is of relevance to the customer.

The result of all this is that organisations build up a resistance to the market-ing concept by dint of their sectionalisation. 'Marketing' becomes a political process, which is rejected by sectional interests striving to retain their power bases. Hence, new procedures, structures and frameworks introduced by mar-keters designed to deliver greater customer satisfaction, are viewed as political processes which are likely to weaken sectional interests and power bases and are, therefore, rejected. An example of this is the introduction of marketing planning procedures involving the formalisation of data and information initiated by managers in a central marketing department. Resistance has got very little to do with rationality. Resistance is based on the subsidiary's conviction that such procedures hand power and control to the marketing department. The marketing department is perceived as having their own agenda, their own power-seeking goals, and their own values, all of which is to do with spreading marketing influence and power and reducing their own priorities and values. The result is that such procedures are rejected as being irrelevant, and a 'battle' starts, in which sectional interests are preserved, priorities protected, departmental culture defended, goals justified and budgets and priorities fought for, all of this being related much more closely to departmental objectives than to the interests of the customer. All new initiatives, therefore, and especially marketing initiatives, are viewed as a weakening of the traditional power base.

It is hardly surprising, then, that the pristine concepts, tools and techniques of marketing taught on marketing courses and written about so profusely in books, take a back seat in such an organisational milieu and are rarely used.

Finally, then, organisational structures will change from their narrow, functional focus, to being orientated towards customers. Teams consisting of managers from several disciplines will focus on customers and markets, so that accountants, for example, will be fighting on behalf of customers rather than on behalf of their functional discipline.

THE FUTURE OF MARKETING

This chapter has attempted to explain why there is such a huge gap between the theory of marketing as taught in universities and what actually happens in the real world. In doing so, many criticisms were levelled at the current state of affairs, and some suggestions were put forward about how some of these barriers can be overcome.

The author has little doubt that attitudes in industry are slowly but surely changing towards marketing, largely as a result of the traumatic market conditions of the past two years, which have forced many well-known companies out of business. Those remaining are beginning to take a cautious look at marketing once again. In future, however, the new breed of marketing director will play a central role in steering the organisation towards the most promising fields. The role of the marketing director has gradually changed from being a dispenser of largesse to grateful consumers to that of a fighter for the consumer's attention. Somewhere along the line, however, the battles for the hearts and minds of his own financial, technical and production people in the difficult process of gaining a sustainable competitive advantage have been lost, and he has often ended up on his own – misunderstood, pilloried and eventually dismissed.

The 1990s, however, will see the emergence of the marketing director to the central, starring role. But he will need to change his ways. Gone are the days when senior company personnel could afford to confuse marketing with sales, product management, advertising and market research. There are still a lot of these characters around, of course, but they will not get very far during the 1990s. The danger of confusing marketing with the American 'Have a nice day' syndrome will soon pass as companies come to realise that they have to get *all* the elements of the offer right to succeed.

People still look incredulously towards the Japanese, even though it is obvious that all they have ever done is to provide value for money by getting all the elements of the offer right, and that everyone in the organisation understands that their success depends on customer satisfaction.

The marketing director of the 1990s, therefore, will have to be a person of both stature and intellect, with appropriate professional marketing training, not a reject from other functions. Marketing is increasingly about focus and concentration. This means an on-going dialogue with specific groups of customers whose needs we must understand in depth, and for whom better offers are developed than those of competitors. A marketing man or woman should only shout when there is something to shout about.

The marketing director will play a central role in directing the organisation's strengths towards the most promising opportunities. He will also have to understand the real meaning of profit, rather than the very narrow financial definition imposed on organisations by accountants. Return on sales, cash flow, net present values, return on investment, asset turnover, and the like, can be disastrous if they are applied equally to everything that moves in an organisation. So the marketing director will have to have a deep understanding of the significance of portfolios of products and markets, and the different policies that emanate from them.

The marketing director will also have to understand the real meaning of intangible assets. Companies are only beginning to realise that much of what appears on their balance sheets is rubbish and that it is brand names and relationships with customers that make profits, not factories and tangible assets.

In addition, the marketing director will have to learn to think strategically rather than being a tactical marketing technician – the preferred mode to date. He will have to learn how to use the principal marketing planning tools to help to create a sustainable competitive advantage and to develop 'global fortresses' for his main products. The entrenched tribal mentality endemic in organisation charts, most of which is alien to the notion of satisfying customer need, must be overcome. In doing so, the marketer will have to redefine his strategic business units around customers rather than around products, functions or geography.

The marketing director will also need to get a much better handle on marketing information about the principal determinants of commercial success (ie, the business environment, the market, competitors and himself). In doing so, he will need to understand better what information technology can do for him. For example, the leaders will surely be developing expert marketing systems (EMS) so that the best marketing expertise in the company can be applied by all executives anywhere in the world, rather than being hoarded inside the heads of a few gifted individuals.

The marketing director will need to think globally. This will entail developing the right skills in all executives involved in marketing, developing the systems to focus on the right issues, and being able to aggregate and synthesise what is fed into global strategies. He will then need to ensure correct priority of objectives and resource allocation. He will also need to recruit properly qualified chartered marketers (the Institute of Marketing is now Chartered).

Lastly, he will have to improve dramatically his communication and political skills. General management skills will also be important, and it is unlikely that anyone not educated to at least MBA standard will succeed.

If all of this is to come to pass, it can be seen that there will be an increasingly major role to be played by marketing teachers. In the UK, we have more than our fair share of world-class educators, as well as a solid base of rising stars. The author's advice to those who will continue to take the brunt of the marketing education workload in the future is:

- Acquire a totally sound theoretical knowledge base in marketing.
- Try to have an even greater in-depth knowledge of certain aspects of marketing.
- Acquire a thorough understanding of other disciplines and where marketing 'fits in'.
- Use and develop innovative teaching/learning methods.
- Get the teaching balance right between knowledge, skills and attitudes.
- Don't believe the saying, 'Those who can, do. Those who can't, teach'. Teaching is a wholly professional job requiring finely honed skills. You don't need to be a millionaire to be a successful marketing teacher.
- Above all, persevere in what will increasingly be a challenging and rewarding profession.

Table 8.2 summarises marketing trends during the past 30 years and summarises the author's prognosis for the remainder of the 1990s.

Table 8.2 Marketing evolution

	1960s	*1970s*	*1980s*	*1990s*
Economy	Growth	Crisis	Flat	Instability • Rapid change • Increased competitiveness (1992)
Product marketing	Brand proliferation	Brand rationalisation	Polarisation	Globalisation • Major brands • Major segments • Major customers • New product development
Consumer requirement	Choice	Price/value	Identity	Service • Quality • Impact of technology
Profit source	Market expansion	Margin improvement	Share shift	Added values • Productivity
Strategy	Diversification	Resource allocation	Competitive strategy	Marketing management • Global integration • Intrapreneurship • Customer/ market force

What to Do to Succeed

In conclusion, the author offers his views on the key change areas in the 1990s, especially those relating to the new Europe, as well as the implications for corporate responses.

Key change areas – the new Europe

End-users

Will our current customer base increase or decrease in numbers, change its purchasing policies, demand different levels of customer service? For example, a movement towards pan-European buying and a change of public procurement practices.

Pricing

How will the likely movement towards pan-European price harmonisation affect us and what will be the effects of trying to maintain price differentiation? For example, growth of international purchasing, stimulation of transnational distribution and expansion of parallel trade.

Distribution

How will the structure and nature of our distribution networks be affected by changing patterns of end-user purchasing, price harmonisation and product availability? For example, fewer, larger distributors, pan-European distribution and increasing demand for distributor own-branding.

Products

How far will our product portfolio be affected by EC legislation and the changing needs of end-users and distributors? For example, EC legislation on specifications, certification, patents and trademarks and demands for common product and service standards.

Competition

What are the likely scenarios post-1992 for current competitors, potential EC competitors and competitors from other parts of the world, notably the USA and the Far East? For example, will the future market environment play to the strengths and weaknesses of these different competitive forces and what will their strategies be?

Corporate response – the new Europe

Strategic implications

Will the key service factors for competitive advantage be changed for or against us as a result of 1992? Should we modify our corporate goals and strategies to take advantage or better defend ourselves in the light of our analysis of the key change areas?

Marketing activities

Are our current databases on end-users, distributors and competitors adequate to enable accurate planning and decision-making? What do we need to do to improve existing products and develop new ones to satisfy a coalescing European market? How can we construct a coherent European pricing strategy recognising the pressure towards harmonisation yet the differences in national customer service costs? How should our marketing communications policy be developed to balance pan-European and local positioning needs through the use of PR, advertising and sales promotion?

Sales activities

How should our key account sales effort be changed to handle larger, pan-European purchasers and the changing requirements of public procurement? What sort of sales-forces will be needed to market through the changing distribution networks? What are the implications of these changes for the numbers, knowledge, skills and attitudes of salespeople and what new policies do we need for their recruitment, training and motivation? Will the nature and scale of sales support need to be changed in terms of the sales office, after-sales service and technical advice?

Organisation

What new tasks need to be performed and thus what human resources will be required to handle pan-European end-users and distributors and to develop consistent product portfolios, pricing and communication programmes? How should these activities be best managed in the future? Do 'home and export' or 'multinational' structures have any relevance in a unifying European market?

Finally, let us consider some very practical ways forward in the difficult years that lie ahead. New challenges face all businesses as they approach the millennium. They were the focus of a special study on the future of marketing carried out by the author for the Chartered Institute of Marketing in 1994 (McDonald, 1994).

This final section distils the author's research, teaching and consultancy during the past 19 years into 12 core marketing guidelines for business. The guidelines build on the author's own practical experience as a marketing and sales director of a major consumer goods company, as the owner of a successful business and as a professor of marketing in one of the world's top business schools.

Although innovation remains a major ingredient in commercial success, there are none the less other challenges which organisations must overcome during the remaining four years of this century.

The challenges which must be addressed by companies include: the pace of change itself; process thinking; market maturity; the expertise and power of customers; and the internationalisation of businesses. These are shown in Tables 8.3–8.7.

Table 8.3 The challenge of rapid change

Pace of change	Marketing challenges
– Compressed time horizons – Shorter product life cycles – Transient customer preferences	– Ability to exploit markets more rapidly – More effective NPD – Flexibility in approach to markets – Accuracy in demand forecasting – Ability to optimise price setting

Table 8.4 Refining the process

Process thinking	Marketing challenges
– Move to flexible manufacturing and control systems – Materials substitution – Developments in microelectronics and robotisation – Quality focus	– Dealing with micro-segmentation – Finding ways to shift from single transaction focus to the forging of long-term relationships – Creating greater customer commitment

Table 8.5 The challenge of the market place

Market maturity	Marketing challenges
– Over capacity – Low margins – Lack of growth – Stronger competition – Trading down – Cost cutting	– Adding value leading to differentiation – New market creation and stimulation

Table 8.6 The customer

Customers' expertise and power	Marketing challenges
– More demanding – Higher expectations – More knowledgeable – Concentration of buying power – More sophisticated buyer behaviour	– Finding ways of getting closer to the customer – Managing the complexities of multiple market channels

Table 8.7 The international dimension

Internationalisation of business	Marketing challenges
– More competitors – Stronger competition – Lower margins – More customer choice – Larger markets – More disparate customer needs	– Restructuring of domestic operations to compete internationally – Becoming customer-focused in larger and more disparate markets

In order to overcome these challenges, the author offers twelve guidelines for developing effective marketing strategies.

TWELVE GUIDELINES FOR EFFECTIVE MARKETING

1. *Understanding the sources of competitive advantage*: Guideline 1 shows a universally recognised list of sources of competitive advantage (Porter, 1980). For small firms, they are more likely to be the ones listed on the left. It is clearly possible to focus on highly individual niches with specialised skills and to develop customer-focused relationships to an extent not possible for large organisations. Flexibility is also a potential source of competitive advantage.

Wherever possible, all organisations should seek to avoid competing with an undifferentiated product or service in too broad a market.

The author frequently has to emphasise to those who seek his advice that, without something different to offer (required by the market, of course!), they will continue to struggle and will have to rely on the crumbs that fall from the tables of others. This leads to the second point.

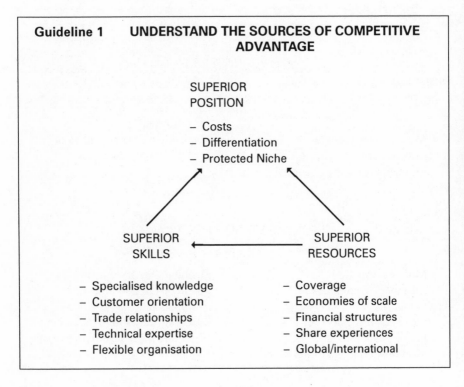

Guideline 1   UNDERSTAND THE SOURCES OF COMPETITIVE ADVANTAGE

SUPERIOR
POSITION

– Costs
– Differentiation
– Protected Niche

SUPERIOR   SUPERIOR
SKILLS   RESOURCES

– Specialised knowledge   – Coverage
– Customer orientation   – Economies of scale
– Trade relationships   – Financial structures
– Technical expertise   – Share experiences
– Flexible organisation   – Global/international

2. *Understanding differentiation*: Guideline 2 takes this point a little further and spells out the main sources of differentiation. One in particular, superior service, has increasingly become a source of competitive advantage. Companies should work relentlessly towards the differential advantage that these will bring. Points 1 and 2 have been confirmed by results from a 1994 3i survey of over 8000 SMEs (Burns, 1994).

Guideline 2 **UNDERSTAND DIFFERENTIATION**

- Superior product quality
- Innovative product features
- Unique product or service
- Strong brand name
- Superior service
  (speed, responsiveness, ability to solve problems)
- Wide distribution coverage

Continuously strive to serve customer needs more effectively.

---

3. *Understanding the environment*: Guideline 3 spells out what is meant by the term environment in the context of companies. There is now an overwhelming body of evidence to show that it is failure to monitor the hostile environmental changes that is the biggest cause of failure in both large and small companies. Had anyone predicted that IBM would lose billions of dollars six years ago, they would have been derided. Yet it was the failure of IBM to respond sufficiently quickly to the changes taking place about them that caused their recent problems.

Clearly, marketing has a key role to play in the process. For all organisations, this means devoting at least some of the key executives' time and resources to monitoring formally the changes taking place about them. Guidelines 3, 4 and 5 comprise the research that is necessary to make a marketing audit. This leads naturally to the next point.

Guideline 3 **UNDERSTAND THE ENVIRONMENT**

(opportunities and threats)

i) MACRO ENVIRONMENT
- Political/regulatory
- Economic
- Technological
- Societal

---

ii) MARKET/INDUSTRY ENVIRONMENT
- Market size and potential
- Customer behaviour
- Segmentation
- Suppliers
- Channels
- Industry practices
- Industry profitability

Carry out a formal marketing audit.

Guideline 4   **UNDERSTAND COMPETITORS**

- Direct competitors
- Potential competitors
- Substitute products
- Forward integration by suppliers
- Backward integration by customers
- Competitors' profitability
- Competitors' strengths and weaknesses

Develop a structured competitor monitoring process. Include the results in the marketing audit.

---

4. *Understanding competitors*: Guideline 4 is merely an extension of the marketing audit. Suffice it to say that if any organisation, big or small, does not know as much about its close competitors as it knows about itself, it should not be surprised if it fails to stay ahead.

5. *Understanding strengths and weaknesses*: Guideline 5 sets out potential sources of differentiation for an organisation. It represents a fairly comprehensive audit of the asset base. Together with written summaries of the other two sections of the marketing audit (Guidelines 3 and 4), there should be a written summary of all the conclusions.

If the sources of the company's own competitive advantage cannot be summarised on a couple of sheets of paper, the audit has not been done properly. If this is the case, the chances are that the organisation is relying on luck. Alas, luck has a habit of being somewhat fickle!

Guideline 5   **UNDERSTAND YOUR OWN STRENGTHS AND WEAKNESSES**

Carry out a formal position audit of your own product/market position in each segment in which you compete, particularly of your own ability to:

- Conceive/design
- Buy
- Produce
- Distribute
- Market
- Service
- Finance
- Manage
- Look for market opportunities where you can utilise your strengths

Include the results in the marketing audit.

---

6. *Understanding market segmentation:* Guideline 6 looks somewhat technical and even esoteric, at first sight. None the less, market segmentation is one of the key sources of commercial success and needs to be taken seriously by all organisations, as the days of the easy marketability of products and services have long since disappeared for all but a lucky few.

The ability to recognise groups of customers who share the same, or similar, needs has always come much easier to SMEs than to large organisations. The secret of success, of course, is to change the offer in accordance with changing needs and not to offer exactly the same product or service to everyone – the most frequent product-oriented mistake of large organisations. Closely connected with this is the next point.

Guideline 6   **UNDERSTAND MARKET SEGMENTATION**

- Not all customers in a broadly defined market have the same needs.
- Positioning is easy. Market segmentation is difficult. Positioning problems stem from poor segmentation.
- Select a segment and serve it. Do not straddle segments and sit between them.

1) Understand how your market works (market structure)
2) List what is bought (including where, when, how, applications)
3) List who buys (demographics, psychographics)
4) List why they buy (needs, benefits sought)
5) Search for groups with similar needs.

**Guideline 7 UNDERSTAND THE DYNAMICS OF PRODUCT/MARKET
EVOLUTION (PRODUCT LIFE-CYCLE ANALYSIS)**

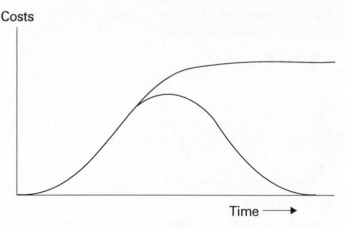

The biological analogy of birth, growth, maturity and decline is apt. Corporate
behaviour – particularly in respect of the marketing mix, must evolve with the
market.

Share building in mature markets is difficult and often results in lower prices.

Those with lower costs have an advantage at the stage of maturity.

Life cycles will be different between segments.

---

7. *Understanding the dynamics of product/market evolution*: While at first
sight Guideline 7 looks as if it applies principally to large companies, few
will need reminding of the short-lived nature of many retailing concepts,
such as the boutiques of the late 1980s. Those who clung doggedly on to a
concept that had had its day lived to regret it.

Few organisations today will need to be reminded of the transitory nature
of their business success.

8. *Understanding a portfolio of products and markets*: Guideline 8 suggests
plotting either products/services or markets (or, in some cases, customers)
on a vertical axis in descending order of market attractiveness. (The potential of each for the achievement of organisational and commercial aims and
objectives should be used as a criterion as, clearly, they cannot all be equal.)
The organisation will obviously have a greater or lesser strength in serving
each of these 'markets', and this will determine their competitive position.
For each location on the graph, a circle, representing the size of current
sales should be drawn.

The graph is divided into a four-box matrix, and each box is assessed for management as suggested in the figure. This will give a reasonably accurate 'picture' of the business at a glance and will indicate whether or not it is a well-balanced portfolio. Too much business in any one box should be regarded as dangerous.

Guideline 8   **UNDERSTAND YOUR PORTFOLIO (OF PRODUCTS AND MARKETS)**

You cannot be all things to all people. A deep understanding of portfolio analysis will enable you to set appropriate objectives and allocate resources effectively. Portfolio logic arrays competitive position against market attractiveness in a matrix form.

	High	Low
High	2	3
Low	1	4

Market attractiveness (vertical axis)

Competitive position (horizontal axis)

Box 1   Maintain and manage for sustained earnings
Box 2   Invest and build for growth
Box 3   Selectively invest
Box 4   Manage for cash

Guideline 9   **SET CLEAR STRATEGIC PRIORITIES AND STICK TO THEM**

- Focus your best resources on the best opportunities for achieving continuous growth in sales and profits.
- This means having a written strategic marketing plan for 3 years containing:
  - A mission statement
  - A financial summary
  - A market overview
  - A SWOT on key segments

- A portfolio summary
- Assumptions
- Marketing objectives and strategies
- A budget
- This strategic plan can then be converted into a detailed one-year plan.
- To do this, an agreed marketing planning process will be necessary.
- Focus on key performance indicators with an unrelenting discipline.

---

9. *Setting clear strategic priorities and sticking to them*: Guideline 9 suggests writing down the results of earlier endeavours in summary form (a marketing/business plan).

While it is not the intention of the author to stifle creativity by suggesting that companies get into a bureaucratic form of planning, it remains a fact that those individuals and organisations who can define their intended sources of revenue and profits, tend to thrive and prosper in the long term (Burns, 1994). This implies something more sophisticated than forecasts and budgets. Commercial history has demonstrated that any fool can spell out the financial results they wish to achieve, but it takes intellect to spell out how they are to be achieved. This implies setting clear strategic priorities and sticking to them.

Guideline 10   UNDERSTAND CUSTOMER ORIENTATION

- Develop customer orientation in all functions. Ensure that every function understands that they are there to serve the customer, not their own narrow functional interests.
- This must be driven from the board downwards.
- Where possible, organise in-cross functional teams around customer groups and core processes.
- Make customers the arbiter of quality.

---

10. *Understanding customer orientation*: Guideline 10 will be familiar to all successful companies. BS5750, ISO9001 and the like, while useful for those with operations such as production processes, in the past have had little to do with real quality, which, of course, can only be seen through the eyes of the customer. (It is obvious that making something perfectly is something of a pointless exercise if no one buys it.)

It is imperative today to monitor customer satisfaction, so this should be done continuously, for it is clearly the only real arbiter of quality.

11. *Being professional*: Guideline 11 sets out some of the marketing skills essential to continuous success. Professional management skills, particularly in marketing, are becoming the hallmark of commercial success in the 1990s. There are countless professional development skills courses available today. Alas, many directors consider themselves too busy to attend, which is an extremely short-sighted attitude. Entrepreneurial skills, combined with hard-edged management skills, will see any company through to the turn of the century.

Guideline 11   **BE PROFESSIONAL**

Particularly in marketing, it is essential to have professional marketing skills, which implies formal training in the underlying concepts, tools and techniques of marketing. In particular, the following are core:

- Market research
- Gap analysis
- Market segmentation/positioning
- Product life cycle analysis
- Portfolio management
- Database management
- The four Ps
  - Product management
  - Pricing
  - Place (customer service, channel management)
  - Promotion (selling, sales force management, advertising, sales promotion)

---

12. *Giving leadership*: Guideline 12 sets out the final factor of success in the 1990s – leadership. Charismatic leadership, however, without the 11 other pillars of success, will be to no avail. Few will need reminding of the charisma of Maxwell, Halpern, Saunders, and countless others during the past decade. Charisma, without something to sell that the market values, will ultimately be pointless. It is, however, still an important ingredient in success.

Guideline 12   **GIVE LEADERSHIP**

- Do not let doom and gloom pervade your thinking.
- The hostile environment offers many opportunities for companies with toughness and insight.
- Lead your team strongly.
- Do not accept poor performance in the most critical positions.

SUMMARY

Lest readers should think that the 12 factors for success in the 1990s are a figment of the imagination there is much recent research to suggest otherwise. Saunders and Wong's study (1993) built on earlier research into the causes of commercial success and confirmed that, in essence, the four ingredients listed in Figure 8.8 are common to all commercially successful organisations, irrespective of their national origin.

From this it can be seen, first, that the core product or service on offer has to be excellent. Secondly, operations have to be efficient and, preferably, state-of-the-art. Thirdly, the research stresses the need for creativity in leadership and personnel, something frequently discouraged by excessive bureaucracy in large organisations. Finally, excellent companies do professional marketing. This means that the organisation continuously monitors the environment, the market, competitors and their own performance against customer-driven standards, and produces a strategic marketing plan which sets out the value that everyone in the organisation has to deliver. This latter point has been the subject of this chapter.

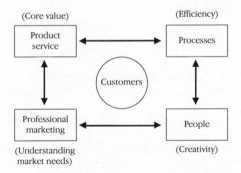

Figure 8.8 Business success

References

Burns, P (1994) 'Growth in the 1990s: Winners and Losers', Special Report 12, 3i European Enterprise Centre.

Doyle, P (1992) 'What makes an excellent company?', *Journal of Marketing Management*, Spring.

Greenley, G (1989) 'An exposition into empirical research into marketing planning', *Journal of Marketing Management*, July.

McDonald, M H B (1990) 'Some methodological problems associated with the directional policy matrix', *MBA Review*, Spring.

Mcdonald, M (1994) 'Marketing – The Challenge of Change', Chartered Institute of Marketing Study.

Pascale, R T (1990) *Managing on the Edge: How Successful Companies Use Conflict to Stay Ahead*, Viking, London.

Porter, M (1980) 'Competitive Strategy: Techniques for Analysing Industries and Competitors', New York Free Press.

Saunders, J and Wong, V (1993) 'Business Orientations and Corporate Success', *Journal of Strategic Marketing*, Vol 1, No 1.

Wong, V, Saunders, J and Doyle, P (1988) 'The quality of British marketing: a comparative investigation of international competition in the UK market', *Proceedings of the 21st Annual Conference of Marketing Education Group*, Huddersfield Polytechnic, July, Butterworth-Heinemann, Oxford.

INDEX